W9-BNR-489

PROFESSIONAL ANDROID™ OPEN ACCESSORY PROGRAMMING WITH ARDUINO™

PROFESSIONAL

Android™ Open Accessory Programming with Arduino™

PROFESSIONAL

Android™ Open Accessory Programming with Arduino™

Andreas Göransson
David Cuartielles Ruiz

WILEY

John Wiley & Sons, Inc.

Professional Android™ Open Accessory Programming with Arduino™

Published by
John Wiley & Sons, Inc.
10475 Crosspoint Boulevard
Indianapolis, IN 46256
www.wiley.com

Copyright © 2013 by John Wiley & Sons, Inc., Indianapolis, Indiana

Published simultaneously in Canada

ISBN: 978-1-118-45476-3
ISBN: 978-1-118-45477-0 (ebk)
ISBN: 978-1-118-49399-1 (ebk)
ISBN: 978-1-118-60554-7 (ebk)

Manufactured in the United States of America

10 9 8 7 6 5 4 3 2 1

No part of this publication may be reproduced, stored in a retrieval system or transmitted in any form or by any means, electronic, mechanical, photocopying, recording, scanning or otherwise, except as permitted under Sections 107 or 108 of the 1976 United States Copyright Act, without either the prior written permission of the Publisher, or authorization through payment of the appropriate per-copy fee to the Copyright Clearance Center, 222 Rosewood Drive, Danvers, MA 01923, (978) 750-8400, fax (978) 646-8600. Requests to the Publisher for permission should be addressed to the Permissions Department, John Wiley & Sons, Inc., 111 River Street, Hoboken, NJ 07030, (201) 748-6011, fax (201) 748-6008, or online at http://www.wiley.com/go/permissions.

Limit of Liability/Disclaimer of Warranty: The publisher and the author make no representations or warranties with respect to the accuracy or completeness of the contents of this work and specifically disclaim all warranties, including without limitation warranties of fitness for a particular purpose. No warranty may be created or extended by sales or promotional materials. The advice and strategies contained herein may not be suitable for every situation. This work is sold with the understanding that the publisher is not engaged in rendering legal, accounting, or other professional services. If professional assistance is required, the services of a competent professional person should be sought. Neither the publisher nor the author shall be liable for damages arising herefrom. The fact that an organization or Web site is referred to in this work as a citation and/or a potential source of further information does not mean that the author or the publisher endorses the information the organization or Web site may provide or recommendations it may make. Further, readers should be aware that Internet Web sites listed in this work may have changed or disappeared between when this work was written and when it is read.

For general information on our other products and services please contact our Customer Care Department within the United States at (877) 762-2974, outside the United States at (317) 572-3993 or fax (317) 572-4002.

Wiley publishes in a variety of print and electronic formats and by print-on-demand. Some material included with standard print versions of this book may not be included in e-books or in print-on-demand. If this book refers to media such as a CD or DVD that is not included in the version you purchased, you may download this material at http://booksupport.wiley.com. For more information about Wiley products, visit www.wiley.com.

Library of Congress Control Number: 2012951521

Trademarks: Wiley, the Wiley logo, Wrox, the Wrox logo, Wrox Programmer to Programmer, and related trade dress are trademarks or registered trademarks of John Wiley & Sons, Inc. and/or its affiliates, in the United States and other countries, and may not be used without written permission. Android is a trademark of Google, Inc. Arduino is a registered trademark of Arduino, LLC. All other trademarks are the property of their respective owners. John Wiley & Sons, Inc., is not associated with any product or vendor mentioned in this book.

To Bobbie for being the only person I know of learning electronics before learning how to read (and for being so extremely patient with her dad).

To Andreas Göransson, co-author and friend because he always exceeds my expectations. I did what I did just because you did what you did.

— DAVID CUARTIELLES RUIZ

ABOUT THE AUTHORS

 **ANDREAS GÖRANSSON** currently works as a lecturer at Malmö University where he teaches programming to design and engineering students; he has also lectured on these subjects at several universities and conferences such as EWSN and Android Only! Andreas actively contributes to various open source projects concerning machine-to-machine communication, which is one of his key research interests.

 **DAVID CUARTIELLES RUIZ** works as a lecturer and runs the Prototyping Laboratory at the School of Arts and Communication at Malmö University. He is a Research Fellow at the Medea Studio looking into two main areas: the Internet of Things and Digital Educational Tools. David is one of the founders of the Arduino project and is currently involved in running different research initiatives for it.

ABOUT THE TECHNICAL EDITOR

 **GREG MILETTE** is a programmer, author, entrepreneur, and musician who loves writing practical Android apps, wiring Arduino hardware, and implementing great ideas. He is the founder of Gradison Technologies, Inc., author of Professional Android Sensor Programming, contributor to StackOverflow, drummer, and father of two.

CREDITS

EXECUTIVE EDITOR
Robert Elliott

PROJECT EDITOR
Ed Connor

TECHNICAL EDITOR
Greg Milette

PRODUCTION EDITOR
Daniel Scribner

COPY EDITOR
Kim Cofer

EDITORIAL MANAGER
Mary Beth Wakefield

FREELANCER EDITORIAL MANAGER
Rosemarie Graham

ASSOCIATE DIRECTOR OF MARKETING
David Mayhew

MARKETING MANAGER
Ashley Zurcher

BUSINESS MANAGER
Amy Knies

PRODUCTION MANAGER
Tim Tate

VICE PRESIDENT AND EXECUTIVE GROUP PUBLISHER
Richard Swadley

VICE PRESIDENT AND EXECUTIVE PUBLISHER
Neil Edde

ASSOCIATE PUBLISHER
Jim Minatel

PROJECT COORDINATOR, COVER
Katie Crocker

PROOFREADER
Scott Klemp, Word One
Josh Chase, Word One

INDEXER
Ron Strauss

COVER DESIGNER
Elizabeth Brooks

COVER IMAGE
"Lottie Lemon" image courtesy of
D. Cuartielles & A. Goransson

ACKNOWLEDGMENTS

THANKS TO FAMILY, friends and colleagues for their support while writing this book; above all a thanks to my co-author David for always pushing me to the next level. Also I'd like to thank Tony Olsson and Fernando Barrajon for their support when writing this book. Special thanks go to Richard Hyndman of Google UK for giving us the opportunity to test the original Google ADK boards when all we had were the "knockoffs," and a big thanks to Mario Böhmer too for sending us photographs of the ADK boards (which we ended up not needing thanks to Richard). Also a big thanks to Eui-Suk Chung and Seowan Kwon of Samsung for so gracefully lending us the latest versions of their Galaxy line phones to build our projects with — and of course Hampus Jacobsson for introducing us to them.

I would also like to extend my gratitude to everyone at Wiley for working so hard. Thanks also to our editors, Ed Connor and Robert Elliot, in particular, for showing such great patience with this, our first, book. I would also like to acknowledge the open source project Fritzing which we used a lot in our writing process. Finally, I'd like to thank Rodrigo Calvo for his assistance in fixing the USB Host libraries to work with the latest Android versions.

—ANDREAS GÖRANSSON

I HAVE TO THANK the whole of the Arduino family: the team, the developers, the members of the forum, all of you that helped us making this project possible. I should also acknowledge the people at Officine Arduino Torino that assisted us with getting materials for the book: Katia, Federico and Cristian jumped in the minute we needed their help.

To Gianluca and Daniela from SmartProjects who fed our pages with boards and sensors. Rodrigo brought to the table the brilliant idea that could patch our library in one line. Hampus introduced us to really nice people at Samsung — Eui-Suk Chung and Seowan Kwon — who kindly lent us the phones that made our experiments possible.

To Twitter, that let us go verbal and get people back to us. One of those was Richard, from Google, who shipped us a Google ADK and Google ADK2. To Mario and his digital camera, it was great to meet up in Berlin! Speaking of Berlin, the open source software Fritzing, the one we used for our schematics, is made there.

To Tony, who made two books before we even thought about making one. You clearly showed us this was possible. And to Malmö University in Sweden, the place where we meet and work every day, the place that makes us think the way we think and brings us opportunities like the one of writing this book (after normal working hours).

—DAVID CUARTIELLES RUIZ

CONTENTS

INTRODUCTION

CONNECTIVITY IS AN EMERGENT TOPIC in home automation. Your tablet should be discovered automatically by your home entertainment system, offering you full control of the film you want to see or the music you want to play. Your refrigerator should be smart enough to keep track of all the groceries in your home and even tell your smartphone what to buy when you arrive at the supermarket. Your car should connect to your cell phone automatically as you turn the ignition on, enabling it to access your music library and all of your contacts — as well as reject incoming phone calls with a pleasant voice, kindly informing whoever is calling that you're currently driving and shouldn't be disturbed.

The idea of a connected life where anything digital sends and receives data from the Internet, and not just your TV or fridge, is something we're both working with on a daily basis as researchers and teachers at Malmö University's School of Arts and Design, Sweden. This research field and new computing paradigm is known as the *Internet of Things*. It centers its efforts on analyzing the implications of connecting our everyday life to the network through a multitude of devices.

We spend our days bringing to life visions of the future. This book is about some hands-on techniques that will help you realize your own ideas. We would love to see you get your hands dirty experimenting with hardware and software, which is why we want to give you that little extra nudge into the Maker movement. In this book you will be building seven different projects using Arduino and Android in different ways, and detailing how you could potentially refine and continue building on them.

WHO THIS BOOK IS FOR

This book is intended for the more seasoned Android developer; you may have already written and published your first application on Google Play and want to explore new frontiers.

In some places we assume you have enough knowledge about the Android frameworks that you feel comfortable browsing classes and libraries you have not yet used.

If you're also familiar with the electronics prototyping platform called Arduino, you can even skip certain parts of Chapters 7 and 8 because those deal with the introduction to electronic sensors and actuators, and connecting those with Arduino.

WHAT THIS BOOK COVERS

The Android operating system offers you, as a developer, the possibility of creating accessories in an open fashion. You can design, manufacture, and sell electronics to be attached to Android phones in a completely standard way that is fully supported by the operating system. The Android Open

Accessory Protocol (AOAP) is the way any Android device connects to accessories, and it has been available since Android's revision 2.3.4. The first part of the book has been made to accommodate any version of Android as long as it supports the AOAP.

You also learn about a much more recent version of Android. The latter chapters explore the use of Jelly Bean (Android's revision number 4), launched in the summer of 2012. It offers high-speed video and some other interesting features needed to build the most advanced projects you will find at the end of the book.

When it comes to the electronics, you will be using the latest revision of the Arduino IDE. At the time of writing it was 1.0.2. You should not try the code provided here with earlier versions because we cannot assure its functionality. This revision of the IDE runs with both the Arduino Mega ADK (compatible with the Google ADK v1) and the Arduino Due (compatible with the Google ADK v2).

We have tried all the examples with the Arduino Mega ADK. We haven't tested them with other compatible boards, but as long as they are compatible, things should run in the very same way. Please take into account that a lot of different manufacturers produce boards and we don't have access to all of them.

HOW THIS BOOK IS STRUCTURED

This book has two major parts with several chapters each. The first part of the book deals with the basics of getting up and running with the Android Open Accessory framework, and building the tools you'll use for the second part. The second part of the book is all about projects — designing and building your Android accessory prototypes using the tools from Part I.

Part I of the book runs from Chapter 1 to Chapter 8.

Chapter 1, "Introduction to Android Open Accessory," introduces you to the two systems you use in the book, Android and Arduino.

Chapter 2, "Setting up the (Arduino) Hardware," is all about electronics, telling you about all the different options available when you want to connect an Arduino-based prototype to your Android phone.

Chapter 3, "Understanding Data Communication," covers the basics of data communication; how data protocols work and are designed. It also introduces the protocol that is used in this book, called P2PMQTT, based on MQTT which is a machine-to-machine messaging protocol designed by IBM.

Chapter 4, "Setting up Development Environments," guides you through setting up the two development environments used in this book: Android and Arduino. In this chapter you also test run your very first Android Accessory.

In **Chapter 5, "Creating the Accessory Library,"** you build the first version of the MQTT-based Android library used to develop all the accessory projects in this book. We strongly recommend that you read Chapter 3 before building the library. Apart from MQTT, you also add the Android Open Accessory-specific code to send and receive messages from and to your Arduino-based accessory.

When you've developed the library in Chapter 5 you can move on to **Chapter 6, "Using Your Accessory Library,"** where you create Android accessory applications for the smaller projects you build in Chapters 7 and 8, using your new library.

Chapter 7, "Digital Arduino," is an introduction to digital sensors and actuators using Arduino. In this chapter you start by learning the basics of Arduino, and finish building smaller accessory-enabled projects that connect to the applications you developed in Chapter 6.

Chapter 8, "Analog Arduino," continues with the introduction from Chapter 7, but in this chapter you switch focus from digital sensors and actuators to the analog counterparts, such as motors and potentiometers. It starts off with some basic Arduino examples, and by the time you're done you should have built two smaller accessory-enabled projects.

Part II of the book deals with three more significant projects, where you use more than one type of sensor or actuator, and exchange information often in both directions between the two devices.

Chapter 9, "Bike Ride Recorder," describes our process of attaching electronic sensors and actuators to a racer bike. You will build an accessory that enables you to record a bike ride with your phone while monitoring your effort in terms of the amount of pedaling you do. At the end of the ride, the phone will render your trip while also displaying your actual speed and the speed detected by your peddling.

The project you build in **Chapter 10, "Kitchen Lamp,"** enables you to control the lighting in a room through your Android device when special events happen on the phone, such as a phone call or SMS, and even change the lighting pattern depending on who is calling or texting you.

Chapter 11, "Mr. Wiley," is the final chapter of the book. In this chapter you build a robot with an "Android brain" that enables it to react in certain ways depending on its environment, such as "running" away from strangers or following a special pattern on the floor.

WHAT YOU NEED TO USE THIS BOOK

To begin creating accessories using the Android Open Accessory framework and Arduino, it's highly recommended that you have at least an Android device running Android 3.1 or above (Andorid 2.3.4 will also work, but it's not recommended) and an Arduino Mega ADK microcontroller board. Without these two components you can't run any of the code examples found in this book.

You also need two different development environments, one for Android and one for Arduino. It's not required that you use the Eclipse or Arduino IDEs, but it's recommended because those are the best documented ways of developing for either platform.

Building Arduino prototypes is more than just code — you need at least the very basic sensors and actuators from each example in the first part of the book to build the mini projects. The Arduino Store has been kind enough to assemble a kit specifically for this book, and you can find it at http://store.arduino.cc. If you check the back of the book you will find a one-stop source for the components to the examples and projects for that first part of the book. The projects in the second half can also be sourced at the same place, but they end up being somehow expensive and therefore it is up to the reader to purchase the components needed in each one of the three projects presented in part two.

However, if you want to acquire the material bit-by-bit, or you just want to buy it elsewhere, you can use the list in Table I-1.

TABLE I-1: Electronic Components Needed for Part I of This Book

ITEM	NAME	DESCRIPTION	CHAPTER
1	Arduino ADK	Original Arduino ADK board	All
2	Workshop kit	Starter kit, breadboard, and wire set	All
3	Extra green LEDs	It's always good to have some extra LEDs when building projects	
4	Extra red LEDs	-	
5	Extra yellow LEDs	-	
6	Extra blue LEDs	-	
7	Resistor kit	To cover most of your prototyping needs	All
8	Potentiometers	To act as inputs to your system	8
9	Continuous-rotation servo motors	Two motors to build the small robot example	8
10	LED display	Two LED displays for a project	7
11	Relay module	Pre-mounted relay module	7
12	Wire	1m-long wire for pre-mounted modules	7, 8
13	Tilt module	Pre-mounted tilt module	7
14	Pushbuttons	Normal pushbuttons that can fit in a breadboard	7
15	Piezo speaker	Piezo speaker or small paper speaker	8
16	Ultrasound sensor	Used to detect distance to objects; MaxBotix is a very common brand that's easy to find more or less anywhere in the world; their MaxSonar EZ1 is a very accurate and simple to use so we recommend it	8
17	Temperature sensor	Inexpensive temperature sensor on Celsius degrees, a good sensor is LM-35 by Texas Instruments	4

Most of these components are completely standard and you can find them at a store close to you. If you happen to be in the US, online stores like `http://adafruit.com` and `http://sparkfun.com` are well known among hobbyists as good places to find parts, Arduino boards and all sorts of materials needed to build projects.

If you are in Europe there is a long list of possible distributors, you can find many of them at your own country. If you want to buy parts saving money on delivery and import taxes, you should check `http://arduino.cc/en/Main/Buy` where you will find a list of possible vendors of Arduino boards as well as many other materials for the projects in this book.

CONVENTIONS

To help you get the most from the text and keep track of what's happening, we've used a number of conventions throughout the book.

> **WARNING** *Boxes like this one hold important, not-to-be-forgotten information that is directly relevant to the surrounding text.*

> **NOTE** *Tips, hints, tricks, and asides to the current discussion are offset and placed in italics like this.*

As for styles in the text:

➤ We *highlight* new terms and important words when we introduce them.

➤ We show keyboard strokes like this: Ctrl+A.

➤ We show filenames, URLs, and code within the text like so: `persistence.properties`.

➤ We present code in two different ways:

```
We use a monofont type with no highlighting for most code examples.
```

```
We use bold to emphasize code that is particularly important in the present context
or to show changes from a previous code snippet.
```

SOURCE CODE

As you work through the examples in this book, you may choose either to type in all the code manually, or to use the source code files that accompany the book. All the source code used in this book is available for download at `www.wrox.com`. Specifically for this book, the code download is on the Download Code tab at:

`www.wrox.com/remtitle.cgi?isbn=1118454766`

You can also search for the book at `www.wrox.com` by ISBN (the ISBN for this book is 978-1-1184-5476-3 to find the code. And a complete list of code downloads for all current Wrox books is available at `www.wrox.com/dynamic/books/download.aspx`.

Most of the code on `www.wrox.com` is compressed in a .ZIP, .RAR archive or similar archive format appropriate to the platform. Once you download the code, just decompress it with an appropriate compression tool.

> **NOTE** *Because many books have similar titles, you may find it easiest to search by ISBN; this book's ISBN is 978-1-118-45476-3.*

Once you download the code, just decompress it with your favorite compression tool. Alternatively, you can go to the main Wrox code download page at `www.wrox.com/dynamic/books/download.aspx` to see the code available for this book and all other Wrox books.

There are also public Git repositories at `https://github.com/aoabook` where all the code for this book is published, and maintained.

ERRATA

We make every effort to ensure that there are no errors in the text or in the code. However, no one is perfect, and mistakes do occur. If you find an error in one of our books, like a spelling mistake or faulty piece of code, we would be very grateful for your feedback. By sending in errata you may save another reader hours of frustration and at the same time you will be helping us provide even higher quality information.

To find the errata page for this book, go to `http://www.wrox.com` and locate the title using the Search box or one of the title lists. Then, on the book details page, click the Book Errata link. On this page you can view all errata that has been submitted for this book and posted by Wrox editors. A complete book list including links to each book's errata is also available at `www.wrox.com/misc-pages/booklist.shtml`.

If you don't spot "your" error on the Book Errata page, go to `www.wrox.com/contact/techsupport.shtml` and complete the form there to send us the error you have found. We'll check the information and, if appropriate, post a message to the book's errata page and fix the problem in subsequent editions of the book.

P2P.WROX.COM

For author and peer discussion, join the P2P forums at p2p.wrox.com. The forums are a web-based system for you to post messages relating to Wrox books and related technologies and interact with other readers and technology users. The forums offer a subscription feature to e-mail you topics of interest of your choosing when new posts are made to the forums. Wrox authors, editors, other industry experts, and your fellow readers are present on these forums.

At http://p2p.wrox.com you will find a number of different forums that will help you not only as you read this book, but also as you develop your own applications. To join the forums, just follow these steps:

1. Go to p2p.wrox.com and click the Register link.

2. Read the terms of use and click Agree.

3. Complete the required information to join as well as any optional information you wish to provide and click Submit.

4. You will receive an e-mail with information describing how to verify your account and complete the joining process.

> **NOTE** *You can read messages in the forums without joining P2P but in order to post your own messages, you must join.*

Once you join, you can post new messages and respond to messages other users post. You can read messages at any time on the web. If you would like to have new messages from a particular forum e-mailed to you, click the Subscribe to this Forum icon by the forum name in the forum listing.

For more information about how to use the Wrox P2P, be sure to read the P2P FAQs for answers to questions about how the forum software works as well as many common questions specific to P2P and Wrox books. To read the FAQs, click the FAQ link on any P2P page.

PART I

Welcome to the Wonderful World of Accessories

Introduction to Android Open Accessory

WHAT'S IN THIS CHAPTER?

➤ Introduction to the Android Open Accessory standard

➤ Getting to know the Arduino project

➤ Understanding the Open Hardware culture

If you ask your colleagues what Android really is, you will probably hear something about Linux, Java Virtual Machines (JVMs), or various devices; you might even hear some statistical reports on market shares of Android in comparison to other mobile operating systems.

We would rather introduce Android as a way to explore the world of connected devices. This is, in essence, what Android Open Accessory (AOA) is all about — making your Android phone connect to, and communicate with, any other device around it!

In this chapter you get a background and overview of the Android project, the Android Open Accessory framework, and the electronics platform called Arduino. All of these technologies are used throughout this book.

I, ANDROID

Technically, there is a lot to know about the Android system and all of its layers and components. But, because several books are already available that thoroughly discuss all the technical aspects of the Android system inside and out, you won't get too much technical information in this chapter. You will, however, become a bit more familiar with the sparks that brought Android to life.

If you want to get deeper into the technical workings of Android, we recommend *Beginning Android 4 Application Development* by Wei Meng-Lee published by Wiley in 2012 if you are a beginner, or *Professional Android Application Development 4* by Reto Meier published by Wiley in 2012 if you are a more seasoned developer; both are excellent books.

The Three Laws of Android

The classic sci-fi author Isaac Asimov created some well-known rules within robotics, called the Three Laws of Robotics. In his fictional stories, these three laws define what a robot can and cannot do when interacting with humans.

Similarly to these laws, the Android Open Source Project (AOSP) is guided by a set of ideals that define why Android exists, how Android will continue to develop, and the roles for all the stakeholders in the project. In this section, you get a brief summary of the ideas that formed Android into what it is today. Just like Azimov created three laws for his robots, in this chapter we summarize the ideals of AOSP into three laws; let's call them the Three Laws of Android.

> **NOTE** *If you're interested in getting more detailed information on the Android Open Source Project and the Open Handset Alliance you should explore these websites in more detail.* `http://source.android.com/about/index.html,` `www.openhandsetalliance.com/` *and* `http://developer.android` `.com/index.html.`

Law #1: Android Must Be Open and Free

The Android project was started back 2003 by a small company called Android, Inc., before the term smartphone was widely recognized by the average user as the device we think of today — a device with a large touchscreen, high-speed Internet connection, GPS, and other fun stuff.

The sole purpose of this company was to create a mobile phone jam-packed with different kinds of sensors that would allow the phone to sense its surroundings. In essence, the company wanted to create a smarter phone.

Some years later, in 2005, Google got involved (actually, Google bought the company and made it a wholly owned subsidiary of Google, as it does in so many cases), and two years after this acquisition (in 2007) the Open Handset Alliance (OHA), which curates the development of Android, was unveiled, sporting a total of 35 initial members. The OHA shared a common idea — the idea that openness improves innovation.

Another important concept of Android is the openness inside the system. Where other competing systems often restrict the capabilities of third-party applications and promote native applications, Android gives you the same freedom as the device manufacturers in developing for the systems.

The OHA has stated that the explicit goal of the Android system is to be the first open, complete, and free platform created specifically for mobile devices.

Law #2: Android Must Be Adaptable

Through this openness and freedom rises the next law of Android; because the system is free for anyone to use, Android must also be highly adaptable. Not adaptable in the sense that anyone can create their own version of the system, but adaptable in the sense that it must be capable of running on many kinds of devices and do it well.

This control of the project is called the Android Compatibility Program, which basically defines what it means for a device to be Android compatible. If a device doesn't comply with the requirements stated in the Android Compatibility Program, it can't take part of the shared ecosystem of Android.

> **NOTE** *You'll actually find Android in just about any type of embedded device. It's used in phones, in tablet computers, and inside TVs. It controls printers and the media system in your car. Heck, you can even find it inside microwave ovens! This means that soon you will be able to write your own app for a microwave oven that sends an image of your cooked meal to your phone when it's ready, and share the app with your friends! Cooked by Android, mmm... yummy!*

This Android ecosystem is the backbone of its great market success over the past years. Because so many devices run Android, the potential number of customers for application developers is far beyond that of other popular systems today.

Law #3: Android Must Be Simple

Because the ecosystem of Android is the backbone of its success, the OHA considers you, the developer, one of its most important assets. If you cannot create stunning and innovative applications for Android, the whole system will fail in competition with other systems.

This is why the alliance strongly believes in empowering the developer, shortening the time from your first app idea to your first market launch. Android achieves this through powerful development frameworks and tools that are both simple in their nature and powerful in their actions.

In addition to the simple frameworks and tools, Android is known for its good documentation and many complete and open-source examples of using the available libraries. If you'd like to know more about using a specific application programming interface (API), you can open the source of the example application through your favorite editor, or browse it online; and because the example applications are all licensed under a very permissive open source license called Apache version 2, you're allowed to use and build upon the example applications in your own commercial projects.

Also, because the Android SDK is built on Java you can often reuse a lot of code from projects you've been involved in before. However, when including code from normal Java projects you should remember that one of the big changes in Android compared to other systems running Java is the rendering. For example, code written using the Swing framework cannot be compiled for Android.

All of these reasons make Android one of the simplest ways of getting started in smartphone application development, even for the complete newcomer.

The Android Philosophy

The Three Laws of Android act as a foundation on which the Android Philosophy is formed — a philosophy that is influenced heavily by the concept called Open Innovation, a term coined by Henry Chesbrough in 2003.

He describes the traditional innovation process that formed most of today's powerful multinational corporations like IBM or General Electric as fortresses in an otherwise barren knowledge landscape.

These fortresses were created out of a necessity; because knowledge was hard to come by, large companies needed to invest heavily in research and development (R&D), an approach where they controlled the entire process of innovation from the very basic science to the finished product.

However, since then we've seen the knowledge landscape change drastically; more than 30 percent of the world's population is now connected to the Internet, workforce mobility has increased, and loyalty to our employers has decreased. This all points in one direction — the traditional R&D departments find themselves in a situation where they stand to lose large resources spent on innovations that someone else is working on as well.

Enter Open Innovation; this new knowledge landscape has seen the corporate giants work more with outside influences than before, either through consulting, the acquisition of new start-up companies, or even cooperation over company borders.

> **NOTE** *Eclipse, the most widely used integrated development environment (IDE) used for Android development, is another project heavily influenced by Open Innovation and Open Source ideas.*
>
> *Eclipse started as a project by IBM in the late nineties to develop a common platform for all IBM businesses, but because its partners weren't so enthusiastic about investing in the project, IBM decided to develop Eclipse under an Open Source license.*
>
> *The move to an Open Source license was well received by the developer community, but it was still an IBM project, and this made many potentially critical contributors reluctant to commit large resources to the project in the event that IBM would close the project again. This marked the beginning of the Eclipse Foundation, an entity separate from IBM with the sole purpose of developing the Eclipse ecosystem.*
>
> *At the time of writing this book, the Eclipse Foundation sported a total of 186 members, which makes it one of the most successful projects based on Open Innovation and Open Source to this day.*

The Open Handset Alliance, and all of its members, sees the idea of Open Innovation as a critical new business model where sharing the risks and the rewards across company borders allows for much faster and broader innovation, and in turn also renders a better experience for the user.

Other Popular Systems

When reviewing the Android system it would be good to compare it to other competing systems to get a better understanding of its place in the market. This section outlines the differences between Android and its most popular competitors, with a focus on developing accessories.

iOS

Based on the system found in other common Apple computer products, such as Mac Book, iOS is the version enhanced for Apple's handheld devices like the iPhone, iPod, and iPad. Although it wasn't the first smartphone system widely available, it was arguably one of the pioneering devices that shaped today's smartphone market.

iOS is built as a proprietary, not licensable, system; this means that only Apple may develop and deploy it. Third-party developers require special developer licenses to create native applications for it and the screening process for an application is also extensive, going as far as the general concept of the application.

Since iOS version 3.0 there is support for external accessories through the External Accessory (EA) framework. However, much like many of Apple's products, developing an accessory is a daunting task that requires approval and often a serious investment by the developer. While this filtering ensures a high-quality product and a style that conforms to Apples ideals with a high finish, this severely limits the possibility of exploration of the field by hobbyists.

Windows Phone

Not to be confused with its predecessor Windows Mobile, Windows Phone is a completely new operating system by Microsoft released in 2010. Notably, the biggest difference is the new user interface developed for the system.

Windows Phone is also a proprietary system owned and developed by Microsoft; however, it can be licensed to device manufacturers for deployment on their handsets — something that made a big buzz in the industry in 2011 when Nokia announced its plans to adopt Windows Phone as its principle smartphone strategy.

As a developer you'll need to acquire a developer license to develop and publish applications for Windows Phone; and the applications also need to pass a validation and certification process by Microsoft. Unfortunately there's no official APIs available to develop external accessories yet, but with the efforts put into the Windows Phone system we can only assume that there will be a framework in the future for connecting your Windows Phone to your environment.

BlackBerry

Developed by Research in Motion, the BlackBerry devices saw great success in the beginning of this millennium because of the emphasis placed on communication. They were among the first mobile devices to focus on e-mail and push notifications on mobile devices, and this has become their signature feature over the years. And there is support for accessories since BlackBerry version 7.0.0.

The BlackBerry operating system is proprietary and non-licensable just like iOS, meaning that only Research in Motion will develop devices with it installed. Developing for BlackBerry is free, however, selling applications on App World requires a vendor license; any applications that are published must also pass a review before they're accepted.

Symbian

With market shares of around 70 percent at its peak, Symbian was the most widespread operating system used for mobile devices; however, it has seen a steady decline over the past few years because of its failure to deliver a compelling user experience in competition with iPhone and Android.

Symbian, in comparison to iPhone and Android, has been deployed mostly on the older-style feature phone, even though it later released an updated smartphone version with all the traditional features you would expect. For the older-style phone, you developed Java Micro Edition programs that would run on top of the Symbian system, which is very different from how Android apps run.

The Symbian system was developed mainly by Nokia until 2011 when the switch with Windows Phone took place; since then the consulting firm Accenture has been charge of the development and maintenance of the Symbian system. Since 2010 the Symbian system has been published under the Eclipse Public License (EPL), this transition was also reported as the largest move from proprietary to Open Source in history.

Preinstalled Applications

Most devices come with a set of preinstalled applications suitable for users new to smartphones. Other mobile operating systems often protect these native applications and hinder any third-party application from taking over. But in Android, you're free to develop an application to replace any existing preinstalled app.

The preinstalled applications include, but are not limited to:

➤ Web browser

➤ E-mail client

➤ Phone

➤ Contacts book

➤ Notepad

➤ Play Store

➤ Camera

➤ Clock

➤ Google Maps

Of course, these applications vary from one device to another; often you'll see some manufacturers providing their own version of any of these applications that they perhaps feel is improved in some fashion or specifically tailored to the look and feel of that specific device.

about the quality of the air in a room, you could use an Arduino Ethernet board connected to a public IP number.

For the purpose of this book, we are going to use the Arduino Mega ADK and the Arduino Due boards as our microcontroller boards. Both boards allow connecting USB devices to the board. In our case we will connect Android devices (phones and tablets) to the circuit. Those boards bring in the possibility of controlling physical objects from a phone or reading a biometric sensor and sending the data to the phone for storage.

Besides the microcontroller boards, you will find the so-called Arduino Shields. The shields are boards to be stacked on top of the Arduino board, offering some more specific functionality. You can find very simple ones including a couple of potentiometers and some buttons, to ones that offer a GPS, gyroscope, and GPRS connectivity.

> **NOTE** *Shields work with almost any kind of Arduino board, but beware that some Arduino boards are developed for specific purposes and because of this the Shields may not fit these boards.*

There is a whole world of possible shields for Arduino out there. They are manufactured by multiple vendors in just about every country in the world. This is also one of the strengths of the Open Source model — because all the software is open, it is possible for anyone to create new hardware add-ons and write drivers for them to run on the Arduino board as libraries.

HOW DOES AOA WORK WITH ARDUINO?

AOA includes a set of libraries that allow bidirectional communication between Android devices and Arduino boards. Arduino boards use the USB port as a way to communicate to computers. It is possible to make a board be listed as USB keyboard or mouse. You can even find examples on how to turn your Arduino board into a USB MIDI device.

> **NOTE** *MIDI stands for Musical Instrument Digital Interface. It's a specification that allows different devices — mainly musical instruments — to connect to one another. In short it is a special modification of a serial port working at 31.250 bps with a set of rules for how to encode different controls and sound actuators.*
>
> *Physically, the different devices connect through 5-pin DIN connectors. It is only since the 2000s that MIDI-to-USB converters have allowed interfacing these devices with state-of-the-art laptop computers. Recently, many of the MIDI instruments implement MIDI over USB and have removed the DIN connectors. Arduino Uno, Mega and Mega ADK can be reprogrammed to become native MIDI over USB devices. You can read more about it at:* `www.arduino.cc/en/Hacking/MidiWith8U2Firmware`.

Some Android devices allow connecting keyboards, mice, and so on, and it should be possible to connect your Arduino board to, for example, your Android tablet that way. Technically, Android devices are computers running a derivative of the Linux operating system. Conceptually, for the final user, tablets and phones aren't computers, or if they are, they cover a different need and therefore they aren't perceived as such.

For this reason, Google introduced the idea of accessories as devices that can be connected to Android devices to enhance their functionality in a slightly different way to how a mouse relates to a PC. At low level, the PC is a USB hub, whereas the mouse acts as USB client. The Android accessory is a USB hub and the phone/tablet is the client.

This makes sense from a conceptual point of view for many reasons. Consider, for example, that you buy an accessory to measure your blood pressure. This is not very far from the kinds of products we are going to see coming to the market soon. Once you get it, you need an application to get it to work. What the accessories do is to inform the phone about the name of the artifact, the manufacturer, the software version, the name of the application, and, most importantly, the URL where you can download the application directly into your phone. You will not need to make a search in the Google Play; the accessory can tell your phone where to search for the app without having to type anything.

In this book we explore the connectivity via a USB cable between your Arduino board and your phone. On the Arduino ADK side there is a library that controls the USB Host functionality. This allows detecting when an Arduino board was connected to your phone. It also allows for sending and receiving data between the two devices. On top of that host functionality there is yet another layer that tells the phone exactly which app should be launched when connecting the accessory, who manufactured it, and the version number. This is the information the phone will use to decide what to launch when and when to launch it.

It is also possible to create Android accessories that work over Bluetooth. You should, however, not confuse a Bluetooth accessory with a USB accessory. Except for the obvious differences in hardware layer, the Bluetooth accessory works with the common Bluetooth API available since Android SDK 5.

WHAT CAN YOU DO WITH AOA?

It is possible to design accessories that will read data from the environment using sensors not included in your Android device, such pulse-rate monitors, air pressure sensors, gyroscopes, or pyroelectric gas detectors.

You can use actuators like servo motors, solenoids, peltier cells, steppers, or piezo-elements. You can build robots using the phone to control them, or you can unlock your apartment door from a distance by sending a text message.

If you want to hook up your phone to control a wireless sensor network communicating over ZigBee, you can use AOA to proxy your communication through an ADK board with a wireless shield on it.

> **NOTE** *ZigBee is a specification for a series of protocols using low-power digital radios. It is intended for personal area networks like a heartbeat sensor communicating with your phone or a wireless temperature sensor to be installed on your balcony.*
>
> *ZigBee devices define mesh networks to transmit data over longer distances. ZigBee networks use intermediate devices to reach more distant ones.*
>
> *ZigBee runs in the same piece of the spectrum as Wi-Fi and Bluetooth. Comparing the features of the three of them, you could conclude that:*
>
> ➤ *Wi-Fi is used for high-speed data transfers like browsing a video archive, where many devices connect simultaneously.*
>
> ➤ *Bluetooth is a one-to-one cable replacement. The latest standard, version 4, allows for very low-power radios, which makes it very suitable for small personal area networks.*
>
> ➤ *ZigBee is used for mid-size networks with low bandwidth requirements and high reconfiguration needs like wirelessly monitoring livestock.*
>
> *You can read more about ZigBee at:* `www.zigbee.org`.

The possibilities are endless, but you want to concentrate on choosing projects that will allow you to learn at the right pace. Therefore, we have selected a series of projects that gradually increase in complexity.

We start with small tasks like reading a temperature sensor and gradually move into controlling motors to then integrate them with distance sensors, adding more intelligence to the system.

In short, AOA allows you to:

➤ Connect external sensors to your Android

➤ Control the world through actuators

➤ Debug your apps from your development environment

WHAT CAN'T YOU DO WITH AOA?

You should avoid building devices that deal with monitoring human constants under critical situations. The tools presented here are not suitable, without the proper level of expertise from your side, to monitor a machine connected to your body. You should take into account that the systems used in this book are not reliable under special circumstances. Neither the Arduino Mega ADK, nor any of the Android phones and tablets presented here were designed to be used in rough environments (like at too high temperatures or under water). The AOA protocol running on top of those systems is a simple communication protocol, not robust enough for those conditions either.

WHY IT MATTERS THAT GOOGLE CHOSE ARDUINO

Open Hardware establishes that individuals, institutions, and companies should have a similar set of rights to create, publish, and share hardware designs as they can within the Open Source/Free Software movements. The big difference is that Open Hardware refers to physical goods, whether circuit boards, chairs, or mechanical parts.

When talking about circuit boards, the Open Hardware movement has been around for a while. Since the first computer clubs in the '80s, people were sharing board designs and firmware. It is the development of computers as a business that brought patents into the game of hardware that affected the way it was used in some fields like education.

The following quote is taken from the OpenSparc project (see www.openspark.net). It represents the understanding of what Open Hardware was meant to be for many until the mid-2000s. Institutions, companies, and other hardware-interested bodies thought that it could be open from the point of view that Field Programmable Gate Arrays (FPGAs) and other chips would represent the configuration of their logical gates in the form of source code. In other words, Open Hardware was perceived as an evolution of open source code, but not as something that would refer to the actual physical object.

> *Small amounts of computer hardware Intellectual Property (IP) have been available for many years in open-source form, typically as circuit descriptions written in an RTL (Register Transfer Level) language such as Verilog or VHDL. However, until now, few large hardware designs have been available in open-source form.*

When Arduino showed up in 2005, it was presented as a piece of Open Hardware. Back then, the Arduino website invited people to download and use the reference design of the board to produce derivatives and learn about hardware by building it themselves. Due to a series of online debates, the Arduino Team (the core group of Arduino designers and maintainers of the project), realized that there was no legal way to protect physical objects like circuit boards. The decision was made to use a Creative Commons (CC) license to protect the digital file or the blueprint that was needed to manufacture the boards.

From a legal point of view, there is no difference between the file or illustration that shows the circuit design and a poem or a musical score. And if the latter could be protected with CC licenses, the boards could as well.

The Arduino CC license allows other designers, educators, and users in general to take the reference design, modify it, manufacture boards, and sell them as long as they respect the Arduino name, which is a trademark registered by the Arduino Team. These terms are very simple and flexible. When taking the reference design to make your own, you just need to credit the initial design team, but you don't need to pay anything, nor do you need to tell them in person.

In May 2011, Google's Accessory Design team came to the point when they needed to exemplify how people could create new accessories for the Android operating system, and Arduino's hardware license made their purpose very simple. Google could take one of the Arduino reference designs (in this case the Arduino Mega) and merge it together with yet another Open Hardware piece, the USB

Host shield by a company called Circuits@home (`www.circuitsathome.com`) to make their Google ADK board.

It is actually an important milestone in the history of Open Hardware because it showed how big corporations could actually become players in the community and contribute back. Google's design was also open and licensed under the same parameters as the original Arduino board; this allowed many taking this new blueprint to use it as a starting point for their work.

In parallel to these series of events, a group of makers and companies had been meeting up in New York since 2010, putting together the Open Source Hardware Definition (see `http://freedomde fined.org/OSHW`) as an attempt to make a declaration of intentions on what Open Hardware should be. A couple of months after Google's announcement, the CERN institute in Switzerland announced the first Open Source Hardware License (see `http://ohwr.org/cernohl`) as a first attempt to produce a legal framework for people to protect hardware in an alternative way.

The Open Hardware culture is a movement growing from the bottom up that is involving entities coming from all countries across the world and that tries to protect designers and makers so that their creations can be made available for others to use. This has a huge impact, especially in fields where cost is an important factor, like education or technological deployment in humanitarian scenarios.

SUMMARY

Android is an operating system developed mainly for use in smartphones, but you can find it in other devices as well such as printers. The way Android is developed and maintained is one of the reasons for this wide range of applications, and it's also one of the main reasons it has excelled on the smartphone marked in the past few years when many proprietary systems are struggling.

Another reason for Android's success is its familiarity; the tools used to develop software are already widespread in industry, education and among hobbyists. Both Android and Arduino rely heavily on Open Source, Open Hardware, and Open Innovation models and thriving communities to develop and maintain.

Qualities of each of these models are leveraged when creating Android accessories, and in time we will hopefully see that the market for accessories will skyrocket because of this.

You also learned some key differences between the Android ecosystem and other popular mobile ecosystems. Where the others often hinder some stakeholders, Android delivers:

- ➤ Freedom for device manufacturers
- ➤ Freedom for application developers
- ➤ And, most importantly, freedom for the user

Hopefully, you will soon start to feel like an integral part of a community that drives the development of smartphone accessories forward... to the future!

2

Setting up the (Arduino) Hardware

WHAT'S IN THIS CHAPTER?

➤ Introducing sensor technology

➤ Using actuators, motors, LEDs

➤ Working with platforms and architectures

➤ Powering up your projects

➤ Using Arduino ADK versus Google ADK boards

➤ Working with add-on boards: shields

This chapter deals with choosing the right physical tools for developing a project. Whether you want to measure the temperature in a room or build a robot, you always have things to take into account. You need to consider what it is you want to monitor, the size of the prototype, or the computing power you need.

You have probably heard the statement that everything is a computer nowadays. The use of microcontrollers responds to the paradigm of so-called ubiquitous computing. Computers are everywhere: the average car has 70 processors, your microwave has one, and your cellphone has a couple of them. You can find general-purpose processors that can be reprogrammed into making almost anything. You can also find purpose-specific processors, aimed at solving a certain type of issue such as USB-serial conversion, decoding MP3 sound files, or controlling the movement of a motor.

In this chapter, you learn about sensor technology. Microcontrollers are just the intelligence of your embedded project. To gather data about the world, you need devices that translate real-world data into digital information. *Sensors* are the interfaces that translate properties of the world such as temperature, acceleration, or intensity of light. These are then translated into a voltage to be read by the microcontroller.

You are also introduced to the concept of an *actuator*. In the same fashion that sensors help in reading the world, actuators "write" to the world. Motors and speakers are probably the most common actuators. Both transform electrical impulses into mechanical movements.

Finally, this chapter discusses the issues with powering up your project: will you make something that runs on batteries or from a power socket? Dealing with power, battery charging, and similar issues is always complex. A full examination of the various options is not within the scope of this book; however, we describe the options for you and suggest an easy way to solve most of your prototypes quickly.

CHOOSING MICROCONTROLLER BOARDS FOR YOUR PROJECT

This book explores the connection between one type of microcontroller ecosystem (Arduino) and the Android operating system for mobile devices. To start with, Arduino is just a microcontroller that can run software made in C. Even if it is possible, Arduino doesn't run an operating system. To keep the system simple, it runs sequential programs performing commands one by one. In contrast, Android is a whole operating system that can run on phones and tablets using many different vendors. An Android device has one or more microcontrollers and runs multiple processes in parallel.

You can find many types of microcontrollers from several different vendors in the market. Don't get confused between the microcontroller platform and the microcontroller itself. Microcontrollers are the chips, the black boxes on the circuits. Platforms are the ecosystem integrated by the microcontroller — its circuit, the programming environment, and the documentation.

In that way, some platforms depend very much on the processor's architecture, whereas others can be implemented on technology from many different vendors. Arduino has been designed to run on different architectures. The API used to program the microcontrollers has been translated into processors coming from a whole series of vendors. Because you learn how to use Arduino boards in this book, we show only a quick analysis of the official Google ADK boards, which are fully compatible Arduino boards.

When you want to add features to your project quickly, instead of building all the parts for it on a breadboard, you can use pre-assembled add-on boards. In the Arduino world, these pre-assembled boards are called *shields*. A few examples of shields that might be of interest to you are described later.

One Platform, Many Architectures

Arduino is a software abstraction that you can apply to many different architectures. You can move the same software seamlessly between boards in an upwards-compatible way. Some of the newest programs might contain features that cannot run on older boards. Different manufacturers (Atmel, Freescale, ST, Microchip, Texas Instruments) are making microcontrollers. Those chips have to be integrated into platforms for people to use them. Those same vendors produce prototyping platforms for engineers to try out the chips and decide whether or not those processors could be used as part of a project.

> **NOTE** *At the time of writing this book, the Arduino project was producing boards using one single manufacturer: Atmel. The platforms made by Arduino made use of two different chip architectures. Some of the boards ran on 8-bit microcontrollers from the ATmega family, whereas the most recent ones ran on 32-bit microcontrollers with ARM Cortex-M3 cores.*

Arduino is an external actor that can use any of those manufacturers to create prototyping boards. One of the main goals when learning about digital technology through Arduino is that it should be easy to use. That ease of use is achieved through a simplified IDE and curated documentation available online. Figure 2-1 shows the Arduino IDE running on a Mac computer. The IDE is cross-platform and can run on Windows, Linux and Mac computers. The code should compile the same way and the board should behave identically.

From an engineering point of view, you would analyze how to solve a project from the technical features in a brief. You would then choose the right microcontroller and IDE to program it.

Choosing a platform like Arduino enables you to start your project with one tool and, if that doesn't completely fulfill your needs in terms of available inputs/outputs, size, or speed, you could move into using a different platform without changing your code. It also enables you to go the other way around: You could start with your most powerful platform and once you are done, trim the project down to make it fit in as small a form factor as you need.

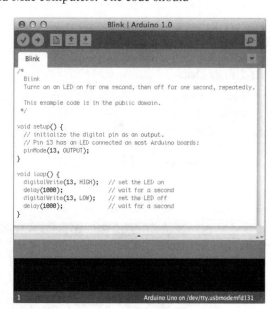

FIGURE 2-1: Arduino IDE v1.0.1 on Mac OSX

Prototyping is an art that you learn by experience. It is very hard to predict everything you need to take into account before you start a project. In many cases, you might get overwhelmed by trying to anticipate everything that could happen. We have seen many projects die prematurely during this initial planning phase. We would recommend you get started building and tinkering and then move between tools as your project evolves. Once you have made a couple of prototypes, you will have a much better understanding of what is possible with each board and you will gradually get better at predicting what you need in each case.

The following sections, as shown in Table 2-1, give an overview of different prototyping boards and examples of using each one. Also, keep in mind that the Arduino boards are open-source hardware, which means that it should be possible to find platform vendors making Arduino-compatible boards with similar or equal functionality to the ones mentioned here.

TABLE 2-1: Comparing the Boards Mentioned in this Chapter

BOARD	ARCHITECTURE	DIGITAL I/O	ANALOG I/O	ADK FUNCTIONALITY	SERIAL PORTS
Arduino Uno	8-bits	14 pins	6 analog inputs, 6 digital pins do PWM	No	1
Arduino Mega ADK	8-bits	54 pins	16 analog inputs, 16 digital pins do PWM	Yes	4
Arduino Due	32-bits	54 pins	12 analog inputs, 12 digital pins do PWM, 2 pins from DAC	Yes	4
Arduino Micro ADK	8-bits	11 pins	6 analog inputs, 6 digital pins do PWM	Yes	1
Google ADK	Arduino Mega ADK compatible				
Google ADK2	Arduino Due compatible				

Arduino Uno

This is the most extended board from the Arduino family. The board carries an 8-bit microcontroller, and it comes with 14 digital input/output pins and 6 analog inputs. Six of the digital pins can be programmed to send pulse width modulation (PWM). The Uno board also comes with internal peripherals able of running the UART, SPI, and I2C communication protocols. Programs using the Arduino Uno board (Figure 2-2) can be as big as 30 Kbytes and run at 16 MHz.

FIGURE 2-2: Arduino Uno board

As you can see, Arduino Uno is a very versatile board that has become the Swiss army knife of the maker community. In literally five minutes you can plug this board into your computer and start programming it. It has a disadvantage, though: You cannot use it to communicate directly with an Android device, because it lacks the USB Host functionality. However, shields are available that can bring the USB Host functionality to the board, as well as some that could add Bluetooth communication. Both methods allow the microcontroller to talk to Android devices.

Arduino Mega ADK

The most extended of all the prototyping boards that can communicate with Android phones is probably the Arduino Mega ADK. This board, shown in Figure 2-3, includes all the functionality of an Arduino Mega 2560 board plus the USB Host. The Arduino Mega 2560, and derivatives, includes a chip with 252 KB of available memory space, 54 digital input/output pins (of which 16 can use PWM), 16 analog inputs, and 4 serial ports (UART). It is very convenient for projects that use sensors to communicate over serial (UART) or systems that require reading many inputs. Like its smaller brother (the Uno) also works at 16 MHz and uses an 8-bit processor.

FIGURE 2-3: Arduino Mega ADK board

As mentioned, the Mega ADK adds to that the USB Host functionality. This means that you can connect a USB device through an on-board female USB connector. It is, of course, possible to connect other USB devices to the board such as Bluetooth dongles, keyboards, or USB drives, but we are not going to explore those possibilities as part of this book. However, you can find multiple examples online on that regard.

Arduino Due

Arduino Due (Figure 2-4) is the first board within the Arduino family to leave the 8-bit realm. It runs an ARM core type Cortex-M3 with 32-bit, internal Digital Signal Processor (DSP), a 12-bit Digital to Analog Converter (DAC), UART, SPI, I2C, and other peripherals. Probably the most interesting of all its capabilities when it comes to the AOA is that the microcontroller has an internal USB OTG (On The Go) peripheral. This is what is used to connect to USB devices either as a host or as a client. In other words, the chip includes the possibility to connect to the Android phone directly.

FIGURE 2-4: Arduino Due board

However, from a programming perspective, the experience is going to be the same as using the Arduino Mega ADK. The same code that runs in one of the boards should run on the other, except for those cases when you might be using some of the extended features from the ARM core like DSP or internal DAC.

Arduino Micro ADK

Probably the only reason to not use any of the previously mentioned boards is their form factor. Both the Arduino Due and the Arduino Mega ADK have the same shape and size (5.33 × 10.16 cm or 2.1 × 4 inch). The Arduino Uno is shorter (6.85 cm or 2.7 inch), but in turn, you need to add the USB Host shield on top of it to achieve the desired functionality. Any of the combinations are optimal in terms of the prototyping experience. They have enough ports and pins to accommodate almost any project you could envision. But when you want to pack your project in a small form factor, you need to rethink how to put things together.

This is where the Arduino Micro ADK board (Figure 2-5) comes in. Its smaller form factor (2.3 × 6.85 cm or 0.9 × 2.7 inch) makes it perfect for many projects. It offers fewer pins and you need to power it up from a battery, but for wearable projects or those where you just want to control a couple of motors and hide everything in a small box, this might be the best tool for you. It also has some really nice features the other boards don't have. Its programming port can transform the board into a computer keyboard or a mouse. You could imagine making an app that would type SMS messages in your computer, or execute certain actions using the command line.

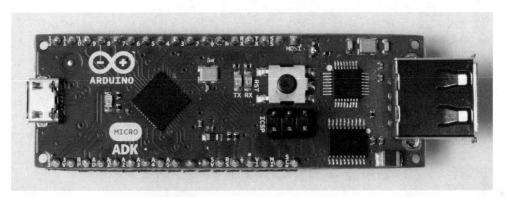

FIGURE 2-5: Arduino Micro ADK board

Arduino ADK vs. Google ADK Boards

Google's official ADK boards (the ADK from 2011 and the ADK2 from 2012) are proofs of concept presented by Google. The company from Mountain View is not interested in manufacturing and selling these platforms — it wants developers to get excited about making accessories for Android devices and therefore make reference designs available for others to take over and bring to the market.

The Google ADK (shown in Figure 2-6) is a development kit presented by Google at its annual conference in May 2011. It is made of two parts:

➤ An Arduino Mega-compatible board that was made by adding a chip with USB Host functionality to the Arduino Mega reference design.

➤ A shield with a series of buttons, LEDs, a touch sensor shaped like the Android OS robot logotype, and a couple of relays to interact with the physical world.

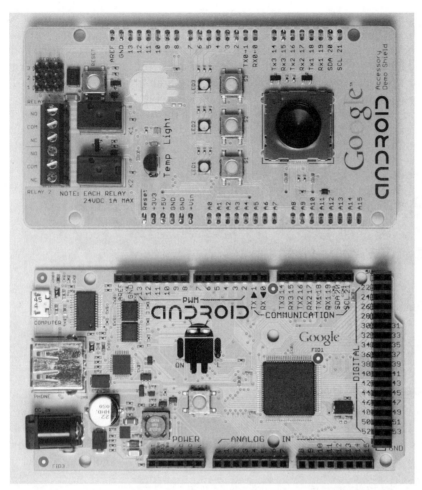

FIGURE 2-6: Google ADK board

> **NOTE** *The first experiments in using USB Host functionality with Arduino boards were made by Oleg Mazurov, who created the USB Host shield for Arduino and wrote the first USB Host library to control it from an Arduino Uno board.*
>
> *For creating the Google ADK, the engineers at Google merged the design of the Arduino Mega 2560 board with Oleg's USB Host shield into one single board.*
>
> *If you want to read more about this shield, visit* www.circuitsathome.com/.

These boards were made in white with a multicolored silkprint showing Google's logotype. The whole kit came in a white cylindrical package. About 1,000 people listened to Google's live official presentation and left the building with one of these boards. If you happen to have one, you should consider yourself lucky because it is a collector's piece and not even the authors of this book own one!

The development kit was made as a one-run production and was priced quite high. Arduino ADK is fully compatible with this system and can be easily obtained from more than 200 distributors around the world.

> **NOTE** *If you are interested in looking for vendors of Google ADK-compatible hardware, visit* http://developer.android.com/tools/adk/adk.html.

On the other hand, the Google ADK2 (shown in Figure 2-7) is an evolution of the previous development kit, and was presented in San Francisco's Google IO of 2012. It is again made of two parts:

➤ An Arduino Due-compatible board with the extra feature of a Bluetooth series 4 chip, which enables you to make wireless accessories and a MicroSD card socket.

➤ A shield with a series of LEDs, inputs, and sound amplifier. It is shaped like a trapezoid.

FIGURE 2-7: Google ADK2 board

This time, Google's design team went for blue (for the microcontroller board) and dark blue (for the shield).

> **NOTE** *As of August 2012 there were no vendors of Google ADK2-compatible hardware. The only board with ADK2 capabilities available was the Arduino Due.*

Shields

Shields are boards put on top of the Arduino board. They enhance the platform's basic functionality by bringing in extra peripherals and sensors. Many shields come with libraries specifically made for them.

> **NOTE** *Arduino's name honors a king named Arduin who lived in Ivrea at the beginning of the eleventh century. Therefore, the term "shield" was chosen to "protect" the king.*

Many different shields are available. Arduino is an open platform, which allows makers and manufacturers to produce their own add-ons to the platform at no fee. You can find specific shields for almost any application out there: controlling motors, reading Real Time Clock (RTC) chips, storing data in SD cards, and so on.

The following sections describe some examples of shields that might be of interest to you. However, keep in mind that the TinkerKit shield is the only one really needed for the examples in this book.

TinkerKit Breakout Shield

For many of the examples in the book, we have chosen to use the TinkerKit breakout shield (Figure 2-8). It consists of a shield that maps the available pins on the Arduino Mega ADK board in a different way. It unfolds all the pins on single molex connectors with independent power and ground for each. This is useful when you want (or are looking for) a mechanically safe way to connect things to your board.

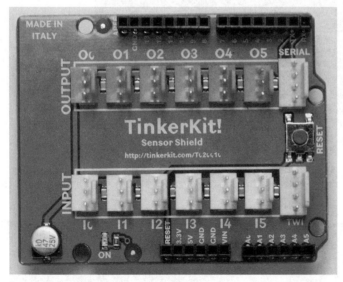

FIGURE 2-8: TinkerKit breakout shield

At the other end, the sensors and actuators (Figure 2-9) that can be used with the TinkerKit shield offer the same types of connectors. You are not required to use this shield or the other tools to complete the examples in this book — you can build all the examples on a breadboard with discrete components. It just takes a little longer.

FIGURE 2-9: Examples of TinkerKit components

USB-Host Shield

The USB Host Shield (Figure 2-10) is a breakout board for the MAX-3421, a chip that can handle the USB protocol to connect any kind of USB device. You can connect a keyboard, mouse, Bluetooth dongle, a 3G modem, or any other USB client and control it from an Arduino Uno or Arduino Mega

2560. The Arduino Mega ADK has this very same chip on board, which renders this shield unnecessary in that case.

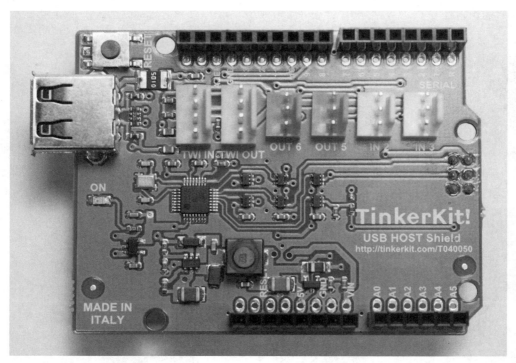

FIGURE 2-10: USB-Host Shield

Remember that, on top of the shield, you will need to install some libraries to make it work. The code to control the MAX-3421 doesn't come by default with the Arduino IDE.

Motor Shield

Many of the projects coming to life focus on making objects move. Many different types of motors exist and each type requires its own way for driving it. A good approach to control both DC and stepper motors is the Arduino Motor shield, shown in Figure 2-11. With it you can either use four solenoids, or control the speed and direction of two DC motors or one stepper as well as measure the motors' feedback current (a feature broadly used in robotics).

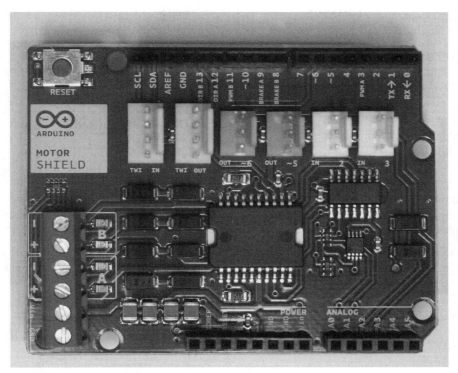

FIGURE 2-11: Arduino Motor shield

In the figure you can also see the characteristic TinkerKit connectors. Moving objects require better ways to secure the sensors, and having these types of connectors will only make things easier.

> **NOTE** *The robotics examples in the book do not use this motor shield, nor any other shield dealing with motors. They use a type of motor called servo motors. You can read more about them in the "Actuators" section later in this chapter. We included this shield here for you to get an overview of which kinds of things can be connected to an Arduino board.*

CHOOSING SENSORS AND ACTUATORS FOR YOUR PROJECT

Do you know where to get parts for your project? Can you just reuse those parts you have in your toolbox?

These are the questions that you will be asking yourself at the beginning of every project. We strongly advise you take the approach of thinking about what is it you want to measure and what is it you want to control. For example, imagine you want to measure "presence." That is a very abstract concept — you first need to determine in which context you want to detect that presence: is it a person in a room, or a person in front of a place, or someone touching an object? These three situations translate in human language into detecting presence, but require completely different sensors.

In addition, when measuring something from the environment, you need to know the kind of precision you can expect from the measurement. Do your sensors need to be expensive in order to give a good response for your project?

Next, we describe some scenarios to help you understand how to approach getting sensors and actuators to build your projects. We have chosen these cases because we think they will give you a good overview about the way we approach making projects.

Sensors

Sensors are electronic components and devices that collect data from the physical world and translate it into electronic impulses or electricity values. With them, you can measure the temperature in a room, the amount of light outdoors, the distance to an object, and so on.

We have chosen two cases to exemplify which kinds of sensors to choose depending on the situation. These are discussed in detail in the following sections:

➤ Detecting presence

➤ Measuring temperature

Detecting Presence

Detecting the presence of a person in a room requires using a sensor that can read whether there is a human being in front of it, up to a certain distance. You can detect presence in many ways, depending on the specifics of the case. The following sections analyze some cases considering different tools.

Passive Infrared Sensors (PIR)

The typical way of detecting presence consists of using a *Passive Infrared Sensor* (PIR), shown in Figure 2-12. These devices measure the amount of infrared light in a room and trigger an event when there is a sudden change in the amount of infrared they detect. These sensors are used everywhere to trigger alarms in buildings or to control whether the light in a room should be on because someone is in there.

The fact that the temperature of the human body is higher than the temperature in a room provokes a heat transfer between the skin and the air. Like anything in nature, heat transfers translate into infrared light transmissions. In other words, the body emits infrared light. This light, which is invisible to our eyes, can be captured by the PIR sensor.

FIGURE 2-12: PIR sensor

PIR sensors cannot tell you the distance the person is from them, nor whether there is more than one person moving at the same time. You should read them as "there is activity in front of me." Thanks to cleverly designed lenses, the PIR sensors can cover very large rooms. Typically, you need only one sensor for a room as big as 100m².

Ultrasound Sensors

On the other hand, imagine a room full of people moving around. How can you detect whether someone is at a specific location? You could use, among other things, an ultrasound sensor (shown in Figure 2-13).

FIGURE 2-13: Ultrasound sensor

Ultrasound is a high-frequency sound. It operates at frequencies beyond the audible range of, for example, 40 KHz. Some animals can hear these kinds of sound beams, so don't be surprised if your dog gets annoyed while you are trying out one of these sensors!

There is a difference in the way infrared and ultrasound sensors work. The former check only the amount of infrared light — therefore, they are called passive. The latter first send a burst of ultrasound and then listen to the echo of the signal after bouncing onto objects.

This technique is very similar to the sonar in submarines, the radar at airports, or the way bats detect obstacles while flying. It gives you precise information about the distance of the object in front of you. Ultrasound is very accurate, but at the same time it has a very reduced coverage area — you need to stand exactly in front of the sensor for it to detect your presence.

Sensing Temperature: Different Tools, Same Goal

Different technologies enable you to map variables from the environment to determine whether something is happening. It is up to you to decide which degree of accuracy you need as offered by each one of the available methods. Also, usually the relationship between accuracy and price tends to be a deciding factor when you are about to build your project. You will have to decide which tools better accommodate your plans each time.

You have many ways to measure the temperature in the environment. This section focuses on three sensors that are easily accessible, because you can purchase them at many different places:

➤ Thermistors (thermal resistors)

➤ Voltage temperature sensors

➤ Infrared temperature sensors

Besides a clear difference in price among the three types of sensors (thermistors are the cheapest ones and infrared are the most expensive), there is a clear difference in precision and speed.

Thermistors

As you know, resistors are components that transform electricity into heat; the higher the resistance value, the bigger the transfer the component can handle for a fixed amount of voltage. Thermistors (Figure 2-14) operate the opposite way around: They change their resistance value depending on the temperature. When placed as part of a voltage divider circuit, the thermistors can be used to measure the temperature. The response time in the thermistor is low, which makes it unsuitable for many situations.

FIGURE 2-14: Thermistor

Voltage Temperature Sensors

In Chapter 4, you see an example of using a silicon-based temperature sensor, also known as a voltage temperature sensor (Figure 2-15). The TMP36 from Analog Devices is the chip we are using. The best way to describe this sensor is to quote its datasheet (www.analog.com/static/imported-files/data_sheets/TMP35_36_37.pdf):

FIGURE 2-15: Voltage temperature sensor

The TMP35/TMP36/TMP37 are low voltage, precision centigrade temperature sensors. They provide a voltage output that is linearly proportional to the Celsius (centigrade) temperature. The TMP35/TMP36/TMP37 do not require any external calibration to provide typical accuracies of ±1°C at +25°C and ±2°C over the −40°C to +125°C temperature range. In Fahrenheit that translates to roughly ±1.8°F at temperatures above 77°F, and ±3.6°F at temperatures in the −40°F to 257°F range.

Datasheets are the technical documents that describe a certain component and they can be a little obscure at first. They describe and praise the goods of electronic components, but are written in a language not meant for the average Joe.

The quote describes three sensors that have similar characteristics. The important feature, when it comes to prototyping, is that they can provide ±1°C accuracy without any calibration. You can test one of these sensors empirically and you will see that they are very responsive (between 3 and 6°C/sec); which translates to between 5.4°F and 10.8°F/sec.

You read them by plugging them into an analog input on your Arduino board without any external components. The main difference between the three sensor types in the series resides in the temperature ranges in which they operate. The TMP36 works in the extended range of between −40°C and +125°C; which in Fahrenheit is −40°F to 257°F.

Infrared Temperature Sensors

Still within the affordable options, but giving a much more accurate series of measurements, are infrared temperature (IR) sensors.

Unlike the thermistors and the voltage temperature sensors, which operate best by touching the surface of the materials whose temperature you are measuring, infrared sensors operate at a certain distance. Yet another difference is that these sensors carry their own intelligence. Figure 2-16 shows an IR capsule that comes with a 17-bit analog-to-digital converter (ADC), which can reach an accuracy of one-tenth of 1°C (roughly translated that's one-tenth of 1.8°F).

FIGURE 2-16: Infrared temperature sensor

IR sensors have two different operation modes. On the one hand, they can serve your microcontroller the data as a PWM signal, which could be filtered using a capacitor into an easy-to-read analog value. However, that would be a waste in accuracy; so therefore, this sensor type also enables you to connect to it via a two-wire communication channel. This allows accessing the sensor's memory directly, getting the value straight from the ADC over a serial connection into the microprocessor.

Actuators

Actuators are components and devices that can transform electricity into light, movement, heat, or any other physical manifestation of energy — for example, lamps, motors, pelzier cells (devices that can change temperature when you apply a current), solenoids, and so on.

As with sensors, how you plan to use your actuator determines which one you choose. This section looks into two cases:

➤   Choosing light for a project

➤   Deciding on a motor type to build a robot

Light

Nowadays, many of the lighting projects you can think of can be solved using light-emitting diodes (LEDs), a variety of which are shown in Figure 2-17. They are available in many form factors as well as ranging from very little to very high power consumption. Usually, power consumption in LEDs represents the amount of light they can generate. LEDs are very efficient in energy transferring — you could say that almost all the power they dissipate is light. That doesn't happen at all with incandescent lamps, which instead transmit a lot of heat.

FIGURE 2-17: Different types of LEDs

One of the nicest things about LEDs is that once you build the control logic for a simple LED, you can easily scale it up by either adding more LEDs or exchanging them for more powerful ones. As long as your power circuitry can carry the amount of current needed for the LEDs to light, the system will allow you to scale up.

LEDs present many other interesting features besides the capability of scaling. It is possible to get LEDs that light up in different colors or that even transmit invisible infrared (IR) or ultraviolet (UV) light. It is also very easy to dim the light from LEDs by using only a signal generated by a microcontroller like Arduino. Actually, the same technique used for fading lights can be used to control the speed of some types of motors or to play tones using a small speaker.

> **NOTE** *The embedded electronics equivalent to the "Hello World" programming example is the so-called "Blink" one and it consists in making an LED go on and off at typically 0.5 Hz.*
>
> *You see more about this later in Chapter 7, where you get the chance to experiment with a single LED but also scale up to controlling hundreds of LEDs in the form of a small screen to display messages coming from your phone or tablet.*

Movement

Getting things to move requires some knowledge about motors, solenoids, and mechanisms. Movement is achieved by provoking changes in the electromagnetic field inside magnets. Depending on the spacial arrangement of those motors, the movement will be linear (like in solenoids) or circular (like, for example, in DC motors).

It is not possible to drive motors directly from a pin on a microcontroller. Digital electronics usually do not carry enough current for getting motors to move. The so-called motor drivers take care of providing the motors with the right values of current and voltage. Many types of motors exist, but when building prototypes, we use mostly one of the three following types:

➤ **DC motor** — This motor is shown in Figure 2-18 and is the cheapest one; you find them inside most of the toys you see in stores. You can easily control its speed and direction of turn, but in order for it to carry weight, you will need to add a gearbox.

➤ **Stepper motor** — This motor, shown in Figure 2-19, is very precise in the amount of degrees it can turn at once. If you apply a pulse to one of its pins, it rotates a fixed amount of degrees. The smaller the resolution (in degrees per pulse), the more expensive it gets. It can carry quite some weight.

➤ **Servo motors** — This motor is shown in Figure 2-20 and is the easiest motor to use. In essence, it's a DC motor with integrated gearboxes and driver circuitry. You use it later in the book to build robots.

FIGURE 2-18: DC motor

FIGURE 2-19: Stepper motor

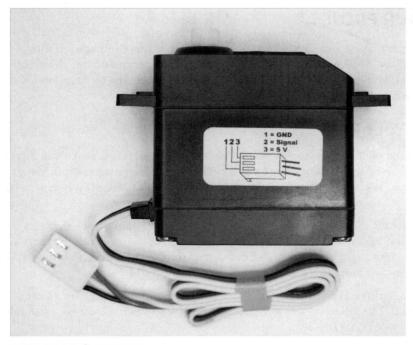

FIGURE 2-20: Servo motor

On top of those, you should add solenoids (Figure 2-21) to the list of relevant components you need when making projects. *Solenoids* are linear actuators that have only two possible positions: in or out. You could use them to make a mechanical finger to press a button or to hit an object at a certain strength.

FIGURE 2-21: Solenoid

POWERING UP YOUR PROJECT

Whether you are planning to make a wearable device or a kitchen appliance, you need to think about how to bring power to your project. When working with digital electronics, one thing you need is a DC (direct current) voltage source. The following sections analyze the different options and how you could approach this issue when building prototypes.

Ways to Power up Your Project

There is a difference between making a prototype and a final product, and it is that you can always oversize your power supply in order to make sure things work. If you were thinking about shipping a new product to the market, you would consider using an optimal circuit to supply power to your project.

When using Arduino, current is the primary thing to consider, and it is recommended that you use a source between 6 VDC and 25 VDC. Making a circuit read a distance sensor is not the same as making one to control two servo motors. Even if both cases need to provide 5 VDC to both a sensor and a motor, the motor demands more current.

When you are focusing on getting a certain set of functions to work, the final thing you need to consider is the power source. The following sections describe the different sources of DC available.

USB Port

You can power your project straight from the USB port. As long as you are not building a robot that needs to move far away from you, it is possible to make your whole prototype work straight out the same USB port that you use to power up your Arduino board.

Arduino boards count with on-board regulators that are designed for prototyping. They are not very efficient when it comes to making systems that run on batteries. On the other hand, they are very robust and can provide enough current to move a couple of motors without trouble.

Therefore, for most of your prototyping needs, you can get your project to run using the USB port (shown in Figure 2-22), or even a USB charger for a phone or a tablet.

FIGURE 2-22: Arduino powered from USB port

> **NOTE** *The USB standard establishes that USB ports should not provide more than 0.5A of current to devices. Empirically we have seen that this varies a lot between computers and operating systems.*
>
> *In general, Linux computers are much more generous when it comes to providing current. Also, some of the operating systems have enabled short-circuit alarms and can block your USB port via software to avoid accidents. If your prototype demands more than 0.5A, Mac OSX will block the USB port and report with a message on the screen. Some Windows computers will happily show the Blue Screen Of Death when overpassing the current limit.*

Power Supply

Most of you will have a ton of old power supplies belonging to old electronic appliances like modems, alarm clocks, and so on stored in boxes. Most of those have a standard DC jack with a 2.1

or 2.5 mm diameter. You can use power supplies (an example is shown in Figure 2-23) with those diameters to power up the Arduino board in the following situations:

➤ Your power supply carries more than 6 VDC: The logics on the Arduino board work at 5 VDC, but the supply circuitry has a fuse, a diode, and a voltage regulator to protect the microcontroller. All those parts require some power to run as well.

➤ The core of the jack is connected to power and the exterior part is the one carrying ground.

➤ The supply can provide enough current for your project: This is the hard part to figure out. I can only recommend that you oversize your supply on this end. A 1A power supply is better than a 500mA one. The system will take as much current as it needs and the fuse on the Arduino board will most likely protect your circuit in case of accident.

FIGURE 2-23: Power supplies

Batteries

On some occasions you might want a project to run on batteries, a variety of which are shown in Figure 2-24. The things to consider when you want to use batteries are very similar to the ones mentioned for the power supply. The main differences are that they:

➤ **Have no DC jack connectors** — You could buy one and add it to the terminals of your battery. Yet another possibility is to connect the positive end of the battery to Arduino's VIN input and the negative end to GND. As long as your battery is providing more than 6 VDC, the system will work fine.

➤ **Do not offer you a value of current as amperes, but as ampere-hour (Ah) or milliampere-hour (mAh)** — This gives you an idea of how long it will take for your battery to discharge according to the amount of current demanded by your system. It also indicates the battery's capability to respond to peaks of current — for example, when a motor starts it demands a peak of current, which is much bigger than current needed during average operation.

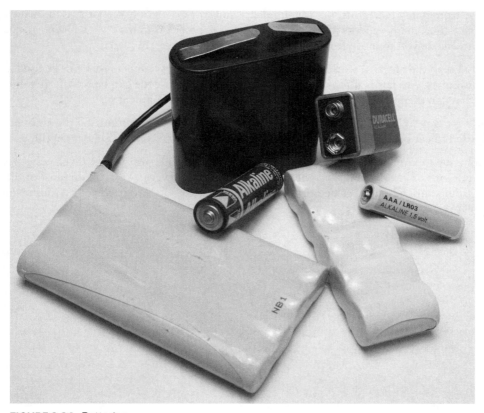

FIGURE 2-24: Batteries

Arduino Feeding Your Phone

The Arduino boards we have chosen for the examples in this book have the capability of offering your Android phone power to recharge the batteries while operating.

Because the Arduino board acts as some sort of USB hub to your phone, the standard establishes the hub should offer the client with power for the device to operate or to recharge its batteries. In this case, if your Arduino project is not consuming all the current offered by your powering method, it should enter the recharge process when connecting the phone to the accessories. The recharge time will depend on how many current-hungry sensors and actuators hang from your Arduino.

SUMMARY

Projects are complex and you will gain experience as you go. Prototyping is an art that you learn by experience. It is important to make some decisions and it is common practice to oversize the needs of the project in order to make a proof of concept and then work to optimize and polish the object.

You can choose from many platforms, but for simplicity you work with only one or two in this book. At the same time, many vendors make chips. Arduino's approach is to have a vendor-independent software core to enable you to move from platform to platform seamlessly.

Sensors help you read the physical world and represent it into series of numbers that can be used as part of your programs. Actuators do the opposite: Values within your code can be transferred into voltage levels that can then operate devices that interact with the environment.

Shields are an easy way to bring sensors and actuators into your projects, minimizing the amount of soldering required to get things done. You can find shields for Arduino that do almost anything.

One important issue to keep in mind is that you need to power up your prototypes. Oversizing the power supply in terms of current is important to avoid surprises. However, you can do most of the work straight from your computer, using one of your USB ports to both program your Arduino and power up your inventions.

3

Understanding Data Communication

WHAT'S IN THIS CHAPTER?

➤ Understanding how data communication works

➤ The basics of how data is structured

➤ The fundamentals of the MQTT messaging protocol

➤ Sketching the P2PMQTT protocol

DATA COMMUNICATION BASICS

Never underestimate the bandwidth of a station wagon full of tapes hurtling down the highway.

—TANENBAUM, ANDREW S. (1996). COMPUTER NETWORKS. NEW JERSEY: PRENTICE-HALL. P. 83. ISBN 0-13-349945-6.

The act of communicating requires having two or more parties exchanging, requesting, sending, and evaluating data. Those involved in the information exchange can be people or machines. Successful exchanges require the use of a predetermined mechanism on how to request data, but also on how to acknowledge the arrival of it. The definition of those mechanisms is made in an abstract way and is independent of the transmission channel. It's what we call a *protocol*.

Different protocols accommodate different scenarios of use. Trying to send data over a 6.000 Km long submarine cable is not the same as using a twisted pair of copper wires between two circuits at 10 cms distance from each other.

Understanding how communication works between two electronic devices requires thinking beyond the bits and electronic components themselves. You need to consider factors like noise, whether the communication happens over wires or in a wireless way, how far the devices are from each other, or how quickly you want data to be sent to the other side.

Sometimes your envisioned application cannot be achieved because of one of the factors is too limiting, but standards exist that can help you get your project done in almost any case.

At the lowest logical level, information is encoded in packages of bits. Most of the existing communication systems use packages of 8 bits (which is the same as 1 byte) as the basic unit for information transfer. Those bytes contain the data you want to send, like the temperature measured by a sensor.

Protocols

Information is seldom sent in its raw form. It is often encapsulated in bigger packages of multiple bytes to include:

➤   Information about the sender

➤   The address to the receiver

➤   Some description of the configuration of the sensor

➤   Error correction bytes

Protocols describe the way information is encoded and encapsulated to provide optimal performance during the communication, but also the way devices take turns in the communication and how they inform the different parties involved that things did or didn't work. In other words, protocols define the way computers talk to each other.

An easy example of a communication between two devices is shown in Figure 3-1. There you see how device #1 starts a communication with device #2, which answers back.

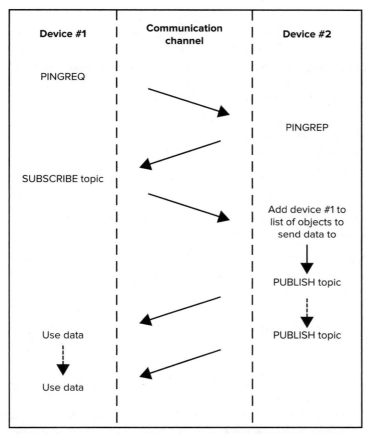

FIGURE 3-1: Example of communication protocol between two devices

Protocols handle about every data exchange in our lives — when sending e-mail, browsing the Internet, making a secure economic transaction at an ATM, receiving SMS, and so on. Some protocols are human-readable, some others are described in bits. MQ Telemetry Transport (MQTT), the protocol we are dealing with in this book, is *not* human-readable, and therefore is not that easy to read at first. However, it is very efficient for small data transactions and portable to a whole series of connected devices.

Terminology

When dealing with computer communications, you are going to find a series of keywords showing up in every document describing a protocol. Table 3-1 gives you a quick look at some basic terms and what they mean, just to get acquainted with them.

TABLE 3-1: Terminology

TERM	MEANING
Data	In a broad sense, data is whatever is sent between two devices. A narrower definition makes data become the actual information, taking away any overhead bytes used in the communication.
Header	Part of the data package containing information about the sender, the type of package, length of the data, and/or other relevant information needed to decode the package upon arrival at the other device.
Payload	Because the word "data" as described earlier can have such a broad meaning, this term is used to very specifically describe the actual information.
Package	The whole series of bytes, including header, payload, and checksum bytes, compose the so-called information packages.
Acknowledgment	Positive response from a receiver when a data package is received and contains no errors. This is usually labeled ACK. The opposite message is labeled NACK (as in Negative ACK) and is sent when an error was detected in a data package and the receiver wants the package sent again.
PING	It is standard procedure to call PING to a method in almost every communication protocol. The idea behind it is to check whether the communication between two points is still functional.
MSB vs. LSB	Most Significant Byte (MSB) vs. Least Significant Byte (LSB) refers to the way the payload or any other data within a package is ordered. This is needed when information is contained in more than one byte. It shouldn't be confused with Most/Least Significant Bit. For example, if the Java short datatype is 16 bit, this means it consists of 2 bytes (2*8bit=16bit). One of these two bytes has a larger impact on the resulting value, and is called Most Significant Byte. Commonly, the Most Significant Byte is the leftmost byte in the order, and the Least Significant Byte is the rightmost byte in the order.
Fixed vs. Variable packages	Some protocols have packages with fixed sizes, thus the same amount of bytes for each package. MQTT has variable package sizes. This makes it harder to encode/decode, but much more efficient in bandwidth.
CRC	Cyclic Redundancy Check, a technique that helps detect errors happening during the transmission of a data package by making a simple mathematical operation on the data upon arrival. The bytes containing the CRC error data are also referred to as checksum.
Encryption	The process of making a message unreadable for anyone without the correct key is called encryption. Some protocols encrypt the payload and any other sensitive information within the data packages, and some others do not encrypt anything.

HARDWARE LAYER FOR THE COMMUNICATION PROTOCOL

You have many different ways to get data from and into your Android device. Both phones and tablets vary in their capabilities — some have 3G wireless communication, some others offer Wi-Fi, Bluetooth, the USB cable — all different technologies that can be used in different ways.

One interesting characteristic of the Android devices is that they are sometimes over-dimensioned from a hardware point of view. They have a whole lot to offer, but the version of the operating system installed in them might not possess the drivers to instantiate some of the hardware peripherals. One example of this is one of the first commercial Android phones, the HTC Hero, which had a Bluetooth chipset inside, but the SDK didn't offer the possibility to program it in any way.

Depending on the device you are experimenting with, you might not have certain hardware peripherals available, and some of them might not be available via software either. Therefore, you should learn about the different techniques you could use when designing and developing your projects.

Lots of cheap devices are available in the market that you could use as an interface to your project, but many of the older ones cannot use the AOA technique we are presenting in this book because it was introduced as a patch to Android API 10 (Android 2.3.4). The following sections take a look at the possibilities for connecting Android devices to physical objects.

ADB

ADB stands for Android Debug Bridge, and it is the original way offered by the Android SDK for you to debug applications both on the SDK's emulator or a real device. ADB is a command-line tool that you can use to install applications on the device, read log files, or simulate real-life uses of the device such as forcing values to the GPS.

A call to the ADB creates a client-server pair that allows communication between the device/emulator and the computer. Your Android phone or tablet runs a daemon that, if enabled in the settings panel, allows ADB servers to connect to them. The data exchange happens through a TCP connection. As a matter of fact, anything capable of handling a TCP connection can potentially communicate to the phone using the ADB.

This is a trick you can use to make your Android device communicate to your Arduino. In essence, you can make your Arduino Mega ADK behave like the ADB server and get them to send data back and forth to the Android phone/tablet that will have the TCP port open and waiting for connections.

At the other end of the communication, you need to enable the debug tools on your device. But instead of logging data from the phone to your ADB terminal in your computer, you will be sending the data back to Arduino.

This technique has some issues:

> ➤ First, you cannot expect this to work in all phones. Google has introduced, together with the AOA, the idea that the phones and tablets will have two different USB identifiers. One of them is going to be used for debugging purposes. In a way, we could expect ADB to be facing technical obsolescence in the near future.

> ➤ Secondly, the use of the ADB requires activating the development mode in your Android device. If you were about to distribute an application together with a physical object working over the ADB, you would have to ask your users to enable that feature manually.

READ MORE ABOUT ADB

You can find the official documentation about the ADB at `http://developer.android.com/tools/help/adb.html`.

If you want to read more about the ADB hack you can explore the IOIO project at `http://ytai-mer.blogspot.se/2011/04/meet-ioio-io-for-android.html`.

Accessory Mode

With AOA, the Android development team introduces the concept of the Accessory mode. Conceptually it is simple: You have an accessory on your Android device and they connect through USB. But, at the same time, that phone will have to be hooked up to a computer at some point to, for example, download the pictures from the SD card to the PC.

One way to solve this situation is to create a way for the Android device to acquire multiple profiles depending on the situation. The USB standard uses a handshake at the beginning of the communication for the different parties to identify each other. If the phone detects it is connected to an accessory, it will behave differently than if it is hooked up to a PC's USB port.

This is what the Accessory mode is all about. It defines the way Android devices have to behave for them to accept accessories and still keep all the other functionality in place. It brings in other features as well:

> ➤ When you create an accessory, you don't need to send its users any software in the first place. The accessory can inform the device about a URL where it can download the application. That app could be stored on any server on the Internet. Your users will just need to activate the option to allow installing software from unknown locations.

> ➤ Multiple apps can access the data from the same accessory; users choose the right one at each occasion. Note though that because of the current state of the Android system there can only be one accessory connected at any time, and just like the camera only one application can connect to that accessory at any one time.

> ➤ Accessories can operate with devices coming from many vendors. The software API is the same for all vendors and is available from version 12 and forward.

Host Mode

Android phones include On The Go (OTG) technology. It is a chip or chip peripheral implementing the USB port that can shift between client and host mode. In other words, more or less any Android device could use the USB connection — with a special USB adapter (see Figure 3-2) — to connect standard HID USB devices like keyboards and mice.

FIGURE 3-2: The cable to use phones under host mode with HID USB devices

Most people identify keyboards as just input devices, but a standard computer keyboard comes with some LEDs used to indicate the status of the different LOCK keys. From this point of view, a computer keyboard is actually an input/output device.

It is possible to reprogram the firmware of your Arduino Uno or Arduino Mega ADK to behave like a keyboard. It is therefore possible to use a self-made keyboard-like device to communicate with your Android device.

Phones are not easy to deal with when it comes to using the Host Mode. This is not a standard feature of the Android OS and the examples you can find are about hacking the phone's kernel. On the other hand, some tablets come equipped with double micro USB connectors, one being the standard Android port and the other one a standard USB Host port. An example of this can be seen in Figure 3-3.

FIGURE 3-3: Tablet with multiple USB connectors with an Arduino Uno acting as a keyboard

GET YOUR ARDUINO MEGA ADK TO BEHAVE LIKE A KEYBOARD

If you are interested in testing how your Arduino Mega ADK (or Arduino Uno) could work as an input device to your tablet configured as an HID keyboard, follow the tutorial at http://hunt.net.nz/users/darran/?tag=keyboard.

TCP/IP

Probably the most obvious way to get your Android device to communicate with the physical world is to get it to talk to a connected object. You could use your Arduino hooked to a series of shields that would offer connectivity to some sort of network.

Among others, you could use:

➤ **An Arduino Ethernet Shield (Figure 3-4) or equivalent.** These boards enable you to connect to a wired network and connect to a server to post data, or even create a small server to which you could connect with your Android device via a browser. An equivalent use scenario would be using an Arduino Ethernet board, which merges an Arduino Uno together with an Ethernet Shield into a single circuit.

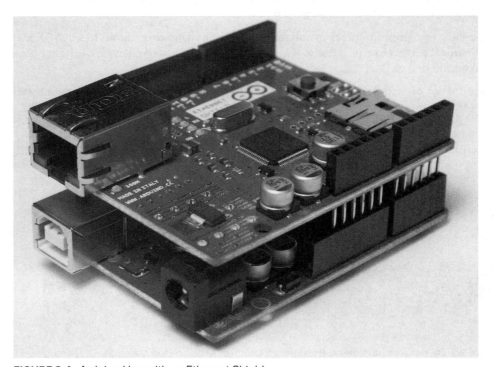

FIGURE 3-4: Arduino Uno with an Ethernet Shield

➤ **An Arduino GSM/GPRS Shield (Figure 3-5) or compatible.** With this you can connect to the Internet to post data to servers. Again, you could connect to the data posted by the board by sending requests to the server. It would also be possible to send data from the phone to the board via the intermediating server.

FIGURE 3-5: Arduino Uno with an GSM/GPRS Shield

➤ **An Arduino Wi-Fi Shield (Figure 3-6).** It is completely equivalent to the Arduino Ethernet Shield case, but operates over a Wi-Fi connection. In the same way as with the Ethernet Shield, you do not necessarily need a server between the Android device and your Arduino board. One of them could operate as server and the other as a client in a typical TCP/IP connection.

FIGURE 3-6: Arduino Uno with a Wi-Fi Shield

Audio Port

Phones have audio ports that include a microphone and two audio out lines (one for the left audio channel and one for the right one). It is therefore possible to create a DTMF-like communication between the Android device and an external circuit.

WHAT IS DTMF?

Dual-Tone Multi-Frequency (DTMF) is a system to encode information using two tones for each symbol. It was originally created to encode the numbers from phones because it is more robust than the previous dialing methods.

This system enables you to easily encode/decode 16 symbols. It should be possible to create tones directly and decode them using an Arduino board; however, it feels unnecessary because multiple low-cost chips are available that can do encoding or decoding of DTMF tones.

Check the DTMF product line of Holtek Semiconductor Inc. for more information at www.holtek.com/english/products/comm_2.htm.

There is a very interesting implementation of this concept of connecting Arduino boards with Android devices over the audio port using frequency-shift keying (FSK)-encoded tones. Visit the Androino Terminal Project on Google Code at `http://code.google.com/p/androino/wiki/AndroinoTerminal` for more information.

Bluetooth Options

The early implementations of the AOA didn't include the possibility of creating accessories over Bluetooth. Also, until the deployment of Froyo (codename for Android's release 2.2), there was no way for the developers to even access the Bluetooth port in the phones and tablets running Android.

From the moment Froyo was released, you could develop applications that could connect to Android devices. The applications could call the basic functions within the operating system to pair to Bluetooth devices and open a transparent serial port connection to them. It is possible to, for example, use the Arduino Bluetooth board to connect to the phone wirelessly. An example of this is shown in Figure 3-7, where you can see the Nexus One, an Arduino Bluetooth board, and a specially made shield to control up to six motors using the PWM-enabled pins on the board.

FIGURE 3-7: Arduino Bluetooth board with homebrew shield.

Any of the above mentioned techniques refer to which is the physical transmission channel the information will be sent through. MQTT operates on top of any of them. MQTT adds structure to the data, in other words, adds headers that will help the receiver classifying the data.

INTRODUCING MQTT

The Message Queue (MQTT) protocol was invented by Andy Standford-Clark and Arlen Nipper at IBM redundant in 1999. Back in those days, as you might recall, bandwidth was quite a scarce commodity, especially the stable kind. If the wired networking was quite poor back then, the wireless was a disaster. This, coupled with the need to remotely monitor and control devices and sensors, led these two gentlemen on a siege to overcome unstable remote monitoring — thus, MQTT came about.

MQTT is a protocol designed for communication on low-bandwidth, high-latency wireless networks. Its properties make it an ideal choice for applications in the world of connected devices, or, as you may know it better, the Internet of Things.

Another key feature of the MQTT protocol is scalability; it supports literally thousands of concurrent connections through a publish/subscribe messaging broker that lies at the heart of the MQTT system. This scalability is one of the reasons that Facebook chose to use it for its instant messaging system. In this book, however, you use just the one connection between an Android device and an accessory built using Arduino.

PUBLISH/SUBSCRIBE

Publish/Subscribe is a one-to-many communications pattern where messages are never sent directly from sender to receiver. Instead, they are sent to a message broker that filters the message and delivers it only to the recipients that have claimed an interest in that message — this is called subscribing, Figure 3-8 shows a typical publish/subscribe topology.

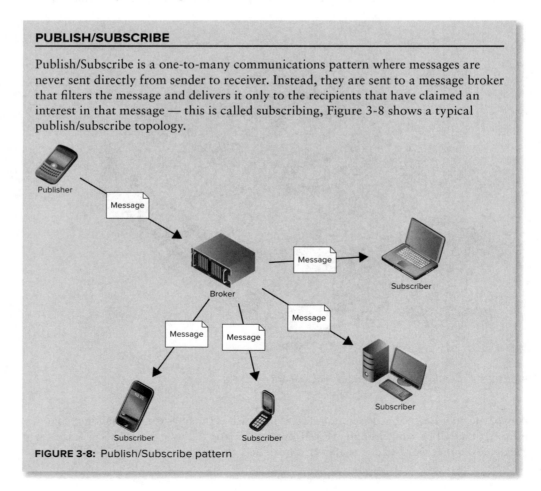

FIGURE 3-8: Publish/Subscribe pattern

Commonly, two types of subscriptions are available to clients: either filtered by the content of the message or based on the message topic. Not all pub/sub systems allow multiple subscription types. MQTT subscriptions are based on topics as you will see shortly.

We thought it would be an interesting challenge to bring it up as a way to implement the data exchanges happening between your accessory (made with an Arduino board) and the phone itself. This one-to-one communication can be seen as a peer-to-peer MQTT (P2P-MQTT), which can transcend beyond devices because the information is already encapsulated in the right format. In other words, you could use the phone to relay the information coming from the sensors to MQTT brokers that are part of a larger infrastructure.

You might ask yourself just how this protocol relates to AOA and Arduino. Because MQTT is designed to be lightweight and with a small footprint, it's an ideal candidate not only for remote monitoring of sensors and instant messaging chat systems, but its specific properties also make it an obvious candidate for the types of projects that you build in this book. Some of the features of MQTT include the following:

➤ To allow for a wide range of applications, the content of the MQTT message that is being sent doesn't matter one little bit (pun intended). The payload of each MQTT message is actually just that, a collection of bits and bytes. You, as the sender/receiver, will decide what those bytes mean.

➤ To limit the amount of data being sent, MQTT has been designed with an overhead of as small as 2 bytes per packet! Don't be fooled, though; although 2 bytes is a very small overhead, most MQTT messages have an overhead that is a little bit bigger than that. The only message that comes to mind with as little as 2 bytes is the PINGREQ message.

➤ You've surely experienced a network disconnection at least once — if it was because of poor wireless coverage or a broken DSL modem, we've all been there. Today, everyone experiences these kinds of seemingly random disconnections, and what's worse is that there's not much you can do to avoid them. MQTT, however, has built-in ways of handling these kinds of disconnections gracefully, which is kind of awesome if you're building an application dependent on networking.

For all of these reasons and more, MQTT makes an excellent candidate for use in many machine-to-machine (M2M) scenarios. You can find more information, and the open specifications, on MQTT at http://mqtt.org/.

Heads Up!

As described earlier, the header of a communications protocol describes how the recipient should decipher the message. In MQTT the overhead actually has two parts. The first part is called the *fixed header* and it's required by all MQTT messages. It's used to describe the general properties of the message. Table 3-2 shows an example of a fixed header.

TABLE 3-2: Fixed Header

BIT	7	6	5	4	3	2	1	0
Byte 1	Message Type				DUP	QoS		RETAIN
Byte 2	Remaining Length							

MQTT V3.1 Protocol Specifications

The first byte of the fixed header has four different values that are interesting to us. First there's the message type, which occupies the last four bits, then three flags that give the message extended properties beyond the message type — DUP, QoS, and RETAIN.

Although MQTT has a very small footprint, it doesn't limit the message size very much; as a matter of fact, you can send single messages that are carrying up to 256MB of payload each. This is possible because of the Remaining Length field that tells you how many bytes the payload contains; this field can extend over 4 bytes in total.

The second part of the overhead is called the *variable header* and it's needed only in certain types of MQTT messages. As the name implies, the format of the variable header doesn't always look the same; it depends on the message being sent. As an example, when attempting to connect to a MQTT broker you also need to say what version of the MQTT protocol you're using. This would be sent as an 8-bit unsigned value in the variable header attached in between the fixed header and the payload.

Message Type

MQTT defines fourteen different message types; each responds to a specific action being taken by one of the parties. For example, if your client application wants to connect to a broker, it would first send the CONNECT message and wait for the CONNACK response from the server before proceeding to publish or subscribe. Table 3-3 lists the different MQTT message types.

TABLE 3-3: MQTT Message Types

MNEMONIC	ENUMERATION	DESCRIPTION
Reserved	0	Reserved
CONNECT	1	Client request to connect to Server
CONNACK	2	Connect Acknowledgement
PUBLISH	3	Publish Message
PUBACK	4	Publish Acknowledgement
PUBREC	5	Publish Received
PUBREL	6	Publish Release
PUBCOMP	7	Publish Complete

SUBSCRIBE	8	Client Subscribe Request
SUBACK	9	Subscribe Acknowledgement
UNSUBSCRIBE	10	Client Unsubscribe Request
UNSUBACK	11	Unsubscribe Acknowledgement
PINGREQ	12	PING Request
PINGRESP	13	PING Response
DISCONNECT	14	Client is Disconnecting
Reserved	15	Reserved

MQTT V3.1 Protocol Specification

Quality of Service (QoS)

Because MQTT has such a wide range of uses, it's imperative that you can choose different service qualities that define how the message will be delivered by the system. Three different levels are defined in MQTT:

➤ **The lowest quality level sees the message sent once, without any sort of confirmation that it has arrived properly.** This quality of service has the value 0 and is called AT MOST ONCE.

➤ **The middle quality level sees the message being delivered at least once.** It manages this by demanding an acknowledgment from the recipient that the message was received; the sender will just keep sending the same message until it gets an acknowledgment. It's called AT LEAST ONCE and has the value 1. As you probably realize, this may cause problems when it comes to funky networking — a message may very well be delivered multiple times.

➤ **The highest quality service level means that the message will be delivered exactly once, not more, not less, using a series of handshakes.** This level is called EXACTLY ONCE and has the value 2.

You can also subscribe to messages based on their Quality of Service (QoS). If you subscribe to the second service level (middle level) you'll only receive messages on that level or below. Any messages above your requested level will be downgraded to match your requested level; this means you will always get all messages on the topic you subscribe, no matter what level they're at.

A published message QoS level may be downgraded by the broker, however it may never be upgraded by the broker.

Duplicate Delivery (DUP)

A message that has already been sent at least once should always be marked as duplicate using the DUP flag in the fixed header. This is used only for certain messages that have QoS level 2 or above; however, not all messages of QoS level 2 or above will be marked as duplicate.

Retain

When publishing a new message the client has the choice to let this message be saved by the broker for some reason. It's important to realize that the broker will retain only one message at a time for a specific topic (often you'd use one topic per sensor, so in reality each sensor can retain its last known value on the broker). If the broker already has a message retained and is asked to retain a new message, the old message is deleted. This can be very useful for sensors that rarely publish new values, but you still want the client to get a value when connecting, or if the value being published is very important.

Remaining Length

This is the last value of the fixed header. In MQTT most messages have a payload, and that payload has a certain size in bytes; this is what the Remaining Length field is used for. It tells the receiver how many bytes to expect after the overhead for a certain message. Be wary, though; the Remaining Length field has some funky rules that you should grasp on at least a basic level:

➤ It's part of the fixed header.

➤ It uses between 1 and 4 bytes.

➤ It represents a payload size of up to 256MB.

The way this works is that if the payload is less than or exactly 127-bytes long, the Remaining Length field uses only 1 byte and it uses all 8 bits of that byte. However, if the payload is anything above 127 bytes, it may use up to 4 bytes, where only 7 bits of each byte is used to describe the length. The eighth bit is used to define if another byte should be expected. Figure 3-9 describes the procedure of calculating the remaining length.

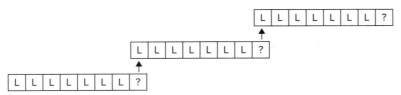

FIGURE 3-9: Remaining length composition

> **NOTE** *The procedure of calculating the remaining length field is described, with code, in chapter 5.*

MQTT Messages

Before moving on to defining the use of your very own protocol based on MQTT, this section reviews a few of the most common messages that you'll use when building the communication library used for this book.

Connect

The CONNECT message is a request sent by a client wanting to connect to the MQTT broker. It should be sent right after the client established a physical connection to the broker; if it's not sent, the broker should terminate the connection. At a very minimum, the CONNECT message contains a unique identifier for the client called the *client ID*. It can also carry more detailed information regarding the client wanting to connect, such as username, password, and so on.

When a broker receives a CONNECT message, it immediately sends a CONNACK message back to the client acknowledging that the first message was received, and some extra information regarding the acceptance of the connection. If the client doesn't get this message, it should terminate the connection. Table 3-4 shows an example variable header for the CONNECT message. Notice that Byte 10 contains settings for the CONNECT message. For example, if the CONNECT message contains a username and password, but it doesn't contain the actual username and password, those are sent as part of the payload.

TABLE 3-4: Example Variable Header for the CONNECT Message

	DESCRIPTION
Protocol Name	
Byte 1	Length MSB (0x00)
Byte 2	Length LSB (0x06)
Byte 3	M (0x4D)
Byte 4	Q (0x44)
Byte 5	I (0x49)
Byte 6	s (0x73)
Byte 7	d (0x64)
Byte 8	p (0x70)
Protocol Version Number	
Byte 9	Version 3 (0x03)
Connect Flags	
Byte 10	Has Username, Has Password, Will Retain, Will QoS, Will, Clean Session (0xCE)
Keep Alive Timer	
Byte 11	Keep Alive MSB (0x00)
Byte 12	Keep Alive LSB (0x0A)

MQTT V3.1 Protocol Specification

Connection Acknowledgment

When the broker receives a connection request, it has to send an acknowledgment of this request back to the client. If it fails to send this acknowledgment within a reasonable timeframe, the client will gracefully disconnect. On the other hand, if the broker doesn't even receive a connect request from a client when connecting, it should also terminate the connection gracefully. This way it's up to both parties to play nice with each other for a connection to happen.

The variable header of the CONNACK message contains a code for the client to decipher, as described in Table 3-5.

TABLE 3-5: CONNACK Response Code

ENUMERATION	HEX	MEANING
0	0x00	Connection Accepted
1	0x01	Connection Refused: unacceptable protocol version
2	0x02	Connection Refused: identifier rejected
3	0x03	Connection Refused: server unavailable
4	0x04	Connection Refused: bad username or password
5	0x05	Connection Refused: not authorized
6-255		Reserved

MQTT V3.1 Protocol Specification

Table 3-6 shows an example variable header for the CONNACK message.

TABLE 3-6: Example Variable Header for the CONNACK Message

	DESCRIPTION
Byte 1	Reserved, not used
Byte 2	Return Code

MQTT V3.1 Protocol Specification

Publish

When the client wants to distribute any type of information, it sends a PUBLISH message to the message broker, which then distributes this message to all clients that are subscribed to that topic.

The QoS for a topic is determined in the fixed header of the PUBLISH message. As mentioned earlier, no matter the QoS for a topic, the subscribers will always receive all the messages for that topic.

The PUBLISH message can take advantage of all the extra parameters in the fixed header, and it also has a variable header with extra information regarding the message being sent; such as the topic and message ID. Table 3-7 shows an example.

TABLE 3-7: Example Variable Header for the PUBLISH Message

	DESCRIPTION
Topic Identifier	
Byte 1	Length MSB (0x00)
Byte 2	Length LSB (0x03)
Byte 3	a (0x61)
Byte 4	/ (0x2F)
Byte 5	b (0x62)
Unique Message Identifier	
Byte 6	Message ID MSB (0x00)
Byte 7	Message ID LSB (0x0A)

MQTT V3.1 Protocol Specification

The message identifier in the variable header is unique only for the client, so it's up to the client to give the message a unique ID number. Because the unique identifier is always 16 bytes long, the system can support up to 65,535 unique messages per client at any one time. The client can, of course, also reuse message IDs that have been sent already, and because of this it's highly unlikely that any two message IDs will interfere with each other.

Publish Acknowledgment

Because the PUBLISH message can have any of the three QoS levels, it must also have different acknowledgment methods. The first quality of service level, 0, has no acknowledgment. The second level, 1, keeps sending the message until an acknowledgment has been received. Table 3-8 shows an example variable header for the PUBACK message.

TABLE 3-8: Example Variable Header for the PUBACK Message

	DESCRIPTION
Byte 1	Message ID MSB (0x00)
Byte 2	Message ID LSB (0x0A)

MQTT V3.1 Protocol Specification

The third level, level 2, has an advanced multi-message handshake to make sure that the message was sent, and received, exactly once. You won't be implementing this level while reading this book. If you're interested in more reliable communication, you should read more about MQTT.

Subscribe

If your application is interested in reading information published by others, it has to subscribe to a certain channel or topic. This tells the message broker that your application is interested in certain information, and if it qualifies for this information based on some criteria such as username and password, it will be eligible for those messages. If, however, the client doesn't fulfill the needed criteria, the broker has no obligation to tell the client this.

The only thing present in the SUBSCRIBE variable header is the message ID; it has this ID because it expects a SUBACK message in response from the broker, meaning that it has QoS level 1. Table 3-9 shows an example variable header for the SUBSCRIBE message.

TABLE 3-9: Example Variable Header for the SUBSCRIBE Message

	DESCRIPTION
Message Identifier	
Byte 1	Message ID MSB (0x00)
Byte 2	Message ID LSB (0x0A)

MQTT V3.1 Protocol Specification

The payload of the subscribe message contains the topics to subscribe to and the quality of service for each of those topics.

Unsubscribe

Unsubscribe is sent by a client that isn't interested in receiving any more updates for a certain topic. It has its own acknowledgment part, which needs to be sent by the broker to acknowledge that the unsubscribe was successful.

The overhead of the unsubscribe message is almost identical to that of the subscribe message. The only difference is the message type in the fixed header; the variable header looks exactly the same as in the subscribe message. The payload, however, has a small difference; where the subscribe message has both Topic and Quality of Service, the unsubscribe message has only the Topic part. This is because the broker doesn't need to know what QoS the client requested for the particular subscription, only that the subscription should be removed.

Ping

Commonly, ping is as tool used to detect broken pipes in networking or to measure latency over connections. In MQTT, the PINGREQ message is used as an indicator that you're still alive, and it's used only when no other information has been sent for a certain period of time. Although the

PINGREQ message expects a response from the broker, it doesn't require one, which is why the QoS isn't used in this message (unlike the SUBSCRIBE message, which is defined as a QoS level 1 message).

The PINGREQ message has no payload or variable header, and it uses none of the extra parameters of the fixed header. This makes it the smallest MQTT message.

P2PMQTT: A MODIFIED MQTT

In this book you'll develop a new protocol called peer-to-peer MQTT (P2PMQTT) based on the standard MQTT v3.1 specification. Because MQTT was originally intended for use in a one-to-many publish/subscribe pattern in which messages always pass through a broker before delivery, you need to modify the use case a little bit before applying it in the new peer-to-peer context.

You won't change the rules of how a message should be packaged. The messages will remain identical to the specification discussed earlier in this chapter, so the major difference lies in how you implement MQTT. Instead of letting a message broker handle the distribution of messages, your two clients — the Android device and the Arduino accessory — each takes some responsibility of the broker, thereby removing the need for having a broker in the system.

Establishing a Connection

In the standard MQTT system, you'd see an always-online message broker at the core of the entire system; MQTT clients would create a connection to this broker. When the client successfully connects to the message broker, meaning the physical connection is established, the client sends a connection request that can contain a number of parameters such as username and password. The broker then responds accordingly.

However, in our slightly modified version of the MQTT protocol, there is no central messaging broker, so the responsibility of handling connections falls to the clients. Each client then needs to do the following:

➤ Send a CONNECT request message when a connection is established.

➤ Terminate connections that aren't followed by a connection request by the other party.

➤ Send the CONNACK message when a CONNECT message is received.

Subscribing to a Topic

Subscribing means the same thing as it does in the normal MQTT system. Each client handles a list of connected peers and their respective subscriptions. If a client isn't interested in a particular topic, the client can at any time during the connection send an unsubscribe message.

Using this approach in an accessory context limits the amount of unnecessary data being transmitted. For example, your particular accessory might support multiple sensors and actuators, but not all the sensors and actuators are active at the same time. In this situation, both the Arduino client and the Android client need to do the following:

➤ Maintain a list of subscriptions for all the other parties connected; right now Android supports only one accessory at a time, but this will likely change in the future.

➤ Send and listen for SUBSCRIBE messages; the client should send a subscribe when interested in receiving messages of a certain topic.

➤ Send UNSUBSCRIBE messages when no longer interested in receiving messages of a certain topic.

➤ Listen for, and send, UNSUBACK when appropriate.

➤ Listen for, and send, SUBACK messages when appropriate.

Publishing a Message

The most interesting message of them all, the PUBLISH message, contains the content of the message in which you're interested. In the normal MQTT system, the broker receives a great deal of messages from clients that care less about who receives it. However, in your broker-less environment the clients will maintain the list of subscriptions themselves, and because of this only publish messages according to that list.

You could of course also make the subscription handling local instead, making each client maintain their own list of subscriptions; only reacting to the messages they're interested in and ignoring all other messages. However, this would potentially add a lot of unnecessary traffic between the devices as the sending party cares less about who is interested in the message and more about sending the message.

Disconnecting

Disconnecting in the P2PMQTT is identical to the DISCONNECT message as defined in the standard specification. Although it's used differently, both sides should send the disconnect when they're about to cancel the connection. A good example of this is in the onDestroy lifecycle method in Android. The party sending the DISCONNECT message shouldn't expect anything in return, it's just a pleasant notice to the other party saying, "Hey dude, I'm about to drop the connection. Clean up after me!"

The "clean up after me" part at the end is fairly important because you should never expect the other party to clean up after itself. All data transfers should be stopped, and sockets should be closed when the DISCONNECT message is received.

SUMMARY

Data communication refers to the exchange of information between systems. The communication itself is commanded by protocols, and different scenarios of use require different techniques. Wireless communication with high environmental noise will, for example, require using more bytes to detect errors, whereas short-distance wired communication will rely on more simple protocols.

Message Queue Telemetry Transport (MQTT) is a messaging system built mainly for low-bandwidth remote sensor systems. While MQTT doesn't inherently contain any package error checking such as a checksum, it has an attribute called Quality of Service (QoS) which defines an expected level of quality for any given message. This quality level will tell both the publisher and the broker (in your context the receiver) how to act to deliver the message properly.

The standard MQTT implementation relies on one central messaging broker that handles connections and distributes all messages to any interested clients. In your context, however, there is no messaging broker, and instead, the two clients of the accessory network will both share the responsibilities of the messaging broker, including handling connections and maintaining subscriptions.

MQTT messages are constructed in three parts:

1. **The fixed header is the first part of the meta-data for the message.** It describes what message is it (publish, subscribe, ping, etc.) and a couple of more attributes shared by every MQTT message. The format of this part is always the same, 1 byte with attributes and between 1 and 4 bytes to describe the length of the message, in bytes.

2. **The second part of the meta-data called variable header is different for all MQTT messages, and some might not even have a variable header.** It contains the message-specific attributes. For example, a connection might require a password and username. The variable header then defines that there is a password and username present in the payload.

3. **The payload is the actual data of the message.** It depends on the message type; in the example of the connect message this could contain the actual password (encoded, of course) and the username.

To enable the best performance on these low-bandwidth and unreliable networks MQTT has been constructed with a set of features. Some of the more important features of MQTT include:

1. **MQTT handles noise, and other complications, by applying the Quality of Service (QoS) attribute to messages being sent.** If the receiver doesn't get the full message, the QoS of that message determines the message's importance and then all parties interested in the message act accordingly; either the client (publisher) resends the message if it wasn't received by the receiver (broker) or it just plain ignores whether the message was or was not received by the broker.

2. **MQTT also allows the unique identification (ID) for each message, and client.** The ID is a two-byte field, which means it can only have 65,536 different values; however, these IDs are managed by the client and should be recycled properly.

3. **MQTT also allows the broker to save (RETAIN) the last known good value for any topic.** This means that any client that subscribes to a topic that has a saved message will get that message instantly delivered to them. This is particularly good for sensors that update infrequently.

4. **The last of the more important features, and certainly not the least of them, is the possible size of a message.**

Of course, MQTT has more features than these, and you should definitely explore the MQTT specification in detail. You can find it at: `http://mqtt.org/`.

Setting up Development Environments

WHAT'S IN THIS CHAPTER?

➤   Setting up the Android development environment

➤   Setting up the Arduino development environment

➤   Hello Android Open Accessory app

WROX.COM CODE DOWNLOADS FOR THIS CHAPTER

The wrox.com code downloads for this chapter are found at www.wrox.com/remtitle
.cgi?isbn=1118454766 on the Download Code tab. The code is in the Chapter 4 download
and individually named according to the names throughout the chapter.

In this chapter you set up the development environments needed to successfully build and
test Android accessories. Because the Android accessory consists of two different artifacts —
the Android application and the Arduino electronics hardware — you have to set up two
different environments.

In addition to setting up the environments, you also take them out for a test run; for this you'll
use some example projects already available.

SETTING UP ANDROID DEVELOPMENT

You have two options when developing for Android. You can choose to do so in Java only, or use
a mix of Java and C through the Android Native Development Kit (Android NDK). However, in
this book you develop in the Java language only, using the Android SDK. But, before you start
writing the code using the SDK you need a development environment to write in.

Most Android developers choose Eclipse for their everyday Android programming. Eclipse has a well-developed and maintained plug-in created by Android, for Android, which makes Android development a breeze. Eclipse is also the environment that is used for the examples and projects throughout this book.

We picked Eclipse for two major reasons: First, it's the best documented way of creating Android applications. Second, the Eclipse project shares some key characteristics of development with the Android Open Source Project — they're both projects built with Open Source licenses and they're developed and maintained in an Open innovation style, something the authors of this book feel very strongly about.

However, if you prefer to work in an IDE other than Eclipse, it's perfectly possible to do so because the Android Eclipse Plugin is little more than a shortcut to the Android SDK Tools. Some of the other popular development environments also have plug-ins for Android development similar to the one available for Eclipse.

ANDROID SDK TOOLS

The Android SDK Tools do all the heavy lifting for you when developing Android applications, it's a series of tools which each serve a special purpose when developing projects using the Android SDK; they are all bundled together using the Apache Ant build system.

This means that you can actually avoid using any special IDE all together if you wish, developing on nothing but the most simple text editor for your system, Notepad (Windows), TextEdit (Mac OS), or gedit (Linux), and then calling the Ant build script to compile the project into a installable Andriod Application Package (apk) file.

Apart from containing the tools to build your projects, the Android SDK Tools also contain a number of programs that help you in your development process, such as debugging or optimizing your project.

Some of the more prominent tools include:

➤ The Hierarchy Viewer which lets you debug and optimize user interfaces.

➤ The Monkey stress tests your user interface by generating a large number of random events (such as touches, gestures and system events).

➤ Traceview gives you a way to profile your applications performance.

➤ Draw 9-patch lets you create scalable bitmaps using a simple WYSIWYG editor.

If you're anything like me, you're probably eager to learn more about this sort of stuff. You should definitely read more about all the tools at `http://developer.android.com/tools/help/index.html`. You'll find some really interesting tools hidden away that you might not find otherwise.

If you're in the mood to explore, you can check any of the following environments; they should all work just fine for Android development:

➤ NetBeans

➤ IntelliJ

➤ JCreator

Because setting up development environments can be a bit of a chore, some device manufacturers, like Motorola and NVidia, have gone through a bit of trouble in creating installers for Android SDK development that contain everything you need for developing Android applications. This way you'll avoid having to go through all the manual steps to install a complete Android development environment. If you would prefer to use any of these prepared packages, feel free to do so. They should work like a charm.

The NVidia installer is specifically targeted at Tegra developers, but will work fine for just about everyone developing Android applications. It's called Tegra Android Developer Pack and you can find it at http://www.nvidia.com/content/devzone/tegra-android-developer-pack.html. The MOTODEV studio is found at http://developer.motorola.com/tools/motodevstudio/ download/ and includes, among other things, customized emulators modeled after Motorola devices. Downloading MOTODEV studio requires a registration, but it is completely free.

Android Development Environment

To get a complete Android development environment up and running, you need the Android SDK and the plug-in in addition to Eclipse to connect the two with each other. To get started installing everything now, you need:

➤ Eclipse for Java Developers, found at http://www.eclipse.org

➤ Android SDK Tools, found at http://developer.android.com/sdk/index.html

➤ Android Development Tools (the Eclipse Plugin), installed from within the Eclipse environment

JAVA DEVELOPMENT KIT

When developing in Java you need something called the Java Development Kit (JDK), which is the key to developing Java applications for any platform. It gives the developer all the necessary tools to write, compile, and debug Java programs. However, in some cases you can develop Java applications with the Java Runtime Environment (JRE) alone, but Android is an exception to this rule — the JRE alone won't cut it.

To develop for Android you'll need version 5 or above of the JDK; anything less than that and your Android applications won't compile. But, because of some major improvements in version 6, there's no reason to use anything lower than that.

continues

continued

Should you decide to install JDK version 7 on your machine, you should be aware that it might be the cause of some minor headaches, especially when importing already created projects into your Eclipse workspace. This is because Android does not work on Java 7, and if it does seem to compile your projects for you it's only working by accident. But this doesn't mean that you shouldn't install JDK 7 on your machine, it only means that you must be aware of what compiler version you've selected for your projects; more on this later. If your computer doesn't have a JDK installed, you can find one here: `http://www.oracle.com/technetwork/java/javase/downloads/index.html`.

Android

Android comes in many versions; not counting the vendor-specific libraries, 14 different Android versions are currently available. These range from API version 3 (codenamed Cupcake) all the way up to Jelly Bean, which is API version 16. Table 4-1 shows all the Android versions currently released.

TABLE 4-1: Android Versions

VERSION	API LEVEL	NAME
4.1, 4.1.1	16	Jelly Bean
4.0.3, 4.0.4	15	Ice Cream Sandwich (MR1)
4.0, 4.0.1, 4.0.2	14	Ice Cream Sandwich
3.2	13	Honeycomb (MR2)
3.1.x	12	Honeycomb (MR1)
3.0.x	11	Honeycomb
2.3.3, 2.3.4	10	Gingerbread (MR1)
2.3, 2.3.1, 2.3.2	9	Gingerbread
2.2.x	8	Froyo
2.1.x	7	Éclair (MR1)
2.0.1	6	Éclair (0.1)
2.0	5	Éclair
1.6	4	Donut
1.5	3	Cupcake
1.1	2	Base (1.1)
1.0	1	Base

http://developer.android.com/guide/topics/manifest/uses-sdk-element.html#ApiLevels

For the purpose of this book you'll work exclusively with two API versions of Android — Gingerbread (MR1) and Jelly Bean. We chose these two versions because Android Open Accessory was first introduced in Gingerbread version 2.3.4 as a back-ported version of the accessory added in Honeycomb. Because we're striving to keep this book current, you'll also work with the latest version of Android; at the time of writing this is Jelly Bean version 4.1.

To begin the installation process, follow these steps:

1. Point your web browser to `http://developer.android.com/sdk/` and download the version of the tools that matches your computer. Figure 4-1 shows the webpage where you download the SDK Manager; it will always try to select to correct installer for your system.

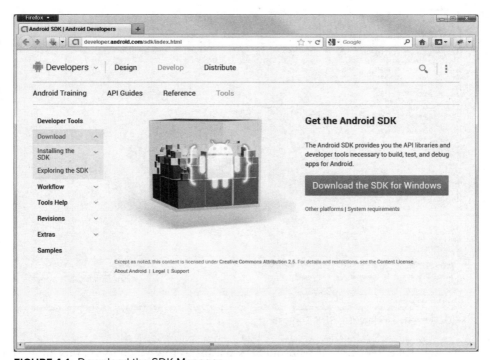

FIGURE 4-1: Download the SDK Manager.

2. Next, install the SDK Manager. If you're working in a Windows environment, this will be easy because it is an executable installation file. If you're running Mac or Linux, you'll have to unarchive the zip or tarball at a desired, secure, place in your filesystem. The default installation directory is always called `android-sdk-mac` on MacOS and `android-sdk-linux` on Linux. When you've installed the SDK, don't move it to another folder.

3. Open the SDK Manager. When you do, it performs a scan of your current Android installation to see what versions of the tools are installed on your system. It also checks the currently available Android platform versions and compares them to the versions you've

installed on your system. On Mac or Linux you need to open the program called android from within folder tools inside the android sdk folder. On Mac this would be `/android-sdk-mac_x86/tools/android`. On Windows you can find the program on your Start Menu, select All Programs ⇨ Android SDK Tools.

4. Update the SDK Tools and SDK Platform-tools, if necessary. At the time of writing this book, the latest SDK Tools are revision 20 and the latest SDK Platform-tools are revision 12. Figure 4-2 shows the SDK Manager with the tools you should install, note that the versions may have changed when you read this and you should always try to have the latest installed version on your system.

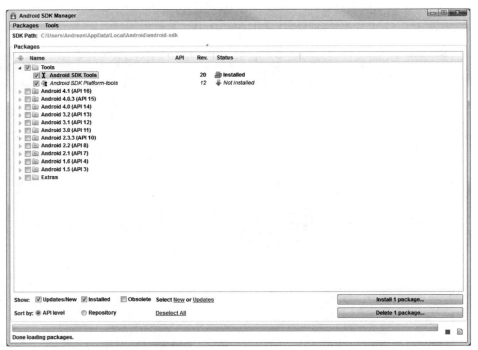

FIGURE 4-2: Update the SDK Tools first.

It's now time to install the Android SDK platforms that you'll use in this book. In the Android SDK Manager window, select the SDK platforms 10 and 16, and their corresponding samples under those categories. You'll notice that some of these platforms have fairly large lists of components available. You don't need to install everything, and we recommend that you select only the bare minimum of what you need. You can always install more components later on as they are needed. However, if you have a lawn to mow or a movie to watch, go ahead and install everything. Chances are it won't be done installing when you're back.

5. Install the SDK Platform, Samples, and Google APIs for version 10 and 16. Figure 4-3 shows which components you should install, at a minimum, for the examples in this book.

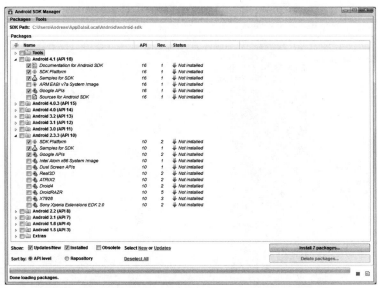

FIGURE 4-3: Select the needed components for platforms 10 and 15.

WARNING *In newer versions of Windows you may run into a problem when installing Android components through the SDK Manager, as shown in Figure 4-4. Most likely this is because you, just like I did, picked the easy executable installation package. Unfortunately, this will sometimes install the SDK Manager into a folder that would normally be protected by the Windows system.*

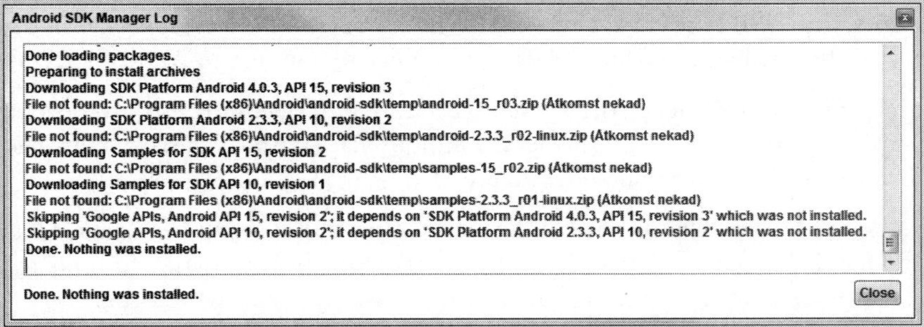

FIGURE 4-4: Common error on Windows

When the SDK Manager tries to install new content into this directory, it'll hit a dead end because Windows won't allow the program to modify the folder. The simple solution is running the SDK Manager as an Administrator rather than your normal user, as shown in Figure 4-5.

continues

continued

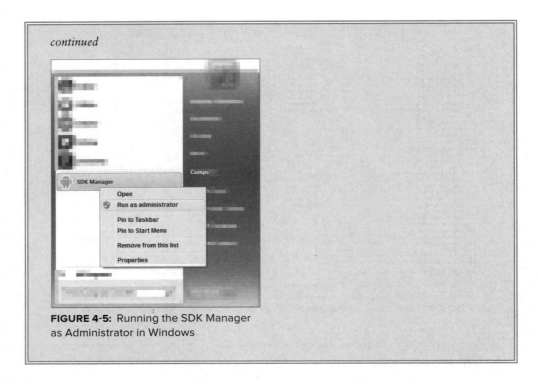

FIGURE 4-5: Running the SDK Manager as Administrator in Windows

USB Drivers

When developing for Android you have the option of working with a virtual device, also called an *emulator*, or a real device. Theoretically, there is no difference between the two; they both run Android. However, the virtual device is just that, virtual. It lacks every physical aspect of the device; sensors, cameras, and USB ports don't exist on a virtual device. However, while the emulator does simulate some of the hardware sensors it lacks the ability to connect to Android accessories.

So, when developing Android accessories you'll need a real device. However, to develop on a real device your development environment needs to communicate with the device by using the Android Debugging Bridge (ADB), as described in Chapter 1.

Connecting a device to the ADB requires a device-specific USB driver; every device manufacturer creates drivers for their own products. You'll find a complete list of download links for USB drivers at http://developer.android.com/tools/extras/oem-usb.html#Drivers.

USB DRIVERS ON MAC OS OR LINUX

You don't need to install a USB driver if you're working with Mac OS or Linux; on Mac "things just work" while on Linux you need to add something called a udev rule.

You can find more information on setting up development on real devices for Mac OS or Linux at http://developer.android.com/tools/device .html#setting-up.

If you're developing on a machine running Mac OS or Linux you should skip the following steps.

> **WARNING** *Make sure to select the correct driver for your device. The driver supplied by Google through the SDK Manager might not work for your device.*

If you are using a Google device, such as Nexus1 or Nexus S use the Android SDK Manager to install the driver. See Figure 4-6 for details. The Galaxy Nexus, however, uses Samsung drivers (it's listed as model SCH-I515).

FIGURE 4-6: Install the Google USB driver.

After you've installed the driver, follow these steps:

1. Make sure your Android device is enabled as a developer device. On devices running Android 4.0 or later you enable this by opening the Settings app.

2. Scroll down to the bottom of the screen and select Developer options.

3. Turn Developer options on using the Toggle button at the top.

4. Make sure the checkbox called USB debugging is selected.

5. Open the Windows Device Manager by typing `mmc devmgmt.msc` in the Windows Start menu. If your device is displayed without a warning symbol in the list, it was installed successfully. If it has a warning symbol, you need to install the driver manually.

6. Right-click the device in the list and select Update Driver Software.

7. Select Browse my computer for driver software, and navigate to the folder where the driver is located. The Google driver is located inside the android-sdk subfolder called extras.

Make sure that your device pops up properly in the Windows Device Manager before continuing.

Eclipse

If you were to draw a painting you would probably start with an empty canvas, and what you can draw on this canvas depends on the brushes you have available. Much like this empty canvas, what you can do with Eclipse depends on the tools that are available to you. To develop for Android you need the Eclipse framework, but you also need the Java Development Tools (JDT) and the Web Standard Tools (WST).

You have two options when downloading Eclipse: either download the bare minimum and install the tools later, or find a package prepared for Java. We recommend either Eclipse Classic or Eclipse for Java Developers. You can find all Eclipse packages at `http://www.eclipse.org/downloads`.

To install Eclipse IDE, follow these steps:

1. Download Eclipse (when writing this book the latest version was Eclipse Juno). Make sure to select the correct version for your computer using the drop-down list. See Figure 4-7.

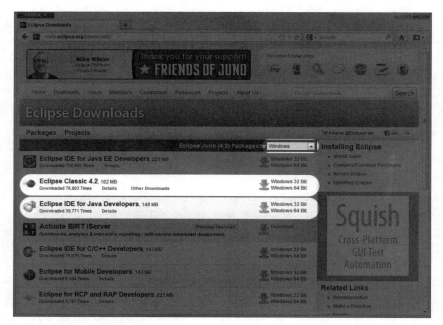

FIGURE 4-7: Download Eclipse IDE for Java Developers.

2. Unzip the downloaded file into a folder of your choice, this will be the location for Eclipse henceforth, so make sure to pick a location on your computer that won't change in the long run.

3. Open the Eclipse IDE; on Windows you double-click the `eclipse.exe` executable and on Mac you open the Application called Eclipse, both are located inside the folder you just extracted.

4. Start a new workspace called **wrox_aoa**.

THE ECLIPSE WORKSPACE

If this is your first time using the Eclipse IDE, you should know that you are using something called a *workspace*. On your computer this may appear as just another folder, but it's actually more than that. For Eclipse the workspace is a logical collection of projects, meaning that one workspace can contain many projects. And Eclipse can also work with multiple workspaces, although it can work with only one workspace at a time.

Android Development Tools (ADT)

Android Development Tools is the Eclipse plug-in, mentioned earlier in this chapter, which enables quick and easy development of Android applications through Eclipse. To install this plug-in you'll need to have Eclipse up and running first:

1. From the Help menu, select Install New Software.

2. Add a new repository by clicking the Add button; set the name to ADT and the location to `https://dl-ssl.google.com/android/eclipse/`, as shown in Figure 4-8.

FIGURE 4-8: Add the new repository.

3. Make sure everything is selected inside Developer Tools, see Figure 4-9. You don't need the NDK unless you specifically want to make use of any native C libraries.

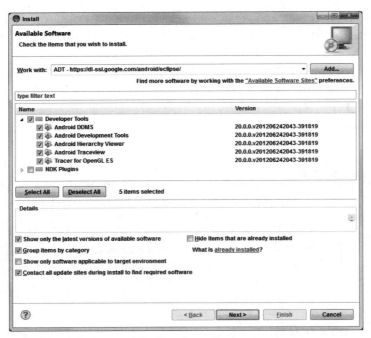

FIGURE 4-9: Select all of the Developer Tools.

4. Restart Eclipse when the plug-in installation has finished.

5. From the Eclipse menu, select Window ➪ Preferences ➪ Android and make sure the SDK Location where you installed Android SDK Tools is filled in and correct. You should see a list of all the installed Android platforms in the list below it, as shown in Figure 4-10.

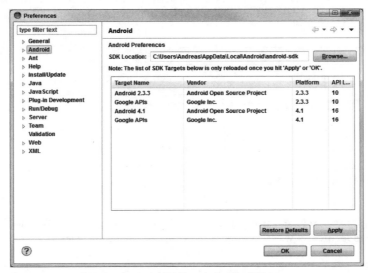

FIGURE 4-10: Set the Android SDK path inside Eclipse.

That's it. You're ready to start developing applications for Android now, but to follow all the examples in this book you need one more development environment installed: the one where you'll program the Arduino microcontroller. But first, test your Android development environment.

Hello, Android!

You're lucky that Android comes with a set of example application projects to test your development environment, this means you can easily test that the environment is working just by using one of these examples.

Another good reason why you should explore all of the example projects is that at some point you'll have to develop something quite complex, and when that time comes it's good to know if it has already been solved in an open source project available to you.

For the purpose of proof testing your development environment, you'll use one of these already available projects:

1. If it's not already opened, open Eclipse.

2. From the File menu select New ⇨ Other.

3. In the dialog box, expand Android and select Android Sample Project.

4. Click Next.

5. Select Android 4.1 as Build Target and click Next, note that not all example projects are available in all API versions.

6. Select the project called ApiDemos and click Finish.

You should now have a new Android project in your Eclipse workspace. This is a project loaded from the Android samples that you downloaded previously through the SDK Manager.

You can test this demo either on an emulator or on a real device. The choice is yours, but you're strongly encouraged to use your real device. Not only is it easier to test all the available technology in the system, but it's also blazingly fast compared to the emulator.

To install the ApiDemos app on your device, follow these steps:

1. Expand the Eclipse project inside the Package Explorer.

2. Open the Run menu and select Run.

FIGURE 4-11: You should see this screen on your device when launching the ApiDemos application for the first time.

When the application has successfully installed you should get the same screen on your device as shown in Figure 4-11.

NOTE *ApiDemos is a project that explores many of the fundamental APIs available in Android, and because of this breadth it's also an excellent source of reusable code for many different kinds of projects.*

SETTING UP ARDUINO DEVELOPMENT

The Android IDE comes in many shapes and forms, from the official text-based version to visual LEGO-like environments where drag-and-drop interactions are used to create the Arduino sketches. The common denominator for all of these different environments is simplicity, which is also one of the objectives of the Arduino platform.

Arduino Development Environment

Arduino comes packaged in an archive, so you'll need to unzip it to a secure location on your computer.

You should also take care when choosing where to install Arduino on a Windows system. If you place it in a protected folder you may run into trouble when updating your installation later on. You need to download and install the following tools:

➤ Arduino IDE

➤ Arduino USB Driver

➤ Arduino ADK Library

Arduino IDE

To install the Arduino IDE follow the steps below:

1. Download the Arduino IDE from `http://arduino.cc/en/Main/Software/`. Figure 4-12 shows the Arduino download page.

FIGURE 4-12: Download Arduino from the Arduino website.

2. Unzip the archive to a suitable folder on your computer.

3. Open Arduino by double-clicking the executable file.

Arduino USB Driver

Just like Android, Arduino requires a specific USB driver to be installed before you can start uploading sketches to it. Some boards share drivers — this is because they're built using the same processors. You can find all the Arduino drivers in a folder called drivers inside the Arduino program folder. If you're on Mac OS or Linux you won't need to install any USB drivers, it should "just work." Follow these steps to install the Arduino USB driver for Windows, if you're using Mac OS or Linux you can skip them:

1. Open the Windows Device Manager by executing the mmc devmgmt.msc command inside the Windows Start menu. Figure 4-13 shows the uninstalled Arduino as "Other Devices."

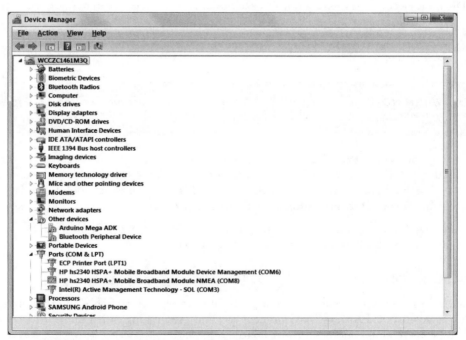

FIGURE 4-13: Install the Arduino Mega ADK driver.

2. Right-click the Arduino Mega ADK item and select Update Driver Software.

3. Search for a driver on your system manually, and navigate to the drivers folder inside the Arduino program folder.

4. You may get a warning saying that the driver can't be verified. Ignore this and install it anyway. You can rest assured that Arduino is not trying to hack your computer!

Your Arduino Mega ADK board should now be installed, and the Windows Device Manager should have been updated, now with a COM X number next to the Arduino Mega ADK line. Remember that number!

USB PORT NUMBERS ON MAC AND LINUX

On computers running Windows the serial ports are numbered in a special manner with a "COM" in front of the number. However, on Mac and Linux these port names look different.

On Mac OS the serial ports for the Arduino boards are called /dev/tty.usbmodem.

ADK Library

The ADK Library contains the functions to use the USB Host mode when developing on the Arduino; to install it follow these steps:

1. Download the `ArduinoADK.zip` file from `http://labs.arduino.cc/ADK/AccessoryMode/`.

WARNING *Beware that this file contains more than just the Arduino ADK files; you should take care to use only the needed files.*

---

2. Copy the folder `<ArduinoADK.zip>\Arduino\libraries` to your `<Arduino Sketchbook>\` folder. On Windows computers you can normally find the sketchbook folder under `C:\Users\<user>\Documents\Arduino\`. On Mac OS the sketchbook folder is placed by default in your Documents folder, the full path is `/<user>/Documents/Arduino/`.

3. Restart Arduino. You need to do this because the Processing IDE, on which Arduino IDE is built, scans for all extras on startup, including extra libraries.

Hello, Arduino!

Just like Android, Arduino comes with a large list of examples for reference and to build upon. To test your newly installed Arduino environment you'll use something called Blink, which just blinks an LED on your Arduino microcontroller board.

1. From the File menu, select Examples ➪ 1.Basics ➪ Blink. This loads the example Blink, which blinks a surface-mounted LED on top of the Arduino board in a certain pattern.

2. Before you compile and upload this sketch to the Arduino board, you need to select the correct board and the correct port. From the Tools menu select Board ➪ Arduino Mega 2560 or Mega ADK.

3. Now you need to select the correct port. This can be a bit tricky if you're not familiar with the Windows system. Open the Start menu and run the command `mmc devmgmt.msc`. On Mac OS you can skip to step 5.

4. Locate the Arduino Mega ADK line and find its port number. In Figure 4-14 the port is COM20.

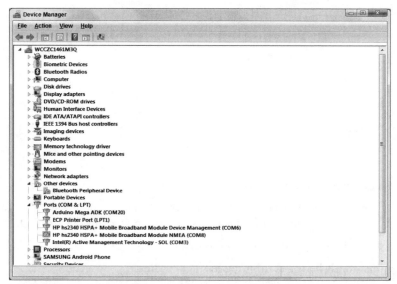

FIGURE 4-14: Find the Arduino Mega ADK port number.

5. Select the correct port in the Arduino IDE from the Tools menu, select Serial Port menu. Replace the X with the number you found in the Device Manager. If you're using Mac you should select the option whose name starts with /dev/tty.usbmodem.

6. To load the sketch onto your Arduino board open the File menu and select Upload. If you've done everything correctly so far, you should see the two small LEDs (named RX and TX) flash; this means that the sketch is uploading properly and will start running shortly. Figure 4-15 shows the RX and TX LEDs on the Arduino MEGA ADK board.

FIGURE 4-15: The sketch is uploading if the LEDs called RX and TX are flashing.

The Arduino Blink example, as shown in Listing 4-1, is really simple.

LISTING 4-1: Arduino Blink

```
int led = 13;
void setup(){
  pinMode( led, OUTPUT );
}
void loop(){
  digitalWrite( led, HIGH );
  delay( 1000 );
  digitalWrite( led, LOW );
  delay( 1000 );
}
```

In fact, the Blink example only has five steps to it:

1. pinMode sets pin number 13 as OUTPUT, meaning that you can send up to 5V to this pin to turn whatever is connected on or off. In this case it's the surface-mounted LED.

2. It then turns the LED on by setting the pin to HIGH.

3. Wait 1000 milliseconds before continuing to the next line.

4. Turn the LED off by setting the pin to LOW.

5. Wait another 1000 milliseconds before starting over from the top.

In between steps 2 and 4 there's also a short delay of 1000 milliseconds. You can change this and see for yourself that the small LED does blink quicker when the delay value is lower.

You may also have noticed that there is a pin labeled 13 on the Arduino board. You might ask yourself if the LED you're playing with now is pin 13, what is this other pin 13? The answer is simply that they're both the same pin and they will both receive the same voltage throughout this sketch. You can test this quickly by connecting a 5mm LED to pin 13 and the ground pin right next to it. See Figure 4-16.

FIGURE 4-16: External 5mm LED connected to pin 13

LIGHT-EMITTING DIODE (LED)

The LED, or light-emitting diode, is a quite robust piece of electronics. However, this doesn't mean that you can treat it in any way you want and still hope that it will work as expected.

First of all you should take care never to exceed the recommended voltage for said LED. Most LEDs require a resistor to work, but fortunately pin 13 also comes with a built-in resistor because of the attached surface-mounted LED. No other pin on the Arduino has a built-in resistor like pin 13, which is why you should always take care to use resistors whenever there's an LED in your circuit.

Secondly, the 5mm LED has two legs, one of which is longer than the other. This longer leg is the positive lead (+) and should be connected to pin 13 in the example; the shorter pin is the negative lead (–) and should be connected to the ground pin (gnd).

Another interesting fact about the LED is that if you look closely inside the bulb you'll see that the two leads are each connected to a little piece of metal. This metal has a very distinctive look, so you can use it to discern between the two leads. See Figure 4-17.

FIGURE 4-17: The common 5mm LED. Notice the inside of the bulb and the length of the legs.

HELLO OPEN ACCESSORY APP

For the purpose of testing your newly installed Android Open Accessory development environment, you'll run a simple test application that reads a temperature sensor connected to Arduino and displays the value in Kelvin on the phone's screen.

The Temperature Sensor

To build the accessory, you need:

➤ 1 Arduino Mega ADK

➤ 1 breadboard

➤ 3 wires

➤ 1 temperature sensor (LM35)

Unlike your common household thermometer, the LM35 has no mercury inside this sensor; instead, it uses the principle that voltage in a diode changes based on the temperature, and it changes at a fixed rate. This behavior makes it really simple to calculate the current ambient temperature with a simple mathematical formula:

$$K = (mV * 100) + 273.15$$

The result of this equation is the ambient temperature in Kelvin; mV (millivolts) is the value read from the analog pin converted to volts. That's delivered as Celcius, adding 273.15 will give you the temperature in Kelvin.

This formula, however, requires that you know what the voltage over the sensor is. To calculate this you'll have to know the voltage you're channeling through the sensor; in the example it's 5000mV, but you can use anything between 3.3V and 5V.

$$mV_{out} = (analogRead * 5.0)/1024$$

You do this calculation to convert the value read from the analog pin to a voltage value. The range for the analog pin is 0 to 1023, and you want to convert it to 0 to 5000mV.

In Figure 4-18 you can see that the sensor is connected to the 5V pin on the Arduino board. This means that the final equation to calculate the temperature in Kelvin is:

$$K = (((analogRead \times (5000/1024)) - 500)/10)\ 273.15$$

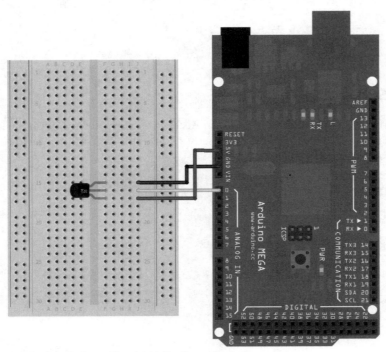

FIGURE 4-18: Circuit for the Hello Open Accessory

The Arduino Sketch

The idea is that the Arduino will keep sending temperature values to the Android device, which will then display the values, and display some suitable graphic.

To do this, the sketch needs to do a few things:

1. Read the analog pin that the sensor is connected to.

2. Convert the read value to a temperature value that is more appropriate; because you are a person who enjoys being scientifically correct, you'll of course convert the value to Kelvin (right?).

3. Write the converted temperature value to the USB.

4. And, because you're not doing rocket science (yet), there's no need to flood the USB connection more than necessary.

The Temperature Sensor example is shown in Listing 4-2.

LISTING 4-2: Arduino Temperature Sensor

```
#include <Max3421e.h>
#include <Usb.h>
#include <AndroidAccessory.h>
char application [] = "wrox_temperature_sensor";
char accessory [] = "wrox_temperature_sensor";
char company [] = "Wiley";
char versionNbr[] = "1.0";
char serialNbr[] = "1";
char url[] = "http://media.wiley.com/product_ancillary/66/11184547/
DOWNLOAD/t.apk";
int sensorPin = 0;
long timer = millis();
AndroidAccessory usb(company, application, accessory, versionNbr, url,
serialNbr);
void setup() {
  usb.powerOn();
}
void loop() {
  if (usb.isConnected()) {
    if( millis() - timer > 10 ) {
      int val = analogRead( sensorPin );
      float voltage = (val * 5.0) / 1024.0;
      float tempCelcius = voltage * 100;
      float tempKelvin = tempCelcius + 273.15;
      byte * b = (byte *) &tempKelvin;
      usb.write(b, 4);
      timer = millis();
    }
  }
}
```

The Android Project

On the Android side you don't actually have to do anything, not even open the project. The compiled app already exists online and the phone will automatically request to download it when connected to the accessory (the Arduino). The Eclipse project for this application is available from the book's website so you can mess around with it on your own, if you want.

Ready to Go

When everything is set — your accessory is all set up and programmed, your phone has a working Internet connection, and you've got a celebratory bottle of champagne — go ahead and hook everything up together in one messy bundle. Hook up the Arduino to the USB port on your computer (for powering only!), the phone to the Arduino, and the champagne to the tall glass.

If everything works well, you should see a request on the Android screen asking if you'd like to install the Temperature Sensor application. Go ahead and say "yes, please, I'd like to know the temperature now." Figure 4-19 shows the assembled temperature sensor accessory.

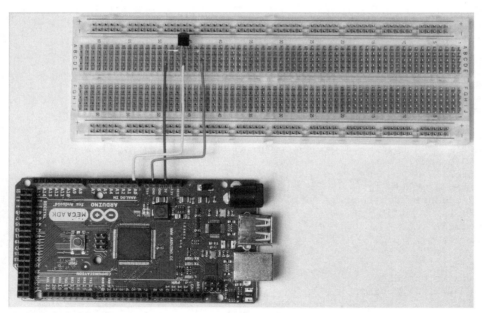

FIGURE 4-19: Your first Android accessory, built and tested.

SUMMARY

In this chapter you finally got the whole development environment up and running. You can now create your own Arduino sketches and upload them to the microcontroller. To do this you need:

➤ The Arduino IDE for your computer

➤ The Arduino USB drivers for your Arduino board

➤ To develop and run Android projects on real devices you need to install a few things: Eclipse IDE with the correct tools installed

➤ Android SDK Tools

➤ Android Development Tools (the Eclipse Plugin)

➤ Android USB drivers to debug applications on a real device

These are all the things you need to get a working environment for Android Open Accessory development. Now you're all set to start experimenting with your own accessories.

Creating the Accessory Library

WHAT'S IN THIS CHAPTER?

➤ A short introduction to Android libraries

➤ Implementing the MQTT protocol

➤ Building a library capable of handling accessory communication

WROX.COM CODE DOWNLOADS FOR THIS CHAPTER

The wrox.com code downloads for this chapter are found at `www.wrox.com/remtitle .cgi?isbn=1118454766` on the Download Code tab. The code is in the Chapter 5 download and individually named according to the names throughout the chapter.

Almost all current mobile applications leverage communication in different formats; however, in many cases as a developer you never have to worry about how the data is passed from point A to point B — it just magically happens. In this chapter you create your first set of Android Open Accessory-enabled applications, but before you get started on the applications you should define the common denominator — the USB communication.

Reusability is an amazing feature of any well-designed software stack; of course, I don't have to tell you this. We've all come in contact with this concept in one way or another when leveraging system libraries or custom additions and plug-ins for various platforms.

Be it web, desktop, or mobile, leveraging reusable software stacks is a key feature of success in our business. For this reason, in this chapter you create an Android library project that handles the communication with the USB accessory, and you use this library in all of the Android Open Accessory (AOA) projects you build while reading this book.

When you've created the USB communications library and made sure it works as intended, you can move forward to the fun stuff — designing and implementing the Android user interfaces for your accessories.

GETTING STARTED WITH ANDROID LIBRARIES

An *Android library* is, like a library in many other programming languages, a set of helpful resources that considerably decreases your development time and enables you to focus on the project at hand instead of spending valuable time on establishing needed infrastructure. In Android you can use two kinds of libraries: system libraries and third-party libraries. The latter are libraries that are not packaged with the Android SDK — they're developed by you or me.

If you've had the opportunity to work with a custom-built Android library in the past, you've undoubtedly noticed the difference between that and its Java counterpart. The Android library is often an Android project specifically marked as a library and added to your Eclipse workspace. It is then referenced inside your application's `project.properties` file, thus making it available to your application on compilation.

Creating a new Android library project is just as simple as creating a normal Android project. The only difference is that you must select the Is Library checkbox in the project properties. When you've selected that checkbox, your new library project is immediately available to your other Android projects.

The library project follows the same format as a normal Android project. For example, any shared components within the Android library project must be declared inside its `AndroidManifest.xml` file. You must then reproduce the shared components you want to use in your Android project inside its own `AndroidManifest.xml` file, or you can merge the two manifests together.

BUILDING THE P2PMQTT LIBRARY

Your P2PMQTT library will inherit all of the message constructs from MQTT specification version 3. Because MQTT messages are so small, you need some knowledge of bitwise operations to understand how each message is constructed.

You should note that although the MQTT specification is a rock-solid protocol, the library you create in this book is just a starting point for building prototype accessories with Arduino; you should not consider using it in release candidate applications, and you should definitely avoid using it in performance-critical applications where people or properties may come in harm's way — such as health care applications, alarms, or control units for large machinery.

Preparing the Library Project

First thing first, you need to create the special Android library type project:

1.   In Eclipse, open the File menu and select New ⇨ Other.
2.   Select Android ⇨ Android Application Project from the list.
3.   Where it says Application Name, enter **WroxAccessories**.
4.   Set the Package Name to **com.wiley.aoa.wroxaccessories**.

5. Select the Mark this project as a library checkbox.

6. Click Next and skip the icon preferences by clicking Next one more time.

7. Because you're making a library without a user interface, you can go ahead and unselect the Create Activity checkbox before you click Finish.

Sketching the API

Before you start to create a library like this one, it's always a good idea to pause for a second and ask yourself the purpose of this library — what tasks should this library make easier for you? In the case of your WroxAccessories library, the answer is quite simple; it should help you create accessory projects at a faster pace. The library should at least perform the following tasks for you:

➤ Simplify the process of adding AOA-specific communications code to your Android project.

➤ Initiate and maintain worker threads for the sockets communications.

➤ Encode and decode MQTT messages from common formats that are easier to understand for you and me.

Creating the Public Library Interface

Now that you know the overall functionality that your library will provide, you need to define the containers where this functionality will go. Start with the library interface — the main class of this library:

1. With your new Android library project selected in Eclipse, open the File menu and choose New ⇨ Class.

2. As the Package Name, enter **com.wiley.wroxaccessories**.

3. Give your new class the name **WroxAccessory**.

4. Check the Constructors from superclass checkbox.

5. Before you click Finish to create the class, make sure that your new class has no specific superclass or interfaces. Also make sure that Eclipse won't create the main method.

Your new class should look something like Listing 5-1 — quite empty! This will be the main entry point for using your new library in your Android projects, so you'll gather most of the public methods in here.

LISTING 5-1: Create the WroxAccessory Library class

```
package com.wiley.wroxaccessories;
public class WroxAccessory {
  public WroxAccessory() {
  }
}
```

Adding a Reference to the Context

Because you'll be working with some context-specific APIs in the Android system, your library needs a reference to the context where it is currently working — the activity or application. However, some pitfalls exist when referencing a context that you should know about:

➤ You should always try to avoid referencing the context whenever you can; in this case, however, you need the reference.

➤ If you really need the context, try to avoid using static references because those might actually outlive the context itself. That's when things get nasty and memory leaks happen.

➤ Another common tip is to avoid referencing the context in non-static inner classes in activities when you're not in control over their life cycle. Use static inner classes and weak references to the activity instead.

➤ Finally, you have two types of contexts: the activity context and the application context. You should consider using the application context if you're unsure about the life cycle of your object because that will always survive through the entire life of the application.

Add the context reference to your library, and also add a `Context` parameter to the library constructor, as shown in Listing 5-2.

LISTING 5-2: Add a reference to the context

```
package com.wiley.wroxaccessories;
import android.content.Context;
public class WroxAccessory {
  private Context mContext;
  public WroxAccessory(Context context) {
    mContext = context;
  }
}
```

Implementing MQTT

To make your library adhere to the MQTT specifications, you need a couple of methods. Even though you might not use some of the methods straight away, it's a good idea to add them now so that it's clearer to you in the future where certain algorithms of the library should go.

Also, you don't need to add methods corresponding to all the messages in the MQTT specification because some of them are responses to other messages. The following is a list of messages that you'll definitely need a public method for in the API:

➤ CONNECT — This is used as a handshake by both the Android and the Arduino device. When the connection is established, both send a CONNECT request, and both should expect a CONNACK response from each other. If either fails to do this, the connection should be closed.

➤ **PUBLISH** — For the sake of simplicity, you use only the lowest Quality of Service (QoS) level for all PUBLISH messages in this tutorial. This means that neither the Arduino nor the Android device will send any responses when receiving a PUBLISH message.

➤ **SUBSCRIBE** — When subscribing you get a simple SUBACK message from the receiver. Subscribing to a topic also means registering a broadcast receiver for each subscription.

➤ **UNSUBSCRIBE** — This is followed by a UNSUBACK message from the receiving end. This also unregisters any broadcast receivers for this subscription.

➤ **PINGREQ** — Gets a PINGRESP as response.

➤ **DISCONNECT** — This message exists to allow for graceful disconnections rather than just dropping the line. Neither end of the communication should expect to get this message, but when it does, it should be happy.

Add the method stubs as shown in Listing 5-3 to your `WroxAccessory.java` class. You modify these stubs more later.

LISTING 5-3: Add the method stubs

```java
package com.wiley.wroxaccessories;
public class WroxAccessory {
  private Context mContext;
  public WroxAccessory( Context context ) {
    mContext = context;
  }
  public void connect(){
  }
  public void publish(){
  }
  public void subscribe(){
  }
  public void unsubscribe(){
  }
  public void pingreq(){
  }
  public void disconnect(){
  }
}
```

Before you can implement your new public API, you need to have your private parts ready (pun intended); that is, the AOA communications and MQTT packaging.

Packaging MQTT

As you read in Chapter 3, MQTT has a very detailed specification of how to package data and how the protocol should be used; for the purpose of your library, you should follow these specifications as closely as possible. In some parts you may follow a different pattern of usage, but the way information is being delivered should strictly follow the MQTT specification.

First, you need to create the `MQTT.java` class:

1. With your new Android library project selected in Eclipse, open the File menu and select New ⇨ Class.

2. As the Package Name, enter **com.wiley.wroxaccessories**.

3. Name your new class **MQTT**.

4. Before you click Finish to create the class, make sure that your new class has no specific superclass or interfaces. Also make sure that Eclipse won't create the main method for this class.

You should end up with something similar to Listing 5-4. Notice that there is no constructor in the `MQTT.java` class; this is because you don't necessarily want to instantiate this class. Instead, you'll create static methods to encode or decode MQTT messages.

Also, go ahead and add the version and protocol name that your library will use. The protocol name will always be P2PMQTT, with that capitalization. Since this is the first time you write this library, set the version to 1.

LISTING 5-4: Create the MQTT.java class

```
package com.wiley.wroxaccessories;
public class MQTT {
  protected static byte VERSION = (byte) 0x01;
  protected static String PROTOCOL_NAME = "P2PMQTT";
}
```

Creating a Dictionary

Your new MQTT encode/decode class must understand MQTT words and terms. The easiest way to help it understand the keywords used is through constants. It is a good idea to make these constants protected so that only the members of the library can access them. Your Android app shouldn't have to know anything about the underlying communication — from its perspective, *things should just work*.

Add the constants shown in Listing 5-5. Notice how the values of these constants correspond to Table 3-3 in Chapter 3.

An alternative approach to this problem would have been to create an MQTT object hierarchy, but because that requires a few more files your best bet is to start off with the dictionary approach.

LISTING 5-5: Add the MQTT message constants

```
package com.wiley.wroxaccessories;
public class MQTT {
  protected static byte VERSION = (byte) 0x01;
  protected static String PROTOCOL_NAME = "P2PMQTT";
  protected static final int CONNECT = 1;
  protected static final int CONNACK = 2;
  protected static final int PUBLISH = 3;
```

```
      protected static final int PUBACK = 4;
      protected static final int PUBREC = 5;
      protected static final int PUBREL = 6;
      protected static final int PUBCOMP = 7;
      protected static final int SUBSCRIBE = 8;
      protected static final int SUBACK = 9;
      protected static final int UNSUBSCRIBE = 10;
      protected static final int UNSUBACK = 11;
      protected static final int PINGREQ = 12;
      protected static final int PINGRESP = 13;
      protected static final int DISCONNECT = 14;
}
```

Encoding an MQTT Message

Your class can now interpret all of the MQTT messages, but it has no idea how to handle that information. Your next step, then, is to start the basic way of encoding a message that adheres to the specific MQTT pattern.

Add the encode method stub as shown in Listing 5-6. The variable header parameters will be sent as a variable string array called `params`.

LISTING 5-6: Add the encode method stub

```
package com.wiley.wroxaccessories;
public class MQTT {
  protected static byte VERSION = (byte) 0x01;
  protected static String PROTOCOL_NAME = "P2PMQTT";
  protected static final int CONNECT = 1;
  protected static final int CONNACK = 2;
  protected static final int PUBLISH = 3;
  protected static final int PUBACK = 4;
  protected static final int PUBREC = 5;
  protected static final int PUBREL = 6;
  protected static final int PUBCOMP = 7;
  protected static final int SUBSCRIBE = 8;
  protected static final int SUBACK = 9;
  protected static final int UNSUBSCRIBE = 10;
  protected static final int UNSUBACK = 11;
  protected static final int PINGREQ = 12;
  protected static final int PINGRESP = 13;
  protected static final int DISCONNECT = 14;
  protected static byte[] encode(int type, boolean retain, int qos, boolean dup,
      byte[]  payload, String... params){
  }
}
```

The Fixed Header

Always start with the bare minimum; in this example, you focus on the CONNECT message as described in Chapter 3. Because the overhead of each message is different, your best bet is to use something called a `ByteArrayOutputStream` because that writes to an expanding byte array that is then returned as the resulting MQTT package, as shown in Listing 5-7.

LISTING 5-7: Add the common components of the encode method

```java
package com.wiley.wroxaccessories;
import java.io.ByteArrayOutputStream;
public class MQTT {
  protected static byte VERSION = (byte) 0x01;
  protected static String PROTOCOL_NAME = "P2PMQTT";
  protected static final int CONNECT = 1;
  protected static final int CONNACK = 2;
  protected static final int PUBLISH = 3;
  protected static final int PUBACK = 4;
  protected static final int PUBREC = 5;
  protected static final int PUBREL = 6;
  protected static final int PUBCOMP = 7;
  protected static final int SUBSCRIBE = 8;
  protected static final int SUBACK = 9;
  protected static final int UNSUBSCRIBE = 10;
  protected static final int UNSUBACK = 11;
  protected static final int PINGREQ = 12;
  protected static final int PINGRESP = 13;
  protected static final int DISCONNECT = 14;
  protected static byte[] encode(int type, boolean retain, int qos, boolean dup,
      byte[] payload, String... params) {
    ByteArrayOutputStream mqtt = new ByteArrayOutputStream();
    switch (type) {
    }
    mqtt.write(payload);
    return mqtt.toByteArray();
  }
}
```

The fixed header will have a minimum of 2 bytes, but it may also grow larger — up to 5 bytes depending on the payload. The first byte contains a number of properties for the message and is fairly easy to encode using straightforward bitwise operations.

OF BITS AND BYTES

Most people with some programming experience are familiar with the concept that computers work with 1s and 0s; however, a large number of these people will never really work with information at that level. Because MQTT is made to transport critical sensor information in even the worst scenarios, there is a need to avoid all excess information, which is why MQTT messages are constructed at the lowest possible level — 1s and 0s.

The Bit

The bit, short for binary digit, is the smallest possible logical unit. It's a binary value, meaning it can have only two possible values: 1 or 0.

The Byte

The byte is the smallest form of primitive information available in Java, and it's a sequence of 8 bits; this means the byte can have 2^8 different combinations. That's 256 different values. A common way to represent the byte is with a table of one row and eight columns; you can see the number 52 represented as one byte in Table 5-1.

TABLE 5-1: The Number 52 Represented as Bits of a Byte

BIT	7	6	5	4	3	2	1	0
Value	0	0	1	1	0	1	0	0

Bitwise Operations

When working at the bit level of information, you must use something called the *bitwise operators*; these are operators much like the common math operators (addition, subtraction, multiplication, and division), but work on bits and bit patterns instead of higher-range values, like the integer. You can use four different bitwise operators: NOT, AND, OR, and XOR.

NOT

The NOT operator (~) performs a logical negation on each bit in the pattern; the result of a NOT operation on the byte from Table 5-1 would look like Table 5-2, and it is the number 203. In Java, however, the byte range is from −128 to 127, which means that in Java the resulting value from this operation would be −53. (Actually, in Java there is no bitwise NOT operation; there is, however, a bitwise complement operator, ~, which does the same as the NOT operator.)

TABLE 5-2: The Number 203 Represented as Bits of a Byte

BIT	7	6	5	4	3	2	1	0
Value	1	1	0	0	1	0	1	1

AND

The bitwise AND operation (&) takes two bit patterns of equal length and performs a multiplication of each bit in the first pattern with the corresponding bit in the second pattern. The bitwise AND operation on the bytes in Tables 5-1 and 5-2 would generate the byte in Table 5-3 — all zeros.

continues

continued

TABLE 5-3: The Result of the Bitwise AND Operation for Tables 5-1 and 5-2

BIT	7	6	5	4	3	2	1	0
Value	0	0	0	0	0	0	0	0

OR

The bitwise inclusive OR operation (|) takes two bit patterns of equal length and then performs an addition on each bit in the first pattern with the corresponding bit in the second pattern; however, if the two bits are both 1, the resulting bit is 1. The result for the bitwise OR operation on the bytes in Tables 5-1 and 5-2 would be the byte in Table 5-4.

TABLE 5-4: The Result of a Bitwise OR Operation for Tables 5-1 and 5-2

BIT	7	6	5	4	3	2	1	0
Value	1	1	1	1	1	1	1	1

XOR

The bitwise exclusive OR operation (^) is similar to the inclusive OR operation; where the inclusive OR performs an addition of each bit in the two patterns, the exclusive OR performs a comparison of the two corresponding bits in the two equal length bit patterns. If either of the bits is 1, and at the same time the other bit is 0, the result is 1. If both bits are 0 or both bits are 1, the result is 0. The bitwise XOR operation between the bytes in Tables 5-1 and 5-4 is displayed in Table 5-5.

TABLE 5-5: The Result of a Bitwise XOR Operation for Tables 5-1 and 5-4

BIT	7	6	5	4	3	2	1	0
Value	1	1	0	0	1	0	1	1

Shift Operations

The bitwise shift operations move the positions of all bits (or just specific bits) in a bit pattern to either the left side or the right side. You can use the shift operation to populate a bit pattern with 1s or 0s to your own preference.

Left Shift

The left shift operation (<<) moves all bits of a pattern to the left. For example, the declaration `byte b = (byte)(1 << 3);` would produce the bit pattern in Table 5-6, which also happens to be the value 8.

TABLE 5-6: The Result of the Left Shift Operation 1 << 3

BIT	7	6	5	4	3	2	1	0
Value	0	0	0	0	1	0	0	0

Right Shift

The right shift operation (>>) works just like the left shift operation, but it moves all the affected bits to the right.

Listing 5-8 shows how to encode multiple parameters into one single byte using bitwise operations. The remaining bytes of the fixed header define the length of the message (including both the variable header and the payload) in bytes and are a little bit more complex to encode.

LISTING 5-8: Write the first byte of the fixed header

```java
package com.wiley.wroxaccessories;
import java.io.ByteArrayOutputStream;
public class MQTT {
  protected static byte VERSION = (byte) 0x01;
  protected static String PROTOCOL_NAME = "P2PMQTT";
  protected static final int CONNECT = 1;
  protected static final int CONNACK = 2;
  protected static final int PUBLISH = 3;
  protected static final int PUBACK = 4;
  protected static final int PUBREC = 5;
  protected static final int PUBREL = 6;
  protected static final int PUBCOMP = 7;
  protected static final int SUBSCRIBE = 8;
  protected static final int SUBACK = 9;
  protected static final int UNSUBSCRIBE = 10;
  protected static final int UNSUBACK = 11;
  protected static final int PINGREQ = 12;
  protected static final int PINGRESP = 13;
  protected static final int DISCONNECT = 14;
  protected static byte[] encode(int type, boolean retain, int qos, boolean dup,
      byte[] payload, String... params) {
    ByteArrayOutputStream mqtt = new ByteArrayOutputStream();
    mqtt.write((byte) ((retain ? 1 : 0) | qos << 1 | (dup ? 1 : 0) << 3 | type << 4));
    switch (type) {
    }
    mqtt.write(payload);
    return mqtt.toByteArray();
  }
}
```

The remaining length field of the fixed header uses between 1 and 4 bytes to encode the maximum length of the payload and the variable header for the message, which can theoretically grow up to 256 MB. For this to work, you'll only use 7 bits of each byte. The last bit defines if the message has another byte in the remaining length field. The basic process of encoding this field is as follows:

1. Find out the length of the payload in bytes and the variable header length; you use this to determine how many bytes are needed for the remaining length field of the fixed header.

2. In a do-while loop, create a new byte that represents the byte you're currently working on in the remaining length field, and assign it the value of the modulus operation of the length and 128.

3. To find out if there should be more bytes to the length value, divide the length by 128. If the length is above 0, this means that you should expect more bytes.

4. Append the current byte to the end of the fixed header. If the length is still above 0, repeat the process until the length is no longer above 0.

Add the algorithm to encode the remaining length field to your `encode` method, as shown in Listing 5-9. For the variable header, you'll use another `ByteArrayOutputStream`.

LISTING 5-9: Add the remaining length field

```
package com.wiley.wroxaccessories;
import java.io.ByteArrayOutputStream;
public class MQTT {
  protected static byte VERSION = (byte) 0x01;
  protected static String PROTOCOL_NAME = "P2PMQTT";
  protected static final int CONNECT = 1;
  protected static final int CONNACK = 2;
  protected static final int PUBLISH = 3;
  protected static final int PUBACK = 4;
  protected static final int PUBREC = 5;
  protected static final int PUBREL = 6;
  protected static final int PUBCOMP = 7;
  protected static final int SUBSCRIBE = 8;
  protected static final int SUBACK = 9;
  protected static final int UNSUBSCRIBE = 10;
  protected static final int UNSUBACK = 11;
  protected static final int PINGREQ = 12;
  protected static final int PINGRESP = 13;
  protected static final int DISCONNECT = 14;
  protected static byte[] encode(int type, boolean retain, int qos, boolean dup,
      byte[] payload, String... params) {
    ByteArrayOutputStream mqtt = new ByteArrayOutputStream();
    mqtt.write((byte) ((retain ? 1 : 0) | qos << 1 | (dup ? 1 : 0) << 3 | type << 4));
    ByteArrayOutputStream variableHeader = new ByteArrayOutputStream();
    switch (type) {
    }
    int length = payload.length + variableHeader.size();
    do {
      byte digit = (byte) (length % 128);
      length /= 128;
      if (length > 0)
```

```
        digit = (byte) (digit | 0x80);
      mqtt.write(digit);
    } while (length > 0);
    mqtt.write(payload);
    return mqtt.toByteArray();
  }
}
```

The Variable Header

Because the structure of the variable header is entirely dependent on the message being sent, the algorithm for compiling it is a lot longer than that of the fixed header. Also, because the content of the variable header is different, you need a way to access different parameters for different messages. You have a number of ways to combat this issue, but in this tutorial you use a list of optional strings that you then parse in different ways depending on the message.

To simplify this process, you implement one message at a time, starting with the CONNECT message, because that will be the first thing happening in the conversation between the two clients. See Listing 5-10 for details.

LISTING 5-10: Create the variable header for the CONNECT message

```
package com.wiley.wroxaccessories;
import java.io.ByteArrayOutputStream;
public class MQTT {
  protected static byte VERSION = (byte) 0x01;
  protected static String PROTOCOL_NAME = "P2PMQTT";
  protected static final int CONNECT = 1;
  protected static final int CONNACK = 2;
  protected static final int PUBLISH = 3;
  protected static final int PUBACK = 4;
  protected static final int PUBREC = 5;
  protected static final int PUBREL = 6;
  protected static final int PUBCOMP = 7;
  protected static final int SUBSCRIBE = 8;
  protected static final int SUBACK = 9;
  protected static final int UNSUBSCRIBE = 10;
  protected static final int UNSUBACK = 11;
  protected static final int PINGREQ = 12;
  protected static final int PINGRESP = 13;
  protected static final int DISCONNECT = 14;
  protected static byte[] encode(int type, boolean retain, int qos, boolean dup,
      byte[] payload, String... params) {
    ByteArrayOutputStream mqtt = new ByteArrayOutputStream();
    mqtt.write((byte) ((retain ? 1 : 0) | qos << 1 | (dup ? 1 : 0) << 3 | type << 4));
    ByteArrayOutputStream variableHeader = new ByteArrayOutputStream();
    switch (type) {
    case CONNECT:
      boolean username = Boolean.parseBoolean(params[0]);
      boolean password = Boolean.parseBoolean(params[1]);
      boolean will = Boolean.parseBoolean(params[2]);
      boolean will_retain = Boolean.parseBoolean(params[3]);
```

continues

LISTING 5-10 *(continued)*

```
        boolean cleansession = Boolean.parseBoolean(params[4]);
        variableHeader.write(0x00);
        variableHeader.write(PROTOCOL_NAME.getBytes("UTF-8").length);
        variableHeader.write(PROTOCOL_NAME.getBytes("UTF-8"));
        variableHeader.write(VERSION);
        variableHeader.write((cleansession ? 1 : 0) << 1 | (will ? 1 : 0) << 2 |
          (qos) << 3 | (will_retain ? 1 : 0) << 5 | (password ? 1 : 0) << 6 |
          (username ? 1 : 0) << 7);
        variableHeader.write(0x00);
        variableHeader.write(0x000A);
        break;
    }
    int length = payload.length + variableHeader.size();
    do {
      byte digit = (byte) (length % 128);
      length /= 128;
      if (length > 0)
        digit = (byte) (digit | 0x80);
      mqtt.write(digit);
    } while (length > 0);
    mqtt.write(payload);
    return mqtt.toByteArray();
  }
}
```

To reduce the level of abstraction for the different messages, you should add another method for each message that the client will send. Add the `connect` method to your `MQTT.java` class as shown in the following code. Notice that, because the `encode` method throws an IOException, you'll have to keep throwing that IOException forward; usually you want the final consumer — your Android app — to decide how to handle these exceptions in try-catch statements.

```
public static byte[] connect() throws UnsupportedEncodingException, IOException {
  String identifier = "android";
  ByteArrayOutputStream payload = new ByteArrayOutputStream();
  payload.write(0);
  payload.write(identifier.length());
  payload.write(identifier.getBytes("UTF-8"));
  return encode(CONNECT, false, 0, false, payload.toByteArray(), "false", "false",
    "false", "false", "false");
}
```

The PUBLISH Message

The CONNECT message really is one of the most complicated messages because it has so many different parameters regarding the connection and the client. The PUBLISH message, however, has far fewer parameters to keep track of and should be easier for you to build, especially because it shares the fixed header with the CONNECT message. Go ahead and add the `publish` method as shown in the following code to your `MQTT.java` class:

```
public static byte[] publish(String topic, byte[] message) throws IOException {
  return encode(PUBLISH, false, 0, false, message, Integer.toString(0), topic);
}
```

For this to work, you also need to add a PUBLISH case to the switch statement in the `encode` method. See Listing 5-11 for how to add the PUBLISH case.

LISTING 5-11: Add the PUBLISH message

```java
package com.wiley.wroxaccessories;
import java.io.ByteArrayOutputStream;
public class MQTT {
  protected static byte VERSION = (byte) 0x01;
  protected static String PROTOCOL_NAME = "P2PMQTT";
  protected static final int CONNECT = 1;
  protected static final int CONNACK = 2;
  protected static final int PUBLISH = 3;
  protected static final int PUBACK = 4;
  protected static final int PUBREC = 5;
  protected static final int PUBREL = 6;
  protected static final int PUBCOMP = 7;
  protected static final int SUBSCRIBE = 8;
  protected static final int SUBACK = 9;
  protected static final int UNSUBSCRIBE = 10;
  protected static final int UNSUBACK = 11;
  protected static final int PINGREQ = 12;
  protected static final int PINGRESP = 13;
  protected static final int DISCONNECT = 14;
  protected static byte[] encode(int type, boolean retain, int qos, boolean dup,
      byte[] payload, String... params) {
    ByteArrayOutputStream mqtt = new ByteArrayOutputStream();
    mqtt.write((byte) ((retain ? 1 : 0) | qos << 1 | (dup ? 1 : 0) << 3 | type << 4));
    ByteArrayOutputStream variableHeader = new ByteArrayOutputStream();
    switch (type) {
    case CONNECT:
      boolean username = Boolean.parseBoolean(params[0]);
      boolean password = Boolean.parseBoolean(params[1]);
      boolean will = Boolean.parseBoolean(params[2]);
      boolean will_retain = Boolean.parseBoolean(params[3]);
      boolean cleansession = Boolean.parseBoolean(params[4]);
      variableHeader.write(0x00);
      variableHeader.write(PROTOCOL_NAME.getBytes("UTF-8").length);
      variableHeader.write(PROTOCOL_NAME.getBytes("UTF-8"));
      variableHeader.write(VERSION);
      variableHeader.write((cleansession ? 1 : 0) << 1 | (will ? 1 : 0) << 2 |
        (qos) << 3 | (will_retain ? 1 : 0) << 5 | (password ? 1 : 0) << 6 |
        (username ? 1 : 0) << 7);
      variableHeader.write(0x00);
      variableHeader.write(0x000A);
      break;
    case PUBLISH:
      int message_id = Integer.parseInt(params[0]);
      String topic_name = params[1];
      variableHeader.write(0x00);
      variableHeader.write(topic_name.getBytes("UTF-8").length);
      variableHeader.write(topic_name.getBytes("UTF-8"));
```

continues

LISTING 5-11 *(continued)*

```
      break;
    }
    int length = payload.length + variableHeader.size();
    do {
      byte digit = (byte) (length % 128);
      length /= 128;
      if (length > 0)
        digit = (byte) (digit | 0x80);
      mqtt.write(digit);
    } while (length > 0);
    mqtt.write(payload);
    return mqtt.toByteArray();
  }
}
```

The SUBSCRIBE Message

This is one of the easier messages to wrap your head around. The only thing the client should do in this message is tell the broker a topic it is interested in and what level of quality it expects. You need yet another `ByteArrayOutputStream` here so you can encode the two payload parameters — the topic and its quality of service — in a proper manner.

Also note that the MQTT specification says that a SUBSCRIBE message can possibly contain more than one subscription topic and corresponding QoS. However, because you're so eager to learn and try things yourself, you'll obviously write the simpler method first, and then explore the next version on your own. Add the following code to your `MQTT.java` class:

```
public static byte[] subscribe(int subscribe_id, String subscribe_topic,
    int subscribed_qos) throws IOException {
  ByteArrayOutputStream payload = new ByteArrayOutputStream();
  payload.write(subscribe_topic.getBytes("UTF-8"));
  payload.write(subscribed_qos);
  return encode(SUBSCRIBE, false, AT_LEAST_ONCE, false, payload.toByteArray(),
    Integer.toString(subscribe_id));
}
```

Add the code in Listing 5-12 to complete your SUBSCRIBE message.

LISTING 5-12: Add the SUBSCRIBE message

```
package com.wiley.wroxaccessories;
import java.io.ByteArrayOutputStream;
public class MQTT {
  protected static byte VERSION = (byte) 0x01;
  protected static String PROTOCOL_NAME = "P2PMQTT";
  protected static final int CONNECT = 1;
  protected static final int CONNACK = 2;
  protected static final int PUBLISH = 3;
  protected static final int PUBACK = 4;
  protected static final int PUBREC = 5;
```

```java
    protected static final int PUBREL = 6;
    protected static final int PUBCOMP = 7;
    protected static final int SUBSCRIBE = 8;
    protected static final int SUBACK = 9;
    protected static final int UNSUBSCRIBE = 10;
    protected static final int UNSUBACK = 11;
    protected static final int PINGREQ = 12;
    protected static final int PINGRESP = 13;
    protected static final int DISCONNECT = 14;
    protected static byte[] encode(int type, boolean retain, int qos, boolean dup,
        byte[] payload, String... params) {
      ByteArrayOutputStream mqtt = new ByteArrayOutputStream();
      mqtt.write((byte) ((retain ? 1 : 0) | qos << 1 | (dup ? 1 : 0) << 3 | type << 4));
      ByteArrayOutputStream variableHeader = new ByteArrayOutputStream();
      switch (type) {
      case CONNECT:
        boolean username = Boolean.parseBoolean(params[0]);
        boolean password = Boolean.parseBoolean(params[1]);
        boolean will = Boolean.parseBoolean(params[2]);
        boolean will_retain = Boolean.parseBoolean(params[3]);
        boolean cleansession = Boolean.parseBoolean(params[4]);
        variableHeader.write(0x00);
        variableHeader.write(PROTOCOL_NAME.getBytes("UTF-8").length);
        variableHeader.write(PROTOCOL_NAME.getBytes("UTF-8"));
        variableHeader.write(VERSION);
        variableHeader.write((cleansession ? 1 : 0) << 1 | (will ? 1 : 0) << 2 |
          (qos) << 3 | (will_retain ? 1 : 0) << 5 | (password ? 1 : 0) << 6 |
          (username ? 1 : 0) << 7);
        variableHeader.write(0x00);
        variableHeader.write(0x000A);
        break;
      case PUBLISH:
        int message_id = Integer.parseInt(params[0]);
        String topic_name = params[1];
        variableHeader.write(0x00);
        variableHeader.write(topic_name.getBytes("UTF-8").length);
        variableHeader.write(topic_name.getBytes("UTF-8"));
        break;
      case SUBSCRIBE:
        message_id = Integer.parseInt(params[0]);
        variableHeader.write((message_id >> 8) & 0xFF);
        variableHeader.write(message_id & 0xFF);
        break;
      }
      int length = payload.length + variableHeader.size();
      do {
        byte digit = (byte) (length % 128);
        length /= 128;
        if (length > 0)
          digit = (byte) (digit | 0x80);
        mqtt.write(digit);
      } while (length > 0);
      mqtt.write(payload);
      return mqtt.toByteArray();
    }
  }
```

Add the PING Message

You can consider the PING message as a sort of heartbeat for the client; if the client hasn't done anything for a while, it should send the PING to let the broker know that it is still alive, and in return the broker should respond with a PINGREQ. This way both parties will get a confirmation that the connection is still open. Add the following method to your `MQTT.java` class:

```
public static byte[] ping() throws IOException {
   return encode(PINGREQ, false, 0, false, new byte[0]);
}
```

Because it has no variable header, you don't actually need to create a case for the PINGREQ message like you've done for the other messages. However, it's not a bad idea to add the empty case to the switch statement just to make it very clear that the PINGREQ doesn't assemble a variable header. Add the following snippet to the end of the switch statement:

```
case PINGREQ:
   // PINGREQ Doesn't have a variable header.
   break;
```

Decoding MQTT

Now that you're done with the most basic encoding functions in MQTT, you can move on to decoding MQTT messages. When decoding complex messages it's always good to have a custom container for them; for this you'll create an `MQTTMessage` class with all the needed attributes.

Follow these steps to create the `MQTTMessage.java` class:

1. With your new Android library project selected in Eclipse, from the File menu, select New ➪ Class.

2. As the Package Name, enter **com.wiley.wroxaccessories**.

3. Name your new class **MQTTMessage**.

4. Before you click Finish to create the class, make sure that your new class has no specific superclass or interfaces. Also make sure that Eclipse won't create the Java main method.

Your new class should look something like Listing 5-13.

LISTING 5-13: Create the MQTTMessage class

```
package com.wiley.wroxaccessories;
public class MQTTMessage {
}
```

You'll fill in this class with all the variables needed to read any MQTT message, but before you do that you should add the decode method stub to your MQTT class as shown in Listing 5-14.

LISTING 5-14: Add the decode method stub

```
public static MQTTMessage decode(final byte[] message) {
  MQTTMessage mqtt = new MQTTMessage();
  return mqtt;
}
```

Decoding the Fixed Header

You'll use a similar approach to decoding the MQTT message as you used when encoding it. Decoding an MQTT message has several steps to it. The first thing you want to find is the fixed header. Add the attributes needed for the fixed header in your MQTTMessage class, as shown in Listing 5-15. Usually you would declare these variables as private and create getter and setter methods, but for simplicity's sake you'll just make them public now.

LISTING 5-15: Add the fixed header attributes

```
package com.wiley.wroxaccessories;
  public class MQTTMessage {
  public int type;
  public boolean DUP;
  public int QoS;
  public boolean retain;
  public int remainingLength;
}
```

First you need to find the message type, and as you'll recall from Chapter 3, the message type is stored in the last four bits of the very first byte of the fixed header. To read only the value from these four bits, you need to remove the first four bits by using a combination of the right shift operation and the AND operator.

You first shift the byte four places to the right and then perform a bitwise AND operation of the remainder with the byte 0x0F (which is the bit pattern 00001111). This effectively queries the status of the first four bits, giving you the value you want. Add the code in Listing 5-16 to your decode method to extract the message type from the received byte array.

LISTING 5-16: Parse the message type

```
public static MQTTMessage decode(final byte[] message) {
  int i = 0;
  MQTTMessage mqtt = new MQTTMessage();
  mqtt.type = (message[i] >> 4) & 0x0F;
  return mqtt;
}
```

Next up is the DUP flag, which exists in bit number 4 of the first byte so you'll need to shift three places to the right and mask everything but that one bit to get the value.

Using a tertiary operator, you'll get the boolean value you so desperately crave. See Listing 5-17.

LISTING 5-17: Parse the DUP flag

```
public static MQTTMessage decode(final byte[] message) {
   int i = 0;
   MQTTMessage mqtt = new MQTTMessage();
   mqtt.type = (message[i] >> 4) & 0x0F;
   mqtt.DUP = ((message[i] >> 3) & 0x01) == 0 ? false : true;
   return mqtt;
}
```

The Quality of Service level takes up two bits of the first byte; this means you'll have to mask everything but the first two bits. The value will then later be compared to your QoS constants: AT_MOST_ONCE, AT_LEAST_ONCE, and EXACTLY_ONCE. Shift the byte three places to the right and then query the first two bits with the bit pattern 00000011, which is the same as the value 0x03. See Listing 5-18.

LISTING 5-18: Read the Quality of Service flag

```
public static MQTTMessage decode(final byte[] message) {
   int i = 0;
   MQTTMessage mqtt = new MQTTMessage();
   mqtt.type = (message[i] >> 4) & 0x0F;
   mqtt.DUP = ((message[i] >> 3) & 0x01) == 0 ? false : true;
   mqtt.QoS = (message[i] >> 1) & 0x03;
   return mqtt;
}
```

Finally, you have to read the RETAIN flag. This is the first bit in the byte so it's fairly simple. You just need to mask the rest of the byte to get the value. Use the tertiary operator to get a Java boolean. See Listing 5-19.

LISTING 5-19: Get the RETAIN property

```
public static MQTTMessage decode(final byte[] message) {
   int i = 0;
   MQTTMessage mqtt = new MQTTMessage();
   mqtt.type = (message[i] >> 4) & 0x0F;
   mqtt.DUP = ((message[i] >> 3) & 0x01) == 0 ? false : true;
   mqtt.QoS = (message[i] >> 1) & 0x03;
   mqtt.retain = (message[i] & 0x01) == 0 ? false : true;
   return mqtt;
}
```

The trickiest part of decoding the fixed header is without a doubt the remaining length field. You need to follow this short procedure to find the number of bytes in the payload.

Add the code in Listing 5-20 to your decode method in order to read the remaining length field of the fixed header.

LISTING 5-20: Parse the message type

```
public static MQTTMessage decode(final byte[] message) {
  int i = 0;
  MQTTMessage mqtt = new MQTTMessage();
  mqtt.type = (message[i] >> 4) & 0x0F;
  mqtt.DUP = ((message[i] >> 3) & 0x01) == 0 ? false : true;
  mqtt.QoS = (message[i] >> 1) & 0x03;
  mqtt.retain = (message[i] & 0x01) == 0 ? false : true;
  i++;
  int multiplier = 1;
  int length = 0;
  byte digit = 0;
  do {
    digit = message[i++];
    length += (digit & 127) * multiplier;
    multiplier *= 128;
  } while ((digit & 128) != 0);
  mqtt.remainingLength = length;
  return mqtt;
}
```

Decoding the Variable Header

Because the variable header has different content depending on the message, you need to store it in a container that isn't bound by a certain type. In this instance you'll use a Map. Add the variable header container to your MQTTMessage class, as shown in Listing 5-21.

LISTING 5-21: Add the variable header container to MQTTMessage

```
package com.wiley.wroxaccessories;
import java.util.Map;
public class MQTTMessage {
  public int type;
  public boolean DUP;
  public int QoS;
  public boolean retain;
  public int remainingLength;
  public Map<String, String> variableHeader;
}
```

Add the switch statement shown in Listing 5-22 to your decode method.

LISTING 5-22: Add the variable header switch statement

```
public static MQTTMessage decode(final byte[] message) {
  int i = 0;
  MQTTMessage mqtt = new MQTTMessage();
  mqtt.type = (message[i] >> 4) & 0x0F;
  mqtt.DUP = ((message[i] >> 3) & 0x01) == 0 ? false : true;
  mqtt.QoS = (message[i] >> 1) & 0x03;
  mqtt.retain = (message[i] & 0x01) == 0 ? false : true;
  i++;
  int multiplier = 1;
  int len = 0;
  byte digit = 0;
  do {
    digit = message[i++];
    len += (digit & 127) * multiplier;
    multiplier *= 128;
  } while ((digit & 128) != 0);
  mqtt.remainingLength = len;
  switch (mqtt.type) {
  case CONNECT:
    break;
  case PUBLISH:
    break;
  case SUBSCRIBE:
    break;
  case PINGREQ:
    break;
  }
  return mqtt;
}
```

According to the MQTT protocol specification, the CONNECT message has a variable header length of 12 bytes, so you know that when the fixed header has ended the next 12 bytes of a CONNECT message belong to the variable header.

Read the properties of the CONNECT message as shown in Listing 5-23.

LISTING 5-23: Read the **CONNECT** message variable header

```
public static MQTTMessage decode(final byte[] message) {
  int i = 0;
  MQTTMessage mqtt = new MQTTMessage();
  mqtt.type = (message[i] >> 4) & 0x0F;
  mqtt.DUP = ((message[i] >> 3) & 0x01) == 0 ? false : true;
  mqtt.QoS = (message[i] >> 1) & 0x03;
  mqtt.retain = (message[i] & 0x01) == 0 ? false : true;
  i++;
  int multiplier = 1;
  int len = 0;
  byte digit = 0;
  do {
    digit = message[i++];
    len += (digit & 127) * multiplier;
```

```
    multiplier *= 128;
  } while ((digit & 128) != 0);
  mqtt.remainingLength = len;
  switch (mqtt.type) {
  case CONNECT:
    int protocol_name_len = (message[i++] << 8 | message[i++]);
    mqtt.variableHeader.put("protocol_name", new String(message, i, protocol_name_len));
    mqtt.variableHeader.put("protocol_version", message[i++]);
    mqtt.variableHeader.put("has_username",
      ((message[i++] << 7) & 0x01) == 0 ? false : true);
    mqtt.variableHeader.put("has_password",
      ((message[i] << 6) & 0x01) == 0 ? false : true);
    mqtt.variableHeader.put("will_retain",
      ((message[i] << 5) & 0x01) == 0 ? false : true);
    mqtt.variableHeader.put("will_qos", ((message[i] << 3) & 0x03));
    mqtt.variableHeader.put("will", ((message[i] << 2) & 0x01) == 0 ? false : true);
    mqtt.variableHeader.put("clean_session",
      ((message[i] << 1) & 0x01) == 0 ? false : true);
    int keep_alive_len = (message[i++] << 8 | message[i++]);
    mqtt.variableHeader.put("keep_alive", new String(message, i, keep_alive_len));
    break;
  case PUBLISH:
    break;
  case SUBSCRIBE:
    break;
  case PINGREQ:
    break;
  }
  return mqtt;
}
```

The PUBLISH message variable header is far shorter, as you probably recall; you really need to read only two things — the topic name and the message ID. Add the code from Listing 5-24 to your decode method.

LISTING 5-24: Read the PUBLISH message variable header

```
public static MQTTMessage decode(final byte[] message) {
  int i = 0;
  MQTTMessage mqtt = new MQTTMessage();
  mqtt.type = (message[i] >> 4) & 0x0F;
  mqtt.DUP = ((message[i] >> 3) & 0x01) == 0 ? false : true;
  mqtt.QoS = (message[i] >> 1) & 0x03;
  mqtt.retain = (message[i] & 0x01) == 0 ? false : true;
  i++;
  int multiplier = 1;
  int len = 0;
  byte digit = 0;
  do {
    digit = message[i++];
    len += (digit & 127) * multiplier;
    multiplier *= 128;
  } while ((digit & 128) != 0);
```

continues

LISTING 5-24 *(continued)*

```
    mqtt.remainingLength = len;
    switch (mqtt.type) {
    case CONNECT:
      int protocol_name_len = (message[i++] << 8 | message[i++]);
      mqtt.variableHeader.put("protocol_name", new String(message, i, protocol_name_len));
      mqtt.variableHeader.put("protocol_version", message[i++]);
      mqtt.variableHeader.put("has_username",
        ((message[i++] << 7) & 0x01) == 0 ? false : true);
      mqtt.variableHeader.put("has_password",
        ((message[i] << 6) & 0x01) == 0 ? false : true);
      mqtt.variableHeader.put("will_retain",
        ((message[i] << 5) & 0x01) == 0 ? false : true);
      mqtt.variableHeader.put("will_qos", ((message[i] << 3) & 0x03));
      mqtt.variableHeader.put("will", ((message[i] << 2) & 0x01) == 0 ? false : true);
      mqtt.variableHeader.put("clean_session",
        ((message[i] << 1) & 0x01) == 0 ? false : true);
      int keep_alive_len = (message[i++] << 8 | message[i++]);
      mqtt.variableHeader.put("keep_alive", new String(message, i, keep_alive_len));
      break;
    case PUBLISH:
      int topic_name_len = (message[i++] << 8 | message[i++]);
      mqtt.variableHeader.put("topic_name", new String(message,i,topic_name_len));
      mqtt.variableHeader.put("message_id", (message[i++] << 8 | message[i++]));
      break;
    case SUBSCRIBE:
      break;
    case PINGREQ:
      break;
    }
    return mqtt;
}
```

The SUBSCRIBE message has only a message ID, and the PINGREQ has no variable header, as shown in Listing 5-25.

LISTING 5-25: Read the **SUBSCRIBE** message variable header

```
public static MQTTMessage decode(final byte[] message) {
  int i = 0;
  MQTTMessage mqtt = new MQTTMessage();
  mqtt.type = (message[i] >> 4) & 0x0F;
  mqtt.DUP = ((message[i] >> 3) & 0x01) == 0 ? false : true;
  mqtt.QoS = (message[i] >> 1) & 0x03;
  mqtt.retain = (message[i] & 0x01) == 0 ? false : true;
  i++;
  int multiplier = 1;
  int len = 0;
  byte digit = 0;
  do {
    digit = message[i++];
    len += (digit & 127) * multiplier;
```

```
    multiplier *= 128;
  } while ((digit & 128) != 0);
  mqtt.remainingLength = len;
  switch (mqtt.type) {
  case CONNECT:
    int protocol_name_len = (message[i++] << 8 | message[i++]);
    mqtt.variableHeader.put("protocol_name", new String(message, i, protocol_name_len));
    mqtt.variableHeader.put("protocol_version", message[i++]);
    mqtt.variableHeader.put("has_username",
      ((message[i++] << 7) & 0x01) == 0 ? false : true);
    mqtt.variableHeader.put("has_password",
      ((message[i] << 6) & 0x01) == 0 ? false : true);
    mqtt.variableHeader.put("will_retain",
      ((message[i] << 5) & 0x01) == 0 ? false : true);
    mqtt.variableHeader.put("will_qos", ((message[i] << 3) & 0x03));
    mqtt.variableHeader.put("will", ((message[i] << 2) & 0x01) == 0 ? false : true);
    mqtt.variableHeader.put("clean_session",
      ((message[i] << 1) & 0x01) == 0 ? false : true);
    int keep_alive_len = (message[i++] << 8 | message[i++]);
    mqtt.variableHeader.put("keep_alive", new String(message, i, keep_alive_len));
    break;
  case PUBLISH:
    int topic_name_len = (message[i++] << 8 | message[i++]);
    mqtt.variableHeader.put("topic_name", new String(message,i,topic_name_len));
    mqtt.variableHeader.put("message_id", (message[i++] << 8 | message[i++]));
    break;
  case SUBSCRIBE:
    mqtt.variableHeader.put("message_id", (message[i++] << 8 | message[i++]));
    break;
  case PINGREQ:
    // PINGREQ has no variable header
    break;
  }
  return mqtt;
}
```

Last, but definitely not least, is the payload. In your MQTTMessage class this will be stored as a primitive byte array because you have no idea what the contents of this is — it could be an integer, but it could also be an image!

Add the payload container to your MQTTMessage class, as shown in Listing 5-26.

LISTING 5-26: Add the payload container to MQTTMessage

```
package com.wiley.wroxaccessories;
import java.util.Map;
public class MQTTMessage {
  public int type;
  public boolean DUP;
  public int QoS;
  public boolean retain;
  public int remainingLength;
  public Map<String, String> variableHeader;
  public byte[] payload;
}
```

Finally, write the payload array to your `MQTTMessage` instance after the switch statement in the `decode` method of the MQTT class, as shown in Listing 5-27.

LISTING 5-27: Write the payload to the MQTTMessage instance

```java
public static MQTTMessage decode(final byte[] message) {
  int i = 0;
  MQTTMessage mqtt = new MQTTMessage();
  mqtt.type = (message[i] >> 4) & 0x0F;
  mqtt.DUP = ((message[i] >> 3) & 0x01) == 0 ? false : true;
  mqtt.QoS = (message[i] >> 1) & 0x03;
  mqtt.retain = (message[i] & 0x01) == 0 ? false : true;
  i++;
  int multiplier = 1;
  int len = 0;
  byte digit = 0;
  do {
    digit = message[i++];
    len += (digit & 127) * multiplier;
    multiplier *= 128;
  } while ((digit & 128) != 0);
  mqtt.remainingLength = len;
  switch (mqtt.type) {
  case CONNECT:
    int protocol_name_len = (message[i++] << 8 | message[i++]);
    mqtt.variableHeader.put("protocol_name", new String(message, i, protocol_name_len));
    mqtt.variableHeader.put("protocol_version", message[i++]);
    mqtt.variableHeader.put("has_username",
      ((message[i++] << 7) & 0x01) == 0 ? false : true);
    mqtt.variableHeader.put("has_password",
      ((message[i] << 6) & 0x01) == 0 ? false : true);
    mqtt.variableHeader.put("will_retain",
      ((message[i] << 5) & 0x01) == 0 ? false : true);
    mqtt.variableHeader.put("will_qos", ((message[i] << 3) & 0x03));
    mqtt.variableHeader.put("will", ((message[i] << 2) & 0x01) == 0 ? false : true);
    mqtt.variableHeader.put("clean_session",
      ((message[i] << 1) & 0x01) == 0 ? false : true);
    int keep_alive_len = (message[i++] << 8 | message[i++]);
    mqtt.variableHeader.put("keep_alive", new String(message, i, keep_alive_len));
    break;
  case PUBLISH:
    int topic_name_len = (message[i++] << 8 | message[i++]);
    mqtt.variableHeader.put("topic_name", new String(message,i,topic_name_len));
    mqtt.variableHeader.put("message_id", (message[i++] << 8 | message[i++]));
    break;
  case SUBSCRIBE:
    mqtt.variableHeader.put("message_id", (message[i++] << 8 | message[i++]));
    break;
  case PINGREQ:
    // PINGREQ has no variable header
    break;
  }
```

```
ByteArrayOutputStream payload = new ByteArrayOutputStream();
for( int b = i; b < message.length; b++)
  payload.write(message[b]);
mqtt.payload = payload.toByteArray();
return mqtt;
}
```

MANAGING OPEN ACCESSORY CONNECTIONS

Although this title uses connections as a plural, currently the system supports only one concurrent accessory connection per Android device. This is because of hardware rather than systemic issues, though. The operating system can theoretically manage more than one USB device; most Android devices, however, come only with one USB port.

Creating the Connection Class

Another important aspect to keep in mind is the different connection alternatives you have when building accessories. When the first AOA framework was released in 2011, there was only one option: USB. Technically speaking, there were two options for connecting depending on your Android version. Both of these versions still work just fine; however, during Google IO 2012 the Bluetooth option was introduced, and you can be sure there will be more options for connecting accessories to your phone in the future. Because of this you'll realize that building a library that is agnostic to the hardware layer is important.

In this section you build an abstract class that represents an accessory connection; this class will serve as the foundation for the three different accessories that your library will support.

1. With your library selected, open the File menu and select New ➪ Class again.

2. Enter the same Package Name as the previous two classes, **com.wiley.wroxaccessories**.

3. Call this class **Connection**.

4. Select the Abstract checkbox and create the class by clicking Finish. You should get an empty class declaration like the one shown in Listing 5-28.

LISTING 5-28: Create the Connection class

```
package com.wiley.wroxaccessories;
public abstract class Connection {
}
```

This abstract `Connection` class will be the description of the common attributes of the connection between an Android device and an accessory. Considering the common denominator for the three available connection types — USB compatibility, USB, and Bluetooth — you'll realize that the input and output streams are the only things that all three share. This is where it gets a bit tricky; the USB accessory uses file streams, whereas the Bluetooth accessory uses the streams found in a `BluetoothSocket`. This means that you can't add the streams themselves to the `Connection` class, but you can add the methods to handle the streams.

Add the input and output stream methods to the `Connection` class, just like in Listing 5-29.

LISTING 5-29: Add the stream methods to the Connection class

```
package com.wiley.wroxaccessories;
import java.io.InputStream;
import java.io.OutputStream;
public abstract class Connection {
    public abstract InputStream getInputStream();
    public abstract OutputStream getOutputStream();
}
```

Because anything related to input and/or output of data can fail miserably, it's important to add some exception handling to these methods so that you can control the failure instead of letting the app crash. Let both methods throw the general IOException as shown in Listing 5-30; this enables you to later catch failures regarding the streams inside your library.

LISTING 5-30: Add the throws declarations

```
package com.wiley.wroxaccessories;
import java.io.IOException;
import java.io.InputStream;
import java.io.OutputStream;
public abstract class Connection {
    public abstract InputStream getInputStream() throws IOException;
    public abstract OutputStream getOutputStream() throws IOException;
}
```

Another important thing to remember about sockets is gracefully closing them, either when a failure happens or when you're done using them, and because it has to do with the sockets you'll need to throw another IOException. All of the three connection types need a `close` method, so go ahead and add that to the abstract `Connection` class as shown in Listing 5-31.

LISTING 5-31: Add the close method

```
package com.wiley.wroxaccessories;
import java.io.IOException;
import java.io.InputStream;
import java.io.OutputStream;
public abstract class Connection {
    public abstract InputStream getInputStream() throws IOException;
    public abstract OutputStream getOutputStream() throws IOException;
    public abstract void close() throws IOException;
}
```

USB Connection

Now it's time to create the USBConnection12 class; this will use the version of the USBManager and USBAccessory classes available in Android SDK 12 and above. As mentioned earlier, the USB accessory connection works over a file stream rather than a socket, so your USBConnection12 class needs to fill in the stream methods from the abstract Connection class using a FileInputStream and a FileOutputStream. See Listing 5-32.

LISTING 5-32: Create the USBConnection12 class

```
package com.wiley.wroxaccessories;

import java.io.FileInputStream;
import java.io.FileOutputStream;
import java.io.InputStream;
import java.io.OutputStream;

public class USBConnection12 extends Connection {
  private FileInputStream mFileInputStream;
  private FileOutputStream mFileOutputStream;
  @Override
  public InputStream getInputStream() {
    return mFileInputStream;
  }
  @Override
  public OutputStream getOutputStream() {
    return mFileInputStream;
  }
  @Override
    public void close() {
  }
}
```

However, getting access to the file streams isn't as straightforward as creating them. First you need something called a FileDescriptor, which is basically the link to a writable file or socket on the filesystem. The FileDescriptor is hidden inside something called a ParcelFileDescriptor, which is a normal FileDescriptor wrapped in the Parcelable interface.

You also need a reference to the USBAccessory to extract the ParcelFileDescriptor; you get the USBAccessory instance by extracting it from the USBManager. Add the constructor for your USBConnection12 class as shown in Listing 5-33.

LISTING 5-33: Add the constructor

```
package com.wiley.wroxaccessories;
import java.io.FileInputStream;
import java.io.FileOutputStream;
import java.io.InputStream;
```

continues

LISTING 5-33 *(continued)*

```java
import java.io.OutputStream;
import com.android.future.usb.UsbAccessory;
import com.android.future.usb.UsbManager;
import android.os.ParcelFileDescriptor;
public class USBConnection12 extends Connection {
  private FileInputStream mFileInputStream;
  private FileOutputStream mFileOutputStream;
  private ParcelFileDescriptor mParcelFileDescriptor;
  private USBAccessory mUsbAccessory;
  public USBConnection12(UsbManager usbmanager) {
    UsbAccessory[] accessories = manager.getAccessoryList();
    UsbAccessory accessory = (accessories == null ? null : accessories[0]);
    if (accessory != null) {
      mUsbAccessory = accessory;
      if (manager.hasPermission(mUsbAccessory)) {
        mFileDescriptor = usbmanager.openAccessory(accessory);
      }
    }
  }
  @Override
  public InputStream getInputStream() {
    return mFileInputStream;
  }
  @Override
  public OutputStream getOutputStream() {
    return mFileOutputStream;
  }
  @Override
  public void close() {
  }
}
```

If the returned `ParcelFileDescriptor` happens to be a null object, it means that it failed to open the descriptor. Make sure to proceed only if it isn't null. Fetch the streams from the `FileDescriptor` as shown in Listing 5-34.

LISTING 5-34: Get the streams from the FileDescriptor object

```java
package com.wiley.wroxaccessories;

import java.io.FileDescriptor;
import java.io.FileInputStream;
import java.io.FileOutputStream;
import java.io.InputStream;
import java.io.OutputStream;

import com.android.future.usb.UsbAccessory;
import com.android.future.usb.UsbManager;
import android.os.ParcelFileDescriptor;
```

```java
public class USBConnection12 extends Connection {
  private FileInputStream mFileInputStream;
  private FileOutputStream mFileOutputStream;
  private ParcelFileDescriptor mFileDescriptor;
  public USBConnection12(UsbManager usbmanager) {
    UsbAccessory[] accessories = manager.getAccessoryList();
    UsbAccessory accessory = (accessories == null ? null : accessories[0]);
    if (accessory != null) {
      mUsbAccessory = accessory;
      if (manager.hasPermission(mUsbAccessory)) {
        mFileDescriptor = usbmanager.openAccessory(accessory);
        if (mFileDescriptor != null) {
          FileDescriptor mFileDescriptor = mFileDescriptor.getFileDescriptor();
          mFileInputStream = new FileInputStream(mFileDescriptor);
          mFileOutputStream = new FileOutputStream(mFileDescriptor);
        }
      }
    }
  }
  @Override
  public InputStream getInputStream() {
    return mFileInputStream;
  }
  @Override
  public OutputStream getOutputStream() {
    return mFileOutputStream;
  }
  @Override
  public void close() {
    if (mFileDescriptor != null) {
      mFileDescriptor.close();
    }
  }
}
```

One of the more compelling ideas of how the accessory should work is the automatic startup of the proper application for a specific accessory. This works using one of the core application components of the Android framework, the BroadcastReceiver. What happens, simply put, is that the system recognizes the USBAccessory by a special accessory handshake defined in the accessory_filter .xml file and initiates a broadcast to open the application/s that are listening for that specific signature broadcast in their IntentFilters. To make your application listen for a USB accessory, you need to add the action android.hardware.usb.action.USB_ACCESSORY_ATTACHED to its IntentFilter, and you also need to specify a meta-data tag for that action, pointing to a special XML file in your resources.

However, what you also want to do is register a receiver that closes the application and all bound resources when the accessory is detached — you do this programmatically in the library because the IntentFilter in the manifest is used to start activities, not kill them (see Listing 5-35). Notice that you'll need a reference to the current activity to register the receiver, so add that as well to your USBConnection12 class.

LISTING 5-35: Add the **ACCESSORY_DETACHED** receiver

```
package com.wiley.wroxaccessories;

import java.io.FileDescriptor;
import java.io.FileInputStream;
import java.io.FileOutputStream;
import java.io.IOException;
import java.io.InputStream;
import java.io.OutputStream;

import android.content.BroadcastReceiver;
import android.content.Context;
import android.content.Intent;
import android.hardware.usb.UsbAccessory;
import android.hardware.usb.UsbManager;
import android.os.ParcelFileDescriptor;

public class USBConnection12 extends Connection {
  private FileInputStream mFileInputStream;
  private FileOutputStream mFileOutputStream;
  private ParcelFileDescriptor mFileDescriptor;
  private Activity mActivity;
  public USBConnection12(UsbManager usbmanager) {
    UsbAccessory[] accessories = manager.getAccessoryList();
    UsbAccessory accessory = (accessories == null ? null : accessories[0]);
    if (accessory != null) {
      mUsbAccessory = accessory;
      if (manager.hasPermission(mUsbAccessory)) {
        mFileDescriptor = usbmanager.openAccessory(accessory);
        if (mFileDescriptor != null) {
          FileDescriptor mFileDescriptor = mFileDescriptor.getFileDescriptor();
          mFileInputStream = new FileInputStream(mFileDescriptor);
          mFileOutputStream = new FileOutputStream(mFileDescriptor);
        }
      }
    }
    IntentFilter mIntentFilter = new IntentFilter();
    mIntentFilter.addAction(UsbManager.ACTION_USB_ACCESSORY_DETACHED);
    mActivity.registerReceiver(mBroadcastReceiver, mIntentFilter);
  }
  @Override
  public InputStream getInputStream() throws IOException {
    return mFileInputStream;
  }
  @Override
  public OutputStream getOutputStream() throws IOException {
    return mFileOutputStream;
  }
  @Override
  public void close() throws IOException {
    if (mFileDescriptor != null) {
```

```
        mFileDescriptor.close();
     }
     mActivity.unregisterReceiver(mBroadcastReceiver);
  }
  private BroadcastReceiver mBroadcastReceiver = new BroadcastReceiver() {
     @Override
     public void onReceive(Context context, Intent intent) {
       if(intent.getAction().equals(UsbManager.ACTION_USB_ACCESSORY_DETACHED)) {
       }
     }
  };
}
```

To utilize the USB accessory library available on some earlier devices running Android 2.3.4, you should create another class called UsbConnection10.java that is almost identical to the USBConnection12.java class. The only difference is the package from which you import the UsbManager class and UsbAccessory class. Find the following import statements in your USBConnection12.java file:

```
import android.hardware.usb.UsbAccessory;
import android.hardware.usb.UsbManager;
```

Replace them with the following import statements in your USBConnection10.java class:

```
import com.android.future.usb.UsbAccessory;
import com.android.future.usb.UsbManager;
```

Bluetooth Connection

Where the USB connections rely on a FileDescriptor object, the Bluetooth connection uses a BluetoothSocket. The socket already contains the two necessary streams so you won't have to instantiate them at all. Create your new BTConnection.java class:

1. With your new Android library project selected in Eclipse, open the File menu and select New ⇨ Class.

2. As the Package Name, enter **com.wiley.wroxaccessories**.

3. Name your new class **BTConnection**.

4. As the Superclass, enter **Connection**.

5. Click Finish to create your new class.

Your new class should come with three methods created automatically: getInputStream, getOutputStream, and close. Before you enter anything in these methods, add the BluetoothSocket instance and the BluetoothAdapter instance. The latter is used to find the BluetoothDevice, which contains the BluetoothSocket. See Listing 5-36.

LISTING 5-36: Add the BluetoothSocket and Adapter

```java
package com.wiley.wroxaccessories;
import java.io.IOException;
import java.io.InputStream;
import java.io.OutputStream;
import android.bluetooth.BluetoothAdapter;
import android.bluetooth.BluetoothSocket;
public class BTConnection extends Connection {
  private BluetoothSocket mBluetoothSocket;
  private BluetoothAdapter mBluetoothAdapter;
  @Override
  public InputStream getInputStream() throws IOException {
    return null;
  }
  @Override
  public OutputStream getOutputStream() throws IOException {
    return null;
  }
  @Override
  public void close() throws IOException {
  }
}
```

Now you have a socket to work with; before you add the code to initialize the socket you can go ahead and fix the three inherited methods, as shown in Listing 5-37.

LISTING 5-37: Fill in the methods inherited from Connection

```java
package com.wiley.wroxaccessories;
import java.io.IOException;
import java.io.InputStream;
import java.io.OutputStream;
import android.bluetooth.BluetoothAdapter;
import android.bluetooth.BluetoothSocket;
public class BTConnection extends Connection {
  private BluetoothSocket mBluetoothSocket;
  private BluetoothAdapter mBluetoothAdapter;
  @Override
  public InputStream getInputStream() throws IOException {
    return mBluetoothSocket.getInputStream();
  }
  @Override
  public OutputStream getOutputStream() throws IOException {
    return mBluetoothSocket.getOutputStream();
  }
  @Override
  public void close() throws IOException {
    mBluetoothSocket.close();
  }
}
```

It's time to add the initialization of the Bluetooth connection. You do this in the class constructor by first finding the `BluetoothAdapter` in the system; from that you'll eventually get a reference to the `BluetoothSocket` you'll use to pass information between your Android device and your accessory. However, to establish a connection to another Bluetooth device you'll first need to know its unique MAC address, and you'll need something called a UUID too.

UNIVERSALLY UNIQUE IDENTIFIER (UUID)

UUID is a way to uniquely identify an object or entity on a network without providing a central administration. In the case of your Bluetooth connection, the UUID must match on both ends of the communication. Normally you'd provide the following UUID to connect to an ArduinoBT board:

```
00001101-0000-1000-8000-00805F9B34FB
```

If, however, you're one of the lucky few in possession of an ADK2012 board, you should use the following UUID:

```
1dd35050-a437-11e1-b3dd-0800200c9a66
```

Add the constructor with the MAC parameter, declare the UUID variable, and then let it initialize the `BluetoothSocket`. See Listing 5-38 for details.

LISTING 5-38: Create the constructor

```
package com.wiley.wroxaccessories;

import java.io.IOException;
import java.io.InputStream;
import java.io.OutputStream;
import java.util.UUID;
import android.bluetooth.BluetoothAdapter;
import android.bluetooth.BluetoothDevice;
import android.bluetooth.BluetoothSocket;
public class BTConnection extends Connection {
  private BluetoothSocket mBluetoothSocket;
  private BluetoothAdapter mBluetoothAdapter;
  private UUID uuid = UUID.fromString("00001101-0000-1000-8000-00805F9B34FB");
  public BTConnection(String address) {
    mBluetoothAdapter = BluetoothAdapter.getDefaultAdapter();
    BluetoothDevice mDevice = mBluetoothAdapter.getRemoteDevice(address);
    try {
      mBluetoothSocket = mDevice.createInsecureRfcommSocketToServiceRecord(uuid);
      mBluetoothSocket.connect();
    } catch (IOException e) {
      e.printStackTrace();
```

continues

LISTING 5-38 *(continued)*

```
      }
    }
    @Override
    public InputStream getInputStream() throws IOException {
      return mBluetoothSocket.getInputStream();
    }
    @Override
    public OutputStream getOutputStream() throws IOException {
      return mBluetoothSocket.getOutputStream();
    }
    @Override
    public void close() throws IOException {
      mBluetoothSocket.close();
    }
}
```

Creating the Connection

Up until now you've only been adding the needed containers for establishing the connection. To create the connection, you'll pass a constant value to the connect method of the WroxAccessory class.

Add the constants to WroxAccessory.java and fill in the connect method as shown in Listing 5-39.

LISTING 5-39: Fill in the connect method

```
package com.wiley.wroxaccessories;
import android.content.Context;
public class WroxAccessory {
  private static final int USB_ACCESSORY_10 = 0;
  private static final int USB_ACCESSORY_12 = 1;
  private static final int BT_ACCESSORY = 3;
  private Context mContext;
  public WroxAccessory(Context context) {
    mContext = context;
  public void connect(int mode, Connection connection) {
  }
  public void publish() {
  }
  public void subscribe() {
  }
  public void unsubscribe() {
  }
  public void pingreq() {
  }
  public void disconnect() {
  }
}
```

In the `connect` method, then, you'll instantiate the thread that will monitor the connection with your accessory. See Listing 5-40 to create the nested thread class that will handle the communication. Notice that this will force you to handle an IOException either in the `connect` method of `WroxAccessories.java`, or in your activity. The latter is preferable.

LISTING 5-40: Add the MonitoringThread

```java
package com.wiley.wroxaccessories;
import java.io.IOException;
import android.content.Context;
public class WroxAccessory {
  public static final int USB_ACCESSORY_10 = 0;
  public static final int USB_ACCESSORY_12 = 1;
  public static final int BT_ACCESSORY = 3;
  private Context mContext;
  private MonitoringThread mMonitoringThread;
  public WroxAccessory(Context context) {
    mContext = context;
  }
  public void connect(int mode, Connection connection) throws IOException {
    mMonitoringThread = new MonitoringThread(mode, connection);
  }
  public void publish() {
  }
  public void subscribe() {
  }
  public void unsubscribe() {
  }
  public void pingreq() {
  }
  public void disconnect() {
  }
  private class MonitoringThread implements Runnable {
    Connection mConnection;
    public MonitoringThread(int mode, Connection connection) {
      mConnection = connection;
    }
    public void run() {
    }
  }
}
```

The `connect` method should also send the first MQTT message so that the accessory doesn't disconnect automatically, as shown in Listing 5-41.

Because the MQTT connection request demands a unique identifier for every client, even if there's just one client, you need to pass that from your activity. You can make this up on your own or use a predefined constant known to be unique — the MAC address. You get more into the specifics how to use this when you build an application using your library later.

LISTING 5-41: Send the MQTT CONNECT request

```java
package com.wiley.wroxaccessories;
import java.io.IOException;
import android.content.Context;
public class WroxAccessory {
  public static final int USB_ACCESSORY_10 = 0;
  public static final int USB_ACCESSORY_12 = 1;
  public static final int BT_ACCESSORY = 3;
  private Context mContext;
  private MonitoringThread mMonitoringThread;
  public WroxAccessory(Context context) {
    mContext = context;
  }
  public void connect(int mode, Connection connection) throws IOException {
    mMonitoringThread = new MonitoringThread(mode, connection);
    Thread thread = new Thread(null, mMonitoringThread, "MonitoringThread");
    thread.start();
    new WriteHelper().execute(MQTT.connect());
  }
  public void publish() {
  }
  public void subscribe() {
  }
  public void unsubscribe() {
  }
  public void pingreq() {
  }
  public void disconnect() {
  }
  private class MonitoringThread implements Runnable {
    Connection mConnection;
    public MonitoringThread(int mode, Connection connection) {
      mConnection = connection;
    }
    public void run() {
    }
  }
}
```

In the preceding code, notice that there's another class that you've still not created called
`WriteHelper`. This only task of this class is to make sure that any threaded calls, such as writing
to the `OutputStream`, are not performed on the UI thread. Create the `WriteHelper` inner class as
shown in Listing 5-42.

LISTING 5-42: Add the WriteHelper class

```java
[...]
public class WroxAccessory {
  [...]
  private class WriteHelper extends AsyncTask<byte[], Void, Void> {
    @Override
    protected Void doInBackground(byte[]... params) {
```

```
      try {
        mMonitoringThread.mConnection.getOutputStream().write(params[0]);
      } catch (IOException e) {
        e.printStackTrace();
      }
      return null;
    }
  }
}
```

Fill in the remaining methods in a similar way using the classes you've built so far. The subscribe and unsubscribe methods should take care of registering and unregistering the receiver for your subscriptions, as shown in Listing 5-43.

LISTING 5-43: Add the remaining methods

```
package com.wiley.wroxaccessories;
import java.io.IOException;
import android.content.Context;
public class WroxAccessory {
  public static final int USB_ACCESSORY_10 = 0;
  public static final int USB_ACCESSORY_12 = 1;
  public static final int BT_ACCESSORY = 3;
  private Context mContext;
  private MonitoringThread mMonitoringThread;
  public WroxAccessory(Context context) {
    mContext = context;
  }
  public void connect(int mode, Connection connection, String ident) throws
      IOException {
    mMonitoringThread = new MonitoringThread(mode, connection);
    mMonitoringThread.mConnection.getOutputStream().write(MQTT.connect(ident));
  }
  public void publish(String topic, byte[] message) throws IOException {
    new WriteHelper().execute(MQTT.publish(topic, message));
  }
  public String subscribe(BroadcastReceiver receiver, String topic, int id) throws
      IOException {
    this.receiver = receiver;
    new WriteHelper().execute(MQTT.subscribe(id, topic, MQTT.AT_MOST_ONCE));
    String sub = WroxAccessory.SUBSCRIBE + "." + topic;
    IntentFilter filter = new IntentFilter();
    filter.addAction(sub);
    mContext.registerReceiver(receiver, filter);
    return sub;
  }
  public void unsubscribe(String topic, int id) throws IOException {
    new WriteHelper().execute(MQTT.unsubscribe(id, topic));
    mContext.unregisterReceiver(receiver);
  }
  public void pingreq() throws IOException {
```

continues

LISTING 5-43 *(continued)*

```
      new WriteHelper().execute(MQTT.ping());
    }
    public void disconnect() throws IOException {
      if (mMonitoringThread.mConnection != null) {
        mMonitoringThread.mConnection.close();
      }
    }
    private class MonitoringThread implements Runnable {
      Connection mConnection;
      public MonitoringThread(int mode, Connection connection) {
        mConnection = connection;
      }
      public void run() {
      }
    }
  }
```

In the `MonitoringThread`, read the incoming data in the `run` method of your thread. Add the code in Listing 5-44 to the `run` method of your `MonitoringThread` inner class; this will try to read all incoming messages on the stream as long as the thread is alive.

LISTING 5-44: Parse the incoming data in the run method

```
    private class MonitoringThread implements Runnable {
      [...]  public void run() {
        int ret = 0;
        byte[] buffer = new byte[16384];
        while (ret >= 0) {
          try {
            ret = mConnection.getInputStream().read(buffer);
          } catch (IOException e) {
            break;
          }
        }
      }
    }
```

Parse the read data using your `decode` method from the `MQTT.java` class. Remember that the accessory can send more than just the PUBLISH message; you should handle all of the different scenarios described in Chapter 3 in the `run` method.

Start by handling the case of an incoming PUBLISH, SUBSCRIBE, or UNSUBSCRIBE message. If your app is reading a subscription request from the accessory, it should try to register the subscription in a list. This list will be used later when your application is attempting to publish information to the accessory. If the topic you're publishing to isn't in the list, the message shouldn't be sent in the first place. See Listing 5-45.

LISTING 5-45: Parse incoming messages

```
private class MonitoringThread implements Runnable {
  Connection mConnection;
  private ArrayList<String> subscriptions;
  public MonitoringThread(int mode, Connection connection) {
    mConnection = connection;
    subscriptions = new ArrayList<String>();
  }
  public void run() {
    int ret = 0;
    byte[] buffer = new byte[16384];
    while (ret >= 0) {
      [...]
      if (ret > 0) {
        MQTTMessage msg = MQTT.decode(buffer);
        if (msg.type == MQTT.PUBLISH) {
          Intent broadcast = new Intent();
          broadcast.setAction(SUBSCRIBE + "." +
            msg.variableHeader.get("topic_name"));
          broadcast.putExtra("topic",
            msg.variableHeader.get("topic_name").toString());
          broadcast.putExtra("payload", msg.payload);
          mContext.sendBroadcast(broadcast);
        } else if (msg.type == MQTT.SUBSCRIBE) {
          String topic = new String(msg.payload);
          if (!subscriptions.contains(topic))
            subscriptions.add(topic);
        } else if (msg.type == MQTT.UNSUBSCRIBE) {
          String topic = new String(msg.payload);
          boolean unsubscribed = subscriptions.remove(topic);
        }
      }
    }
  }
}
```

SUMMARY

The Android accessory communication always happens on an input stream and an output stream. However, depending on the type of accessory — Bluetooth or USB — the streams take different forms. Where the USB accessory uses a `FileDescriptor`, the Bluetooth accessory uses a `BluetoothSocket`.

Reading and writing data to streams can be a perilous task, and should never be done on the UI thread. Whenever you are dealing with exchanging data between devices, be it over WiFi, Bluetooth, or USB, you should avoid writing directly to the `InputSocket` or `OutputSockets` from your activity.

It's up to the two clients to encode and decode the primitive byte array data that is being passed back and forth on the streams. In the library you built throughout this chapter, the messages are encoded according to your own defined P2PMQTT protocol, which inherits from the MQTT v3.1 Protocol Specification, as discussed in Chapter 3.

You're now set to build your own Android accessory applications, with very little effort.

Using Your Accessory Library

WROX.COM CODE DOWNLOADS FOR THIS CHAPTER

The wrox.com code downloads for this chapter are found at www.wrox.com/remtitle .cgi?isbn=1118454766 on the Download Code tab. The code is in the Chapter 6 download and individually named according to the names throughout the chapter.

In this chapter you familiarize yourself in more detail with the Android Open Accessory (AOA) framework and what it means to use accessories in your apps; in particular, all the different steps you need to take to use accessories in your app and the different things you need to think about.

In this chapter you also use the WroxAccessories library that you developed in Chapter 5 to build four accessory-enabled apps for the mini projects introduced in Chapters 7 and 8. Using your library implies understanding how to add custom libraries to your application, so you'll start off by exploring what a library is from the point of view of the Android application.

USING CUSTOM ANDROID LIBRARIES

You've already used Android libraries in your project; in fact, the Android SDK itself is a library! You can find the Android library inside any Android project. If you're using the latest SDK (at the time of writing this was Android SDK 16, or 4.1), you can see it in the subfolder called "Android 4.1" in your Android project. The Android library file is called `android.jar` and contains all the compiled classes available in that particular SDK version. You can even browse the constants and methods available for each class from the Package Explorer.

The Android Support Libraries have been available since Android 3.1. You'll often see them in projects developed to be compatible with Android versions earlier than 3.1. The Android Support Libraries enable you to use new components in old projects, without having to do much magic in your code; the most obvious example that is (or at least should be) used a lot by many developers is the Fragment. You can find the support library for your project (if it has one) under the Android Dependencies folder, and the file is called `android-support-v?.jar`.

You don't need to worry about either of these libraries as they're both added automatically to your build path in Eclipse. Adding custom libraries is slightly trickier, depending on your approach. In general, you can add custom libraries to your projects in two ways: either as compiled collections of class files (as in the example of `android.jar` and `android-support-v?.jar`) or by using the new Android-specific way, which is adding a special Android library project to your workspace. In this approach, Eclipse automatically builds the referenced libraries at the same time when building your application.

ANT IS SMART, SOMETIMES TOO SMART

Usually, Ant (or rather Apache Ant, the tool used to compile Android projects) manages to rebuild and compile only the files that changed in your projects. Ant is great — it does the heavy lifting of organizing your compilation and does it in a smart way by compiling only the files that need to be compiled.

However, sometimes Ant is so smart it gets lazy and seems to ignore some changes, or fails to update the compiled version of your library in your Android project. A general tip when working with Android libraries, then, is to clean both the Android application project and the Android library project when changes have been made; cleaning your projects like this forces Eclipse to do a complete rebuild of your projects.

1. To clean a project, open the Project menu and select Clean.

   In the dialog box that pops up, you can either select to clean your entire workspace (not recommended if you have a lot of projects open) or to clean only the selected projects in the list.

2. Choose "Clean projects selected below" and then select the project you're currently working on.

The WroxAccessories Library

The WroxAccessories library handles the communication with your accessory using the well-known MQTT protocol standard. However, it doesn't define exactly how, or where, you should use it. The most obvious way to use your WroxAccessories library is within an activity that is closely linked to the communication, such as a control UI for a robot or a chat view; however, for the communication to work in these circumstances your activity needs to be visible in the foreground.

At times you want your accessory to work even if the accessory application isn't in the foreground, or you want to share the accessory connection between multiple activities. In these circumstances it makes sense to push the communication to a service running in the background.

The Activity Approach

Because your accessory library already handles the communication in a thread different from the UI thread, the heavy lifting is done. The activity approach, then, means that you'll instead focus your efforts on quickly building a working UI prototype without putting much consideration into creating services in which to run the communication.

This approach is suitable mostly for accessories that require only one user interface to work.

The Service Approach

In the service approach, you would first create an Android service running in either the local process or a process of its own, and then hook your Android user interface to that service using a Binder. This allows the accessory to run continuously regardless of the state of the user interface. It is a fair bit more complex than the previous approach, in that it requires at least a basic understanding of the service component in the Android system; it's also intended for use in a completely different scenario.

As an example, consider a clock application that includes an alarm function. The clock must manage at least two basic functions: show the time when the application is in the foreground and at any time be able to alert the user of an alarm event. The second function needs to run both when the clock application is active in the foreground and, even more importantly, when the clock application isn't in the foreground.

CONNECTING TO AN ANDROID ACCESSORY

Establishing an accessory connection can happen in two ways: either by detecting a system-wide broadcast or by manually requesting permission from the user to use to a connected accessory. Both ways require the user to manually select your application to handle the accessory.

The first option is the most intriguing because it automatically attempts to launch the appropriate application for the connected accessory, and it's also the option used in the examples in this book. What's important to note, though, is that the only component that can receive this system-wide broadcast is the activity. As you can imagine, this limitation causes some headaches when you want to use the accessory connection in a service because the activity needs to act as a proxy in setting up the connection.

Unfortunately, it's not enough to just rely on the underlying mechanics of the WroxAccessories library you've developed; you still need to add some special components when you want to use Android accessories in your app.

The Manifest

The first thing you need to add to your manifest of any accessory-enabled application is the `<uses-feature>` element. This element declares what software or hardware features your app relies on. The Google Play store uses this element to filter available applications for your device. Some of the more common `uses-feature` declarations include hardware features like the camera or sensors such as the gyroscope.

You should add the highlighted code in the following snippet to the `AndroidManifest.xml` of any application that uses accessories; it's a direct child of the `<manifest>` tag:

```
<manifest ...>
  <uses-feature
    android:name="android.hardware.usb.accessory"
    android:required="true" />
</manifest>
```

Moving on, to make your launcher activity (often called `MainActivity.java`) attempt to start when the system fires the `USB_ACCESSORY_ATTACHED` broadcast, you need to modify the `<intent-filter>` element of that activity. See the following code snippet for a typical accessory-enabled filter.

```
<intent-filter>
  <action android:name="android.intent.action.MAIN" />
  <category android:name="android.intent.category.LAUNCHER" />
  <action android:name="android.hardware.usb.action.USB_ACCESSORY_ATTACHED" />
</intent-filter>
```

However, just making your application react to the `USB_ACCESSORY_ATTACHED` broadcast isn't enough; each accessory is uniquely identified by the manufacturer, the model, and its version. This information is sent by the accessory when it connects to the Android device and you need to know this identification to let your app react properly to the accessory.

Create a new XML file with the root element `<resources>` containing only one child element, `<usb-accessory>`. See the following snippet for a typical declaration of this filter:

```
<?xml version="1.0" encoding="utf-8"?>
<resources>
  <usb-accessory model="Android Application Name" manufacturer="You" version="1.0"/>
</resources>
```

The model name is the most important part; that is the name you have to use inside your accessory firmware (the Arduino). You learn more about this in Chapters 7 and 8.

To make your activity use this filter you have to add a `<meta-data>` element to your activity; this lets the activity know that there's extra data it should take into consideration. You define the data, and what action the meta-data is and what action the meta-data belongs to. See the following snippet for a typical declaration:

```
<meta-data
    android:name="android.hardware.usb.action.USB_ACCESSORY_ATTACHED"
    android:resource="@xml/accessory_filter" />
```

Note that it defines a resource file; this needs to correspond to the aforementioned XML filter where you defined which accessory you wanted to connect to.

BUILDING THE MINI PROJECTS

In this section you build the four mini projects: the Large SMS Display (LSMSD), the Sampler, the Parking Assistant, and the Basic Robot. These projects are meant as simple illustrations on how to build basic accessories using common sensors, actuators, and Arduino. In this chapter you focus on building the Android applications; you build the physical accessories in Chapters 7 and 8.

The LSMSD

The Large Short Message Service Display (LSMSD) is a large LED display connected to an Android accessory that displays incoming SMS messages. Because this application has no real user interface — it just prints a received SMS message on the LED display — you'll build a service that runs in the background listening for new SMS messages. You can see the finished accessory in Figure 6-1.

FIGURE 6-1: The finished LED display

Create the Project

First, create the Eclipse project by following these steps:

1. From the File menu, select New ⇨ Android Application Project.

2. Enter **LSMSD** as the Application Name.

3. For the Package Name, enter **com.wiley.aoa.lsmsd**.

4. Select Android SDK 12 or above; if you want to use the earlier version of the USB Accessory you should select Google SDK 10 or above.

5. Click Next.

6. Style the launcher icon to your preference, using either an image or the supplied clipart resources.

7. Let Eclipse create the BlankActivity; this will only be used as an interface to start or stop the service.

8. Click Next.

9. Change the title of your activity to **LSMSD**, and leave everything else as is. Make sure Hierarchical Parent is empty.

10. Click Finish to create the project.

Eclipse should automatically load the layout for your `MainActivity` with the text "Hello world!" printed in the center. Go ahead and delete the text and replace it with a button instead, as shown in Figure 6-2.

FIGURE 6-2: The LSMSD user interface

Usually you'd change the ID of all UI widgets in your application, but because your entire interface consists of just this one button, you can skip that if you want.

Fix the Manifest

Before going further, make sure you add the `<uses-feature>` declaration to your manifest so that devices without support can't install and run the app. See Listing 6-1.

LISTING 6-1: Add the uses-feature declaration

```xml
<manifest xmlns:android="http://schemas.android.com/apk/res/android"
  package="com.wiley.aoa.lsmsd"
  android:versionCode="1"
  android:versionName="1.0" >
<uses-feature android:name="android.hardware.usb.accessory" android:required="true" />
<uses-sdk
    android:minSdkVersion="12"
    android:targetSdkVersion="15" />
<application
    android:icon="@drawable/ic_launcher"
```

```
      android:label="@string/app_name"
      android:theme="@style/AppTheme" >
      <activity
        android:name=".MainActivity"
        android:label="@string/title_activity_main" >
        <intent-filter>
          <action android:name="android.intent.action.MAIN" />
          <category android:name="android.intent.category.LAUNCHER" />
          <action android:name="android.hardware.usb.action.USB_ACCESSORY_ATTACHED" />
        </intent-filter>
        <meta-data
          android:name="android.hardware.usb.action.USB_ACCESSORY_ATTACHED"
          android:resource="@xml/accessory_filter" />    </activity>
    </application>
</manifest>
```

Create the accessory_filter.xml

The `accessory_filter` defines what accessory your application can connect to. It's a resource file often located in the `/res/xml` folder. Follow these steps to create a new Android XML Resources file:

1. From the File menu, select New ⇨ Other.

2. Expand the Android category in the dialog box.

3. Select Android XML Values File and click Next.

4. In the File box, enter **accessory_filter**.

5. Select resources as the Root Element and click Next.

6. Change the folder name to **/res/xml** and click Finish. If this fails, change it back to /res/values and simply move the file later by dragging it to the `/res/xml` folder.

Open your new XML file, located inside the `/res/xml` folder, and add the `<usb-accessory>` element as shown in Listing 6-2.

LISTING 6-2: Add the <usb-accessory> element

```
<?xml version="1.0" encoding="utf-8"?>
<resources>
  <usb-accessory manufacturer="Wiley" model="Large SMS Display" version="1.0" />
</resources>
```

Create the Service

Before you make any changes to the `MainActivity` class, you should create the service; after all, the `MainActivity` just starts and stops the service.

1. In the Package Explorer, expand the src folder and select the package called com.wiley.aoa.lsmsd.

2. From the File menu, select New ⇨ Class.

3. Call the service **AoaService**.

4. As the superclass, enter **android.app.Service**.

5. Uncheck the public static void main checkbox to make sure you do not create the Main method.

6. Click Finish to create the class.

You should end up with something similar to Listing 6-3.

LISTING 6-3: Create the AoaService

```
package com.wiley.aoa.lsmsd;
import android.app.Service;
import android.content.Intent;
import android.os.IBinder;
public class AoaService extends Service {
  @Override
  public IBinder onBind(Intent intent) {
    return null;
  }
}
```

Opening the Service for Connections

The way services work is that they run in a process; either the same process as the user interface (called the local service) or a process of its own (called a remote service). Though slightly different, the two service types share the idea of allowing other Android application components to bind to them. Add the local binder for the service as shown in Listing 6-4.

LISTING 6-4: Add the binder interface

```
package com.wiley.aoa.lsmsd;
import android.app.Service;
import android.content.Intent;
import android.os.Binder;
import android.os.IBinder;
public class AoaService extends Service {
  private final IBinder mBinder = new AoaBinder();
  public class AoaBinder extends Binder {
    AoaService getService() {
      return AoaService.this;
    }
  }
  @Override
  public IBinder onBind(Intent intent) {
    return mBinder;
  }
}
```

Reading Incoming SMS Messages

When the Android device receives an SMS message, it automatically publishes a device-wide broadcast with all the details for that SMS. The only thing your service needs to do to get messages is register a receiver for those broadcasts. Add the BroadcastReciever as shown in Listing 6-5.

LISTING 6-5: Add the SMS receiver

```
package com.wiley.aoa.lsmsd;
import android.app.Service;
import android.content.BroadcastReceiver;
import android.content.Context;
import android.content.Intent;
import android.content.IntentFilter;
import android.os.Binder;
import android.os.Bundle;
import android.os.IBinder;
import android.telephony.SmsMessage;
import android.util.Log;
import android.widget.Toast;
public class AoaService extends Service {
  private final IBinder mBinder = new AoaBinder();
  public class AoaBinder extends Binder {
    AoaService getService() {
      return AoaService.this;
    }
  }
  @Override
  public void onCreate() {
    super.onCreate();
    IntentFilter filter = new IntentFilter();
    filter.addAction("android.provider.Telephony.SMS_RECEIVED");
    registerReceiver(smsReceiver, filter);
  }
  @Override
  public void onDestroy() {
    super.onDestroy();
    unregisterReceiver(smsReceiver);
  }
  @Override
  public IBinder onBind(Intent intent) {
    return mBinder;
  }
  private BroadcastReceiver smsReceiver = new BroadcastReceiver() {
    @Override
    public void onReceive(Context context, Intent intent) {
      Bundle pudsBundle = intent.getExtras();
      Object[] pdus = (Object[]) pudsBundle.get("pdus");
      SmsMessage messages = SmsMessage.createFromPdu((byte[]) pdus[0]);
      String sms = messages.getMessageBody();
    }
  };
}
```

Add the WroxAccessory Instance

Having created the core background service, all that's left is to hook it up to the WroxAccessory and send the SMS message as it arrives. Add the WroxAccessory instance as shown in Listing 6-6.

LISTING 6-6: Add the WroxAccessory instance

```java
package com.wiley.aoa.lsmsd;import java.io.IOException;
import android.app.Service;
import android.content.BroadcastReceiver;
import android.content.Context;
import android.content.Intent;
import android.content.IntentFilter;
import android.os.Binder;
import android.os.Bundle;
import android.os.IBinder;
import android.telephony.SmsMessage;
import android.widget.Toast;
import android.hardware.usb.UsbManager;
import com.wiley.wroxaccessories.UsbConnection12;
import com.wiley.wroxaccessories.WroxAccessory;
public class AoaService extends Service {
  private final IBinder mBinder = new AoaBinder();
  private WroxAccessory mAccessory;
  private UsbConnection12 mConnection;
    public class AoaBinder extends Binder {
    AoaService getService() {
      return AoaService.this;
    }
  }
  @Override
  public void onCreate() {
    super.onCreate();
    IntentFilter filter = new IntentFilter();
    filter.addAction("android.provider.Telephony.SMS_RECEIVED");
    registerReceiver(mReceiver, filter);
    if (mAccessory == null)
      mAccessory = new WroxAccessory(this);
    UsbManager manager = (UsbManager) getSystemService(USB_SERVICE);
    if (mConnection == null)
      mConnection = new UsbConnection12(this, manager);
    try {
      mAccessory.connect(WroxAccessory.USB_ACCESSORY_12, mConnection);
    } catch (IOException e) {
      e.printStackTrace();
    }
  }
  @Override
  public boolean onUnbind(Intent intent) {
    return super.onUnbind(intent);
  }
  @Override
```

```
    public void onDestroy() {
      super.onDestroy();
      unregisterReceiver(mReceiver);
      try {
        mAccessory.disconnect();
      } catch (IOException e) {
        e.printStackTrace();
      }
    }
    @Override
    public IBinder onBind(Intent intent) {
      return mBinder;
    }
    private BroadcastReceiver mReceiver = new BroadcastReceiver() {
      @Override
      public void onReceive(Context context, Intent intent) {
        Bundle pudsBundle = intent.getExtras();
        Object[] pdus = (Object[]) pudsBundle.get("pdus");
        SmsMessage messages = SmsMessage.createFromPdu((byte[]) pdus[0]);
        String sms = messages.getMessageBody();
      }
    };
}
```

Pass the SMS to Your Accessory

The final thing to do is to send the MQTT message to your accessory. Publish the message as shown in Listing 6-7.

LISTING 6-7: Publishing an SMS

```
package com.wiley.aoa.lsmsd;
import java.io.IOException;
import android.app.Service;
import android.content.BroadcastReceiver;
import android.content.Context;
import android.content.Intent;
import android.content.IntentFilter;
import android.os.Binder;
import android.os.Bundle;
import android.os.IBinder;
import android.telephony.SmsMessage;
import android.hardware.usb.UsbManager;
import com.wiley.wroxaccessories.UsbConnection12;
import com.wiley.wroxaccessories.WroxAccessory;
public class AoaService extends Service {
  private final IBinder mBinder = new AoaBinder();
  private WroxAccessory mAccessory;
  private UsbConnection12 mConnection;
  public class AoaBinder extends Binder {
    AoaService getService() {
      return AoaService.this;
    }
```

continues

LISTING 6-7 *(continued)*

```
      }
    @Override
    public void onCreate() {
      super.onCreate();
      IntentFilter filter = new IntentFilter();
      filter.addAction("android.provider.Telephony.SMS_RECEIVED");
      registerReceiver(mReceiver, filter);
      if (mAccessory == null)
        mAccessory = new WroxAccessory(this);
      UsbManager manager =(UsbManager) getSystemService(USB_SERVICE);
      if (mConnection == null)
        mConnection = new UsbConnection12(this, manager);
      try {
        mAccessory.connect(WroxAccessory.USB_ACCESSORY_12, mConnection);
      } catch (IOException e) {
        e.printStackTrace();
      }
    }   @Override
    public boolean onUnbind(Intent intent) {
      return super.onUnbind(intent);
    }   @Override
    public void onDestroy() {
      super.onDestroy();
      unregisterReceiver(mReceiver);
      try {
        mAccessory.disconnect();
      } catch (IOException e) {
        e.printStackTrace();
      }
    }
    @Override
    public IBinder onBind(Intent intent) {
      return mBinder;
    }
    private BroadcastReceiver mReceiver = new BroadcastReceiver() {
      @Override
      public void onReceive(Context context, Intent intent) {
        Bundle pudsBundle = intent.getExtras();
        Object[] pdus = (Object[]) pudsBundle.get("pdus");
        SmsMessage messages = SmsMessage.createFromPdu((byte[]) pdus[0]);
        String sms = messages.getMessageBody();
        try {
          mAccessory.publish("sms", sms.getBytes());
        } catch (IOException e) {
          e.printStackTrace();
        }
      }
    };
  }
```

You're now ready to build the Arduino accessory in Chapter 7, and then you'll have your very own LSMSD to publicize all the fancy SMS messages you receive.

Improving the Prototype

Some SMS messages just aren't meant to be displayed publicly, so the first possible improvement to the LSMSD would be a filter of some sort. Perhaps only displaying messages sent from contacts that the user manually selects in a list is a wise improvement.

You could also add extra information to the display, such as time since you received a message or showing multiple messages after each other.

Another improvement would be letting the user interact with messages by pressing buttons or pulling levers on the accessory, so that he or she doesn't need to open the phone to mark a message as read.

The Parking Assistant

The Parking Assistant is intended to help you avoid hitting things as you reverse your car. Most modern cars have this already built in — they emit sound beeps, and the interval between them defines the distance to an object behind your car.

In this mini project, however, you build a visual aid to parking your car; obviously not the best idea if you consider the project from an interaction design perspective. But you'll find that out as you try the prototype yourself on your car. For clarity, do not use this aid in a "live" setting without having tested it in controlled environments first.

Figure 6-3 shows the finished, mounted prototype.

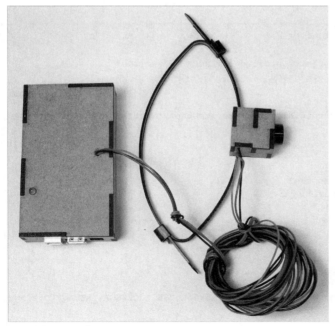

FIGURE 6-3: The finished Parking Assistant

Create the Project

Follow these steps to create the Eclipse project:

1. From the File menu in Eclipse, select New ⇨ Android Application Project.

2. Enter **Parking Assistant** as the Application Name.

3. For the Package Name, enter **com.wiley.aoa.parking_assistant**.

4. Select Android SDK 12 or above. If you want to work with the older USB Accessory, select Google SDK 10.

5. Click Next.

6. Style the launcher icon to your preference, using either an image or the supplied clipart resources.

7. Let Eclipse create the BlankActivity.

8. Click Next.

9. Change the title of your activity to **Parking Assistant**, and leave everything else as is.

10. Click finish to create the project.

Because you're building the Parking Assistant as a USB accessory, remember to add the required elements to the manifest: the `<uses-feature>` declaration, the extra action to your `<intent-filter>`, and the `<meta-data>` element defining which accessory you'll connect to. See Listing 6-8 for details.

LISTING 6-8: Add the needed manifest changes

```xml
<manifest xmlns:android="http://schemas.android.com/apk/res/android"
  package="com.wiley.aoa.parking_assistant"
  android:versionCode="1"
  android:versionName="1.0" >
<uses-feature android:name="android.hardware.usb.accessory" android:required="true" />
<uses-sdk
    android:minSdkVersion="12"
    android:targetSdkVersion="15" />
<application
    android:icon="@drawable/ic_launcher"
    android:label="@string/app_name"
    android:theme="@style/AppTheme" >
    <activity
      android:name=".MainActivity"
      android:label="@string/title_activity_main" >
      <intent-filter>
        <action android:name="android.intent.action.MAIN" />
        <category android:name="android.intent.category.LAUNCHER" />
        <action android:name="android.hardware.usb.action.USB_ACCESSORY_ATTACHED" />
```

```
        </intent-filter>
        <meta-data
          android:name="android.hardware.usb.action.USB_ACCESSORY_ATTACHED"
          android:resource="@xml/accessory_filter" />
      </activity>
    </application>
  </manifest>
```

Create the accessory_filter.xml

The `accessory_filter` defines what accessory your application can connect to. It's a resource file often located in the `/res/xml` folder. Follow these steps to create a new Android XML Resources file:

1. From the File menu, select New ⇨ Other.

2. Expand the Android category in the dialog box.

3. Select Android XML Values File and click Next.

4. In the File box, enter **accessory_filter**.

5. Select resources as the Root Element and click Next.

6. Change the folder name to **/res/xml** and click Finish. If this fails, change it back to /res/values and simply move the file later by dragging it to the /res/xml folder.

Open your new XML file, located inside the /res/xml folder, and add the `<usb-accessory>` element as shown in Listing 6-9.

LISTING 6-9: Add the <usb-accessory> element

```
<?xml version="1.0" encoding="utf-8"?>
<resources>
  <usb-accessory manufacturer="Wiley" model="Parking Assistant" version="1.0" />
</resources>
```

Link Your WroxAccessories Library

To connect to the `WroxAccessory` you need to link the library to your build path. You do this by using the project context menu:

1. Select your project in the Package Explorer, and in the Eclipse File menu select Properties.

2. Select Android on the left side.

3. Click the Add button on the right side within the Library panel.

4. Select WroxAccessories in the dialog box that pops up.

5. Click Apply and close the dialog box by clicking OK.

Build the User Interface

Eclipse should automatically load the layout for your `MainActivity` with the text "Hello world!" printed in the center. Go ahead and delete the text and replace it with a `ProgressBar` that expands over the whole screen. This will visualize the distance to the objects behind the vehicle. Over the `ProgressBar` you should place a `TextView`, centered in the screen, that will display the distance with more detail. See Listing 6-10.

LISTING 6-10: The Parking Assistant user interface

```
<RelativeLayout xmlns:android="http://schemas.android.com/apk/res/android"
  xmlns:tools="http://schemas.android.com/tools"
  android:layout_width="match_parent"
  android:layout_height="match_parent" >
  <ProgressBar
    android:id="@+id/progressBar1"
    style="?android:attr/progressBarStyleHorizontal"
    android:layout_width="match_parent"
    android:layout_height="match_parent"
    android:layout_centerHorizontal="true"
    android:layout_centerVertical="true"
    android:layout_margin="5dp" />
  <TextView
    android:id="@+id/textView1"
    android:layout_width="wrap_content"
    android:layout_height="wrap_content"
    android:layout_centerHorizontal="true"
    android:layout_centerVertical="true"
    android:text="Large Text"
    android:textAppearance="?android:attr/textAppearanceLarge" />
</RelativeLayout>
```

The standard `ProgressBar` is horizontal, however, and that's just not very suitable for this application. To make the `ProgressBar` vertical instead, you should create a custom drawable:

1. From the File menu, select New ➪ Other.

2. Select Android XML File.

3. Set the Resource Type to Drawable.

4. Enter **myprogress** as the File name.

5. Select layer-list as the Root Element.

Add the items from Listing 6-11 to your new `myprogress.xml` file. The names of the `<item>` elements are important in this file because the `ProgressBar` expects them to match a certain pattern.

LISTING 6-11: Create the vertical progress bar

```xml
<?xml version="1.0" encoding="utf-8"?>
<layer-list xmlns:android="http://schemas.android.com/apk/res/android" >
  <item android:id="@android:id/background">
    <shape>
      <solid android:color="#FFFFFF" />
    </shape>
  </item>
  <item android:id="@android:id/secondaryProgress">
    <clip
        android:clipOrientation="vertical"
        android:gravity="bottom" >
      <shape>
        <corners android:radius="5dip" />
        <solid android:color="#00FF00" />
      </shape>
    </clip>
  </item>
  <item android:id="@android:id/progress">
    <clip
        android:clipOrientation="vertical"
        android:gravity="bottom" >
      <shape>
        <corners android:radius="5dip" />
        <solid android:color="#00FF00" />
      </shape>
    </clip>
  </item>
</layer-list>
```

To make your `ProgressBar` use this new drawable, add the `android:progressDrawable` attribute to the `<ProgressBar>` element. See the following code snippet for details:

```xml
<ProgressBar
    android:id="@+id/progressBar1"
    style="?android:attr/progressBarStyleHorizontal"
    android:layout_width="match_parent"
    android:layout_height="match_parent"
    android:layout_centerHorizontal="true"
    android:layout_centerVertical="true"
    android:layout_margin="5dp"
    android:progressDrawable="@drawable/myprogress" />
```

The finished layout should look something like Figure 6-4.

Load the User Interface

Now, because you want to update this UI you need some references to it. Declare the `ProgressBar` object and the `TextView` object in your `MainActivity` class. See Listing 6-12.

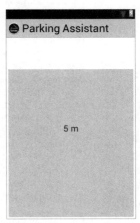

FIGURE 6-4: The user interface for the Parking Assistant

LISTING 6-12: Load the user interface

```
package com.wiley.aoa.parking_assistant;
import android.app.Activity;
import android.os.Bundle;
import android.widget.ProgressBar;
import android.widget.TextView;
public class MainActivity extends Activity {
  private ProgressBar mProgressBar;
  private TextView mTextView;
  @Override
  public void onCreate(Bundle savedInstanceState) {
    super.onCreate(savedInstanceState);
    setContentView(R.layout.activity_main);
    mProgressBar = (ProgressBar) findViewById(R.id.progressBar1);
    mProgressBar.setMax(6);
    mProgressBar.setProgress(0);
    mTextView = (TextView) findViewById(R.id.textView1);
  }
}
```

Create the WroxAccessory Instance

You need an instance of the library interface for handling the connection to your accessory. Add it to your MainActivity.java class as shown in Listing 6-13, passing the current context as an argument.

LISTING 6-13: Add the WroxAccessory instance

```
package com.wiley.aoa.parking_assistant;
import com.wiley.wroxaccessories.WroxAccessory;
import android.app.Activity;
import android.os.Bundle;
import android.widget.ProgressBar;
import android.widget.TextView;public class MainActivity extends Activity {
  private ProgressBar mProgressBar;
  private TextView mTextView;
  private WroxAccessory mWroxAccessory;
  @Override
  public void onCreate(Bundle savedInstanceState) {
    super.onCreate(savedInstanceState);
    setContentView(R.layout.activity_main);
    mProgressBar = (ProgressBar) findViewById(R.id.progressBar1);
    mProgressBar.setMax(6);
    mProgressBar.setProgress(0);
    mTextView = (TextView) findViewById(R.id.textView1);
    mWroxAccessory = new WroxAccessory(this);
  }
}
```

Connecting

The WroxAccessory constructor initiates all the necessary framework for establishing a connection, but it doesn't create the connection itself. For that you'll need another object, the Connection object. Depending on the type of accessory you're building the Parking Assistant to be — USB or Bluetooth — instantiate a Connection object as shown in Listing 6-14.

LISTING 6-14: Create the connection

```
package com.wiley.aoa.parking_assistant;
import com.wiley.wroxaccessories.UsbConnection12;
import com.wiley.wroxaccessories.WroxAccessory;
import android.app.Activity;
import android.hardware.usb.UsbManager;
import android.os.Bundle;
import android.widget.ProgressBar;
import android.widget.TextView;public class MainActivity extends Activity {
  private ProgressBar mProgressBar;
  private TextView mTextView;
  private WroxAccessory mWroxAccessory;
  private UsbManager mUsbManager;
  private UsbConnection12 mUsbConnection12;
    @Override
  public void onCreate(Bundle savedInstanceState) {
    super.onCreate(savedInstanceState);
    setContentView(R.layout.activity_main);
    mProgressBar = (ProgressBar) findViewById(R.id.progressBar1);
    mProgressBar.setMax(6);
    mProgressBar.setProgress(0);
    mTextView = (TextView) findViewById(R.id.textView1);
    mWroxAccessory = new WroxAccessory(this);
    mUsbManager = (UsbManager) getSystemService(USB_SERVICE);
    mUsbConnection12 = new UsbConnection12(this, mUsbManager);
    try {
      mAccessory.connect(WroxAccessory.USB_ACCESSORY_12, connection);
    } catch (IOException e) {
      e.printStackTrace();
    }
  }
}
```

Make sure to disconnect as well. See Listing 6-15.

LISTING 6-15: Disconnect from the accessory

```
package com.wiley.aoa.parking_assistant;
import com.wiley.wroxaccessories.UsbConnection12;
import com.wiley.wroxaccessories.WroxAccessory;
import android.app.Activity;
import android.hardware.usb.UsbManager;
import android.os.Bundle;
import android.widget.ProgressBar;
```

continues

LISTING 6-15 *(continued)*

```java
import android.widget.TextView;
public class MainActivity extends Activity {
  private ProgressBar mProgressBar;
  private TextView mTextView;
  private WroxAccessory mWroxAccessory;
  private UsbManager mUsbManager;
  private UsbConnection12 mUsbConnection12;
  @Override
  public void onCreate(Bundle savedInstanceState) {
    super.onCreate(savedInstanceState);
    setContentView(R.layout.activity_main);
    mProgressBar = (ProgressBar) findViewById(R.id.progressBar1);
    mProgressBar.setMax(6);
    mProgressBar.setProgress(0);
    mTextView = (TextView) findViewById(R.id.textView1);
    mWroxAccessory = new WroxAccessory(this);
    mUsbManager = (UsbManager) getSystemService(USB_SERVICE);
    mUsbConnection12 = new UsbConnection12(this, mUsbManager);
    mWroxAccessory.connect(WroxAccessory.USB_ACCESSORY_12, mUsbConnection12);
  }
  @Override
  protected void onDestroy() {
    super.onDestroy();
    try {
      mAccessory.disconnect();
    } catch (IOException e) {
      e.printStackTrace();
    }
  }
}
```

Interacting with the WroxAccessory

You're building an application that will listen for information from the accessory, not the other way around. This means you need to subscribe to a topic on the Android side; otherwise, you won't receive any data from the accessory. Add the subscription as shown in Listing 6-16.

LISTING 6-16: Subscribe to the "us" topic

```java
package com.wiley.aoa.parking_assistant;
import com.wiley.wroxaccessories.UsbConnection12;
import com.wiley.wroxaccessories.WroxAccessory;
import android.app.Activity;
import android.hardware.usb.UsbManager;
import android.os.Bundle;
import android.widget.ProgressBar;
import android.widget.TextView;
public class MainActivity extends Activity {
  private ProgressBar mProgressBar;
  private TextView mTextView;
```

```
    private WroxAccessory mWroxAccessory;
    private UsbManager mUsbManager;
    private UsbConnection12 mUsbConnection12;
    private int id = 0;
    @Override
    public void onCreate(Bundle savedInstanceState) {
      super.onCreate(savedInstanceState);
      setContentView(R.layout.activity_main);
      mProgressBar = (ProgressBar) findViewById(R.id.progressBar1);
      mProgressBar.setMax(6);
      mProgressBar.setProgress(0);
      mTextView = (TextView) findViewById(R.id.textView1);
      mWroxAccessory = new WroxAccessory(this);
      mUsbManager = (UsbManager) getSystemService(USB_SERVICE);
      mUsbConnection12 = new UsbConnection12(this, mUsbManager);
      mWroxAccessory.connect(WroxAccessory.USB_ACCESSORY_12, mUsbConnection12);
    }
    @Override
    protected void onResume() {
      super.onResume();
      try {
        subscription = mAccessory.subscribe(receiver, "us", id++);
      } catch (IOException e) {
        e.printStackTrace();
      }
    }
    @Override
    protected void onDestroy() {
      super.onDestroy();
      try {
        mAccessory.disconnect();
      } catch (IOException e) {
        e.printStackTrace();
      }
    }
    private BroadcastReceiver receiver = new BroadcastReceiver() {
      @Override
      public void onReceive(Context context, Intent intent) {
        if (intent.getAction().equals(subscription)) {
          byte[] payload = intent.getByteArrayExtra(subscription + ".payload");
          mProgressBar.setProgress(payload[0]);
          mTextView.setText(payload[0] + " m");
        }
      }
    };
  }
```

Possible Improvements

The most obvious improvement to this mini project is to fix the dangerous interaction; you should never talk on your phone as you drive your car, and you should *definitely* not look on the phone's screen as you try to reverse your car! So, instead of using a visual feedback you should add sound to the application, and change a variable in the sound playback (interval, pitch, volume, or other) depending on the distance.

The Basic Robot

Building a robot isn't as hard as it may seem. Of course, if you want your robot to be as brilliant as Data, or as fierce as the Terminator, you'll find yourself taking on quite a challenge. The little robot you build for this application won't be as impressive as those sci-fi alternatives; it will have no intelligence of its own, and will only be able to take simple movement commands from you. You can see the final prototype in Figure 6-5.

FIGURE 6-5: The Basic Robot

Create the Project

To create the Basic Robot project, follow these steps:

1. In the Eclipse menu, select File ⇨ New ⇨ Android Application Project.

2. Enter **Basic Robot** as the Application Name.

3. For the Package Name, enter **com.wiley.aoa.basic_robot**.

4. Select Android SDK 12 or above. If you want to use the first version of the Accessory library, select Google SDK 10 or above instead.

5. Click Next.

6. Style the launcher icon to your preference, using either an image or the supplied clipart resources.

7. Let Eclipse create the BlankActivity; this will only be used as an interface to start or stop the service.

8. Click Next.

9. Change the title of your activity to **Basic Robot**, and leave everything else as is.

10. Click Finish to create the project.

Like with all accessory-enabled projects, you need to add some attributes and elements to the manifest. See Listing 6-17.

LISTING 6-17: Add the needed manifest changes

```xml
<manifest xmlns:android="http://schemas.android.com/apk/res/android"
  package="com.wiley.aoa.basic_robot"
  android:versionCode="1"
  android:versionName="1.0" >
<uses-feature android:name="android.hardware.usb.accessory" />
<uses-sdk
  android:minSdkVersion="12"
  android:targetSdkVersion="15" />
<application
  android:icon="@drawable/ic_launcher"
  android:label="@string/app_name"
  android:theme="@style/AppTheme" >
  <activity
    android:name=".MainActivity"
    android:label="@string/title_activity_main" >
    <intent-filter>
      <action android:name="android.intent.action.MAIN" />
      <category android:name="android.intent.category.LAUNCHER" />
      <action android:name="android.hardware.usb.action.USB_ACCESSORY_ATTACHED" />
    </intent-filter>
    <meta-data
      android:name="android.hardware.usb.action.USB_ACCESSORY_ATTACHED"
      android:resource="@xml/accessory_filter" />
  </activity>
</application>
</manifest>
```

Create the accessory_filter.xml

The `accessory_filter` defines what accessory your application can connect to. It's a resource file often located in the /res/xml folder. Follow these steps to create a new Android XML Resources file:

1. From the File menu, select New ⇨ Other.

2. Expand the Android category in the dialog box.

3. Select Android XML Values File and click Next.

4. In the File box, enter **accessory_filter**.

5. Select resources as the Root Element and click Next.

6. Change the folder name to **/res/xml** and click Finish. If this fails, change it back to /res/values and simply move the file later by dragging it to the /res/xml folder.

Open your new XML file, located inside the `/res/xml` folder, and add the `<usb-accessory>` element as shown in Listing 6-18.

LISTING 6-18 Add the `<usb-accessory>` element

```xml
<?xml version="1.0" encoding="utf-8"?>
<resources>
  <usb-accessory manufacturer="Wiley" model="Basic Robot" version="1.0" />
</resources>
```

Link Your WroxAccessories Library

To connect to the `WroxAccessory` you need to link the library to your build path. You do this by using the project context menu:

1. Select your project in the Package Explorer and in the File menu, select Properties.

2. Select Android on the left side.

3. Click the Add button on the right side within the Library panel.

4. Select WroxAccessories in the dialog box that pops up.

5. Click Apply and exit by clicking OK.

Build the User Interface

The user interface to control Basic Robot is quite simple; it contains five different buttons placed in a cross, as you can see in Figure 6-6.

The central button tells the robot to stop everything it is currently doing; in essence, it tells the robot to stop moving because it can't do anything else. The button to the north tells Basic Robot to move forward, the button to the south tells Basic Robot to move backward, and the two buttons on the side tell him to move to the left or right.

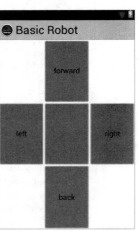

FIGURE 6-6: The Basic Robot interface

NESTED WEIGHTS

You can achieve this layout in a number of ways; one easy way is using LinearLayouts with nested weights. Although this will work, it's also going to be costly for your app, so in general it's not recommended to use the weight attribute. But because it's such a simple app with no real other performance issues, you can safely use it in this example.

You can, of course, try other alternatives. GridLayout (requires API 14 or above) or TableLayout are the two primary alternatives to nested weights.

Build the user interface as shown in Listing 6-19.

LISTING 6-19: Basic Robot user interface

```xml
<RelativeLayout xmlns:android="http://schemas.android.com/apk/res/android"
  xmlns:tools="http://schemas.android.com/tools"
  android:layout_width="match_parent"
  android:layout_height="match_parent" >
  <LinearLayout
    android:layout_width="match_parent"
    android:layout_height="match_parent"
    android:layout_alignParentLeft="true"
    android:layout_alignParentTop="true"
    android:orientation="vertical" >
    <LinearLayout
      android:layout_width="match_parent"
      android:layout_height="match_parent"
      android:layout_weight="1" >
      <View
        android:id="@+id/view1"
        android:layout_width="match_parent"
        android:layout_height="match_parent"
        android:layout_weight="1" />
      <Button
        android:id="@+id/button_north"
        android:layout_width="match_parent"
        android:layout_height="match_parent"
        android:layout_weight="1"
        android:text="Button" />
      <View
        android:id="@+id/view2"
        android:layout_width="match_parent"
        android:layout_height="match_parent"
        android:layout_weight="1" />
    </LinearLayout>
    <LinearLayout
      android:layout_width="match_parent"
      android:layout_height="match_parent"
      android:layout_weight="1" >
      <Button
        android:id="@+id/button_west"
        android:layout_width="match_parent"
        android:layout_height="match_parent"
        android:layout_weight="1"
        android:text="Button" />
      <Button
        android:id="@+id/button_stop"
        android:layout_width="match_parent"
        android:layout_height="match_parent"
        android:layout_weight="1"
        android:text="Button" />
      <Button
        android:id="@+id/button_east"
```

continues

LISTING 6-19 *(continued)*

```
            android:layout_width="match_parent"
            android:layout_height="match_parent"
            android:layout_weight="1"
            android:text="Button" />
    </LinearLayout>
    <LinearLayout
      android:layout_width="match_parent"
      android:layout_height="match_parent"
      android:layout_weight="1" >
      <View
        android:id="@+id/view3"
        android:layout_width="match_parent"
        android:layout_height="match_parent"
        android:layout_weight="1" />
      <Button
        android:id="@+id/button_south"
        android:layout_width="match_parent"
        android:layout_height="match_parent"
        android:layout_weight="1"
        android:text="Button" />
      <View
        android:id="@+id/view4"
        android:layout_width="match_parent"
        android:layout_height="match_parent"
        android:layout_weight="1" />
    </LinearLayout>
  </LinearLayout>
</RelativeLayout>
```

When you have the layout you want, it's time to apply a little bit of style. Much like before, you use a selector drawable for all your buttons. Create the selector as shown in Listing 6-20.

LISTING 6-20: The Basic Robot selector

```
<?xml version="1.0" encoding="utf-8"?>
<selector xmlns:android="http://schemas.android.com/apk/res/android" >
  <item android:state_pressed="true">
    <shape android:shape="rectangle">
      <corners android:radius="5dp" />
      <solid android:color="#043C6B"/>
      <stroke android:width="2dp" android:color="#25547B"/>
      <padding
        android:left="5dp" android:top="5dp"
        android:right="5dp" android:bottom="5dp" />
    </shape>
  </item>
  <item android:state_focused="true">
    <shape android:shape="rectangle">
      <corners android:radius="5dp" />
      <solid android:color="#043C6B"/>
```

```
            <stroke android:width="2dp" android:color="#25547B"/>
            <padding
             android:left="5dp" android:top="5dp"
             android:right="5dp" android:bottom="5dp" />
          </shape>
        </item>
        <item>
          <shape android:shape="rectangle">
            <corners android:radius="5dp" />
            <solid android:color="#0B5FA5"/>
            <stroke android:width="2dp" android:color="#25547B"/>
            <padding
              android:left="5dp" android:top="5dp"
              android:right="5dp" android:bottom="5dp" />
          </shape>
        </item>
      </selector>
```

You also want to add some text to the buttons to make it even more clear what each button does. Open the `strings.xml` file in your project; it's located inside the `/res/values` folder. Add the strings as shown in Listing 6-21.

LISTING 6-21: Create the button labels

```
<resources>
  <string name="app_name">Basic Robot</string>
  <string name="hello_world">Hello world!</string>
  <string name="menu_settings">Settings</string>
  <string name="title_activity_main">Basic Robot</string>
  <string name="north">forward</string>
  <string name="east">right</string>
  <string name="stop">stop</string>
  <string name="west">left</string>
  <string name="south">back</string>
</resources>
```

With all the UI styles complete, you can go ahead and apply them to the buttons, as shown in Listing 6-22.

LISTING 6-22: Apply the styles

```
<RelativeLayout xmlns:android="http://schemas.android.com/apk/res/android"
    xmlns:tools="http://schemas.android.com/tools"
    android:layout_width="match_parent"
    android:layout_height="match_parent" >
    <LinearLayout
      android:layout_width="match_parent"
      android:layout_height="match_parent"
      android:layout_alignParentLeft="true"
      android:layout_alignParentTop="true"
      android:orientation="vertical" >
```

continues

LISTING 6-22 *(continued)*

```xml
<LinearLayout
  android:layout_width="match_parent"
  android:layout_height="match_parent"
  android:layout_weight="1" >
  <View
    android:id="@+id/view1"
    android:layout_width="match_parent"
    android:layout_height="match_parent"
    android:layout_weight="1" />
  <Button
    android:id="@+id/button_north"
    android:layout_width="match_parent"
    android:layout_height="match_parent"
    android:layout_weight="1"
    android:background="@drawable/mybutton"
    android:text="@string/north" />
  <View
    android:id="@+id/view2"
    android:layout_width="match_parent"
    android:layout_height="match_parent"
    android:layout_weight="1" />
</LinearLayout>
<LinearLayout
  android:layout_width="match_parent"
  android:layout_height="match_parent"
  android:layout_weight="1" >
  <Button
    android:id="@+id/button_west"
    android:layout_width="match_parent"
    android:layout_height="match_parent"
    android:layout_weight="1"
    android:background="@drawable/mybutton"
    android:text="@string/west" />
  <Button
    android:id="@+id/button_stop"
    android:layout_width="match_parent"
    android:layout_height="match_parent"
    android:layout_weight="1"
    android:background="@drawable/mybutton"
    android:text="@string/stop" />
  <Button
    android:id="@+id/button_east"
    android:layout_width="match_parent"
    android:layout_height="match_parent"
    android:layout_weight="1"
    android:background="@drawable/mybutton"
    android:text="@string/east" />
</LinearLayout>
<LinearLayout
  android:layout_width="match_parent"
  android:layout_height="match_parent"
  android:layout_weight="1" >
```

```
        <View
          android:id="@+id/view3"
          android:layout_width="match_parent"
          android:layout_height="match_parent"
          android:layout_weight="1" />
        <Button
          android:id="@+id/button_south"
          android:layout_width="match_parent"
          android:layout_height="match_parent"
          android:layout_weight="1"
          android:background="@drawable/mybutton"
          android:text="@string/south" />
        <View
          android:id="@+id/view4"
          android:layout_width="match_parent"
          android:layout_height="match_parent"
          android:layout_weight="1" />
      </LinearLayout>
    </LinearLayout>
</RelativeLayout>
```

Connect to the WroxAccessory

Create the connection to your `WroxAccessory` as shown in Listing 6-23.

LISTING 6-23: The WroxAccessory connection

```java
package com.wiley.aoa.basic_robot;
import java.io.IOException;
import android.app.Activity;
import android.hardware.usb.UsbManager;
import android.os.Bundle;
import com.wiley.wroxaccessories.UsbConnection12;
import com.wiley.wroxaccessories.WroxAccessory;
public class MainActivity extends Activity {
  private WroxAccessory mWroxAccessory;
  private UsbManager mUsbManager;
  private UsbConnection12 mUsbConnection12;
  @Override
  public void onCreate(Bundle savedInstanceState) {
    super.onCreate(savedInstanceState);
    setContentView(R.layout.activity_main);
    mWroxAccessory = new WroxAccessory(this);
    mUsbManager = (UsbManager) getSystemService(USB_SERVICE);
    mUsbConnection12 = new UsbConnection12(this, mUsbManager);
    try {
      mWroxAccessory.connect(WroxAccessory.USB_ACCESSORY_12, mUsbConnection12);
    } catch (IOException e) {
      e.printStackTrace();
    }
  }

  @Override
```

continues

LISTING 6-23 *(continued)*

```
  protected void onPause() {
    try {
      mWroxAccessory.disconnect();
    } catch (IOException e) {
      e.printStackTrace();
    }
    super.onPause();
  }
}
```

Hook Up the User Interface

You need to create an `OnClickListener` for your buttons and attach it. The listener will then determine which button it received an event from and publish the appropriate message to the accessory. See Listing 6-24.

LISTING 6-24: The OnClickListener

```
package com.wiley.aoa.basic_robot;
import java.io.IOException;
import android.app.Activity;
import android.hardware.usb.UsbManager;
import android.os.Bundle;
import android.view.View;
import android.view.View.OnClickListener;
import android.widget.Button;
import com.wiley.wroxaccessories.UsbConnection12;
import com.wiley.wroxaccessories.WroxAccessory;
public class MainActivity extends Activity {
  private WroxAccessory mWroxAccessory;
  private UsbManager mUsbManager;
  private UsbConnection12 mUsbConnection12;
  @Override
  public void onCreate(Bundle savedInstanceState) {
    super.onCreate(savedInstanceState);
    setContentView(R.layout.activity_main);
    mWroxAccessory = new WroxAccessory();
    mUsbManager = (UsbManager) getSystemService(USB_SERVICE);
    mUsbConnection12 = new UsbConnection12(this, mUsbManager);
    Button button = (Button) findViewById(R.id.button_north);
    button.setOnClickListener(buttonListener);
    button = (Button) findViewById(R.id.button_east);
    button.setOnClickListener(buttonListener);
    button = (Button) findViewById(R.id.button_south);
    button.setOnClickListener(buttonListener);
    button = (Button) findViewById(R.id.button_west);
    button.setOnClickListener(buttonListener);
    button = (Button) findViewById(R.id.button_stop);
    button.setOnClickListener(buttonListener);
```

```
      }
      @Override
      protected void onResume() {
        try {
          mWroxAccessory.connect(WroxAccessory.USB_ACCESSORY_12, mUsbConnection12);
        } catch (IOException e) {
          e.printStackTrace();
        }
        super.onResume();
      }
      @Override
      protected void onPause() {
        try {
          mWroxAccessory.disconnect();
        } catch (IOException e) {
          e.printStackTrace();
        }
        super.onPause();
      }
      private OnClickListener buttonListener = new OnClickListener() {
        public void onClick(View v) {
          byte[] message = new byte[1];
          switch (v.getId()) {
          case R.id.button_north:
            message[0] = 1;
            break;
          case R.id.button_east:
            message[0] = 2;
            break;
          case R.id.button_south:
            message[0] = 3;
            break;
          case R.id.button_west:
            message[0] = 4;
            break;
          case R.id.button_stop:
            message[0] = 0;
          }
          try {
            mWroxAccessory.publish("mv", message);
          } catch (IOException e) {
            e.printStackTrace();
          }
        }
      };
    }
```

Possible Improvements

The first thing that comes to mind when thinking of improvements for the Basic Robot is more actuators on the accessory. You could, for example, add some LEDs in the front and back of the robot that would act as headlights and brakelights, and then turn them on or off depending on how you steer.

Another improvement is in the way you interact with the robot. Instead of using buttons you could build a software joystick, like the ones you find in many popular games for handheld devices.

The Sampler

The Sampler is a project that turns the phone into a music machine, giving you a way to play sounds on the device by pressing physical buttons — turning it into a sampler or keyboard, if you will. This is by far the easiest of all the mini projects, using built-in sounds effectively through the RingtoneManager.

Figure 6-7 shows the finished Sampler prototype.

FIGURE 6-7: The Sampler

Create the Project

Start by creating a new Eclipse project. Follow these steps:

1. From the File menu, select New ⇨ Android Application Project.
2. Enter **The Sampler** as the Application Name.
3. For the Package Name, enter **com.wiley.aoa.the_sampler**.
4. Select Android SDK 12 or above. If you want to use the first version of the Accessory library, select Google SDK 10 or above instead.

5. Click Next.

6. Style the launcher icon to your preference, using either an image or the supplied clipart resources.

7. Let Eclipse create the BlankActivity; this will only be used as an interface to start or stop the service.

8. Click Next.

9. Change the title of your activity to **The Sampler,** and leave everything else as is.

10. Click Finish to create the project.

Don't forget to make the required changes to the manifest. See Listing 6-25.

LISTING 6-25: Add the needed manifest changes

```xml
<manifest xmlns:android="http://schemas.android.com/apk/res/android"
  package="com.wiley.aoa.basic_robot"
  android:versionCode="1"
  android:versionName="1.0" >
  <uses-feature android:name="android.hardware.usb.accessory" />
  <uses-sdk
    android:minSdkVersion="12"
    android:targetSdkVersion="15" />
  <application
    android:icon="@drawable/ic_launcher"
    android:label="@string/app_name"
    android:theme="@style/AppTheme" >
    <activity
      android:name=".MainActivity"
      android:label="@string/title_activity_main" >
      <intent-filter>
        <action android:name="android.intent.action.MAIN" />
        <category android:name="android.intent.category.LAUNCHER" />
        <action android:name="android.hardware.usb.action.USB_ACCESSORY_ATTACHED" />
      </intent-filter>
      <meta-data
        android:name="android.hardware.usb.action.USB_ACCESSORY_ATTACHED"
        android:resource="@xml/accessory_filter" />
    </activity>
  </application>
</manifest>
```

Create the accessory_filter.xml

The `accessory_filter` defines what accessory your application can connect to. It's a resource file often located in the `/res/xml` folder. Follow these steps to create a new Android XML Resources file:

1. From the File menu, select New ⇨ Other.

2. Expand the Android category in the dialog box.

3. Select Android XML Values File and click Next.

4. In the File box, enter **accessory_filter**.

5. Select resources as the Root Element and click Next.

6. Change the folder name to **/res/xml** and click Finish. If this fails, change it back to /res/values and simply move the file later by dragging it to the /res/xml folder.

Open your new XML file, located inside the /res/xml folder, and add the <usb-accessory> element as shown in Listing 6-26.

LISTING 6-26 Add the <usb-accessory> element

```xml
<?xml version="1.0" encoding="utf-8"?>
<resources>
  <usb-accessory manufacturer="Wiley" model="The Sampler" version="1.0" />
</resources>
```

Add the WroxAccessory object, the Connection object, and the UsbManager to your MainActivity.java class. You'll use these to interact with the accessory. See Listing 6-27.

LISTING 6-27: Add the WroxAccessory variables

```java
package com.wiley.aoa.the_sampler;
import android.app.Activity;
import android.hardware.usb.UsbManager;
import android.os.Bundle;
import com.wiley.wroxaccessories.UsbConnection12;
import com.wiley.wroxaccessories.WroxAccessory;
public class MainActivity extends Activity {
  private WroxAccessory mAccessory;
  private UsbManager mUsbManager;
  private UsbConnection12 connection;
  @Override
  public void onCreate(Bundle savedInstanceState) {
    super.onCreate(savedInstanceState);
    setContentView(R.layout.activity_main);
  }
}
```

Perform the connection inside the onCreate life-cycle method, and disconnect inside onDestroy. The connect method sets up the communication and starts the threads, and the disconnect method effectively kills the communication, so you don't want to do that before you know that your app is dying. See Listing 6-28.

LISTING 6-28: Let the accessory connect and disconnect

```java
package com.wiley.aoa.the_sampler;
import android.app.Activity;
import android.hardware.usb.UsbManager;
```

```
import android.os.Bundle;
import com.wiley.wroxaccessories.UsbConnection12;
import com.wiley.wroxaccessories.WroxAccessory;
public class MainActivity extends Activity {
  private WroxAccessory mAccessory;
  private UsbManager mUsbManager;
  private UsbConnection12 connection;
  @Override
  public void onCreate(Bundle savedInstanceState) {
    super.onCreate(savedInstanceState);
    setContentView(R.layout.activity_main);
    mUsbManager = (UsbManager) getSystemService(USB_SERVICE);
    connection = new UsbConnection12(this, mUsbManager);
    mAccessory = new WroxAccessory(this);
    mRingtoneManager = new RingtoneManager(this);
    try {
      mAccessory.connect(WroxAccessory.USB_ACCESSORY_12, connection);
    } catch (IOException e) {
      e.printStackTrace();
    }
  }
  @Override
  protected void onDestroy() {
    super.onDestroy();
  }    try {
      mAccessory.disconnect();
    } catch (IOException e) {
      e.printStackTrace();
    }
}
```

In this mini project you use the RingtoneManager to play short sounds when the pushbuttons on the prototype are pressed. It might not be the best choice in performance and options, but it's a quick way of utilizing already available audio on every device. Notice that in onPause you stop the previously played RingTone; if you didn't it would just keep playing. Listing 6-29 shows you how to get a reference to the RingtoneManager.

LISTING 6-29: Add the RingtoneManager

```
package com.wiley.aoa.the_sampler;
import java.io.IOException;
import android.app.Activity;
import android.hardware.usb.UsbManager;
import android.media.RingtoneManager;
import android.os.Bundle;
import com.wiley.wroxaccessories.UsbConnection12;
import com.wiley.wroxaccessories.WroxAccessory;
public class MainActivity extends Activity {
  RingtoneManager mRingtoneManager;
  private WroxAccessory mAccessory;
  private UsbManager mUsbManager;
  private UsbConnection12 connection;
```

continues

LISTING 6-29 *(continued)*

```java
@Override
public void onCreate(Bundle savedInstanceState) {
  super.onCreate(savedInstanceState);
  setContentView(R.layout.activity_main);
  mUsbManager = (UsbManager) getSystemService(USB_SERVICE);
  connection = new UsbConnection12(this, mUsbManager);
  mAccessory = new WroxAccessory(this);
  try {
    mAccessory.connect(WroxAccessory.USB_ACCESSORY_12, connection);
  } catch (IOException e) {
    e.printStackTrace();
  }
  mRingtoneManager = new RingtoneManager(this);
}
@Override
protected void onPause() {
  super.onPause();
  mRingtoneManager.stopPreviousRingtone();
}
@Override
protected void onDestroy() {
  super.onDestroy();
  try {
    mAccessory.disconnect();
  } catch (IOException e) {
    e.printStackTrace();
  }
}
}
```

Finally, subscribe to messages from the accessory on the topic "ts," as shown in Listing 6-30.

LISTING 6-30: Subscribe to messages on the topic "ts"

```java
package com.wiley.aoa.the_sampler;

import java.io.IOException;
import android.app.Activity;
import android.content.BroadcastReceiver;
import android.content.Context;
import android.content.Intent;
import android.hardware.usb.UsbManager;
import android.media.RingtoneManager;
import android.os.Bundle;
import com.wiley.wroxaccessories.UsbConnection12;
import com.wiley.wroxaccessories.WroxAccessory;
public class MainActivity extends Activity {
  RingtoneManager mRingtoneManager;
  private WroxAccessory mAccessory;
  private UsbManager mUsbManager;
```

```java
private UsbConnection12 connection;
private String subscription;
private int id = 0;
@Override
public void onCreate(Bundle savedInstanceState) {
  super.onCreate(savedInstanceState);
  setContentView(R.layout.activity_main);
  mUsbManager = (UsbManager) getSystemService(USB_SERVICE);
  connection = new UsbConnection12(this, mUsbManager);
  mAccessory = new WroxAccessory(this);
  try {
    mAccessory.connect(WroxAccessory.USB_ACCESSORY_12, connection);
  } catch (IOException e) {
    e.printStackTrace();
  }
  mRingtoneManager = new RingtoneManager(this);
}
@Override
protected void onResume() {
  super.onResume();
  try {
    subscription = mAccessory.subscribe(mReceiver, "ts", id++);
  } catch (IOException e) {
    e.printStackTrace();
  }
}
@Override
protected void onPause() {
  super.onPause();
  mRingtoneManager.stopPreviousRingtone();
}
@Override
protected void onDestroy() {
  super.onDestroy();
  try {
    mAccessory.disconnect();
  } catch (IOException e) {
    e.printStackTrace();
  }
}
private BroadcastReceiver mReceiver = new BroadcastReceiver() {
  @Override
  public void onReceive(Context context, Intent intent) {
    if (intent.getAction().equals(subscription)) {
      byte[] payload = intent.getByteArrayExtra(subscription + ".payload");
      mRingtoneManager.stopPreviousRingtone();
      mRingtoneManager.getRingtone(payload[0]).play();
    }
  }
};
}
```

Possible Improvements

You can easily enhance The Sampler, both visually and technically. First of all is the obvious: Instead of using `RingtoneManager`, use the `SoundPool` or `JetPlayer` because those are much more suited for playing multiple sounds concurrently.

Secondly, you could create a visual feedback for the user giving certain sounds a certain visual feel — turn your phone into a disco!

SUMMARY

Although the WroxAccessories library helps you in dealing with the communication, it can't determine what accessory you want to use currently. You need to choose the correct `Connection` object to instantiate for your setup; some phones may not even support the USB accessory connection.

Because of this, make sure to add the `<uses-feature>` declaration in your manifest if the USB accessory is required; this will help the device determine if it should even try to install this application. If you're building accessories for Bluetooth, you should instead use the feature `android.hardware.bluetooth`.

Currently, you have three types of connections to choose from:

➤ UsbConnection10 is the first version, sometimes called the backport ADK. This uses an add-on library from Google and therefore requires the `<uses-library>` declaration in your manifest as well as the `<uses-feature>`.

➤ UsbConnection12 is the real accessory version available from the standard Android libraries. It was introduced in SDK 12 Honeycomb, and because it's part of the core libraries, it doesn't require the extra `<uses-library>` declaration. You should, however, use the `<uses-feature>` declaration to filter out any device not capable of USB accessory connections.

➤ BluetoothConnection was introduced as an accessory during Google IO 2012. However, the BluetoothAccessory is built on top of the common Bluetooth library in Android, available from SDK 5 and forward. You don't need any extra library declarations to use Bluetooth, but you do need the `<uses-feature>`.

Another key feature is the way you use the WroxAccessories library. It will create an extra thread for the communication to happen in, but it won't push it to another process or automatically create a service that runs in the background. Consider the scenario for your accessory before you start building it — will the user interact with the accessory actively all the time, or will she only use it on certain occasions while it's still running in the background?

Finally, remember to disconnect the accessory when you don't need it anymore by calling `WroxAccessory.disconnect()`. This will close the streams used, and it will also unregister any `BroadcastReceiver` used for subscriptions.

7

Digital Arduino

WHAT'S IN THIS CHAPTER?

➤ Building Arduino prototypes

➤ Digital signals vs. voltage levels

➤ Digital actuators: LEDs and lamps

➤ Digital sensors: buttons, switches, and tilt sensors

WROX.COM CODE DOWNLOADS FOR THIS CHAPTER

The wrox.com code downloads for this chapter are found at www.wrox.com/remtitle
.cgi?isbn=1118454766 on the Download Code tab. The code is in the Chapter 7 download
and individually named according to the names throughout the chapter.

In the broadest sense, digital electronics deal with circuits that can perform logic operations,
such as comparisons between variables, mathematical ones, like multiplications or subtrac-
tions, and reading/writing ones, as in checking whether a pin is HIGH or LOW or turning
one of those pins ON or OFF. The Arduino prototyping platform runs on top of a digital
brain, which enables the different pins on an Arduino board to read and write digital
signals.

Typically, the existing digital technologies map the two binary levels to 0 Volts (logic 0)
and 5 Volts (logic 1). They correspond to the logical levels of LOW and HIGH, but also to the
boolean values FALSE and TRUE, respectively.

You can control LEDs, servo motors, and other devices directly from the pins on the Arduino
board. If you want to drive devices that demand more current or work at higher voltages, like
lamps or powerful motors, you will need to use either transistors or relays.

With sensors, you can read an input from any device that puts out voltage levels between 0 and Voltage In (Vin), where Vin is the value of the voltage at which a certain technology is powered up. Traditionally, CMOS technology has been powered at 5 Volts; recently we see more and more chips being powered at 3.3 Volts. Up to a certain voltage, typically around half of Vin, the signal is interpreted as logic 0. Anything higher than half of Vin is interpreted as logic 1.

We are seeing a migration toward lower voltage levels both in microcontrollers and in sensors. Most mobile devices have already done a migration to the so-called 3.3 Volts logic. The Arduino Mega ADK works at 5 Volts, and the Arduino Due is already one of those boards working at 3.3 Volts.

This chapter introduces you to the basics of working with digital signals, which can either be HIGH or LOW. You are going to be reading those into your Arduino microcontroller and compute their values to determine which actions to perform. You will learn the difference between sensors and actuators, turn LEDs ON and OFF, send data through a serial port, and control a lamp from your computer. You will connect buttons and tilt sensors to your Arduino board, make the physical interface to a music sampler, and send information to a big LED screen.

DIGITAL ACTUATORS

Actuators are those devices that use electricity to generate some sort of action in the physical world. From lights to motors, you will use a whole series of actuators when building different projects.

Digital actuators are those devices that can be triggered using basic digital signals. A light-emitting diode (LED) is a good example of a digital actuator; in essence, they are either ON or OFF.

Based on our experience, it is good to have different LEDs in your toolbox with different sizes, form factors, and colors. Whenever you are building anything using a digital output, you can use LEDs to check whether the intelligence in your circuit is working as it should.

Imagine you are building a robot using two motors. You can test whether the motors will get the right signal from the logics using LEDs. Once you are sure the pin that will activate the motor in your robot is working as expected, you can just connect the wires to the motor instead of the LED.

You are first going to experiment with turning a LED ON and OFF. As we assume that this might be a completely new experience for you, we are going to guide you through the process of plug-in components to your board, uploading code to it, etc.

The Blinking LEDs

The most basic example when building a prototype with Arduino is without a doubt the blinking LED. For the most common blink example you'll find yourself using the built-in LED on pin 13, meaning you won't need anything but the Arduino board itself to build it — you've even done it once in Chapter 4. However, this time around — as shown on Figure 7-1 — you'll avoid using the built-in LED and instead use a series of LEDs that light up in a pattern. More specifically, they'll mimic the flashing light from K.I.T.T., the intelligent sports car from the hit 1980s TV show *Knight Rider*.

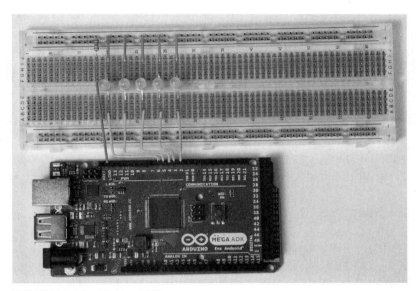

FIGURE 7-1: The blinking LEDs

Gathering Components

You need at least a couple of components before you start building this example. See Figure 7-2 and the following list for details.

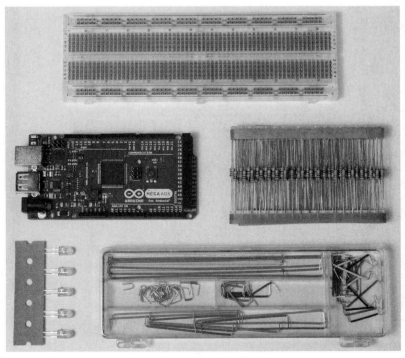

FIGURE 7-2: Components needed for the blinking LEDs

➤ An Arduino board. Any board should work, but it's preferable to start with something that is easy to work with, like the Arduino Mega or Arduino Uno.

➤ A USB cable. Which type of USB cable you need depends on the Arduino board you're using. The most common Arduino boards require a USB A-B cable, just like the one used by many home office printers.

➤ A breadboard.

➤ Some wires.

➤ A few resistors; 220 Ω will do fine. The lower the value the brighter your LED will shine, but will also reduce the LED's effective life. At bigger values the light dims and could even become invisible.

➤ And last but not least, the LEDs.

Assembling the Prototype

Building this prototype is quite straightforward. You need to connect each LED between a digital pin on the Arduino and the ground pin, thus creating a complete circuit. Because LEDs are quite fragile, even at the low voltage used in the Arduino board, you need a resistor somewhere in this circuit to avoid burning them. Figure 7-3 shows the whole schematic for this example; you see there that you have to connect one resistor per LED. Please note that for the schematic we chose to use the Arduino Uno, but it will work the same with the Arduino Mega ADK we chose for the book.

FIGURE 7-3: The Knight Rider example

Writing the Arduino Program

Just like with all programming, you can write Arduino programs in many different styles. The most common way of writing this particular program involves a lot of if-statements and individual delays. You'll find it more soothing, of course, to limit the code a little bit.

The process of making this program is simple, just start the Arduino IDE and, if needed, create an empty new Sketch using the File ➪ New menu.

The first thing you need to do for your Arduino Sketch to even compile is to add the setup and loop functions, as shown in Listing 7-1.

LISTING 7-1: Start the Arduino Sketch

```
void setup(){
}
void loop(){
}
```

You use the setup function to define what pins you're using for your example and how you're using them — that is, are you writing to them or reading from them? Declare the pins you're using in your circuit as OUTPUT. In the circuit from Figure 7-3 you can see that pins 2 through 6 are used, and the easiest way to enable these is by using a for loop. See Listing 7-2.

LISTING 7-2: Declare pins as OUTPUT

```
void setup(){
  for( int i = 2; i < 7; i++ )
    pinMode( i, OUTPUT );
}
void loop(){
}
```

THE RX AND TX PINS

The microcontrollers running on the Arduino boards have many different internal peripherals. This gives the boards extra features like I2C, SPI ports, or multiple UART ports. Those extra ports are mapped on top of the normal pins on the board.

Arduino Uno, Arduino Mega, Arduino Mega ADK, and compatible boards share the digital pins labeled 0 and 1 with the RX and TX pins that are used by the microcontroller to reprogram its firmware. You should never use those pins if you plan on using the serial communication back to your PC from your prototype.

continues

continued

If you are in a situation in which you really need to use those pins and your device will never use the serial communication, you should remember to disconnect whatever is plugged into them when uploading your program to the Arduino board. Otherwise, the IDE will throw an error indicating it is not possible to upload the code.

Just note that connecting anything to pins 0 and 1 is not dangerous, it just limits the communication to the PC through the USB cable, meaning that you won't be able to reprogram the board.

That takes care of declaring what pins you'll use and how you'll use them, but you still need a way to actually use them. When it comes to writing to digital pins you have two modes to choose from — HIGH and LOW — like the switch you have in your living room for controlling the lights (unless you have a dimmer, but that's a whole other story).

In the Knight Rider example you want to have only one LED turned on at a time, so you need a pointer to the LED that should currently be turned on. Add the pointer as shown in Listing 7-3, and give it the starting value of 2 because that's the first LED in the order.

LISTING 7-3: Add the LED pointer

```
int led = 2;
void setup(){
  for( int i = 2; i < 6; i++ )
    pinMode( i, OUTPUT );
}
void loop(){
}
```

Turn the LEDs on or off using the `digitalWrite()` function, as shown in Listing 7-4. In this code you use a tertiary operation to determine if the current LED in the loop should be HIGH or LOW; you could, of course, use `if` statements instead.

LISTING 7-4: Set the pins to HIGH or LOW

```
int led = 2;
void setup(){
  for( int i = 2; i < 6; i++ )
    pinMode( i, OUTPUT );
}
void loop(){
  for( int i = 2; i < 7; i++ )
    digitalWrite( i, (i == led ? HIGH : LOW) );
}
```

Unfortunately, as you probably realize, this isn't enough. This simply sets pin 2 as HIGH and the rest of the pins (3, 4, 5, and 6) as LOW. What you need is to change the `led` pointer, as shown in Listing 7-5.

LISTING 7-5: Change the LED pointer

```
int led = 2;
void setup(){
  for( int i = 2; i < 6; i++ )
    pinMode( i, OUTPUT );
}
void loop(){
  for( int i = 2; i < 7; i++ )
    digitalWrite( i, (i == led ? HIGH : LOW) );
  ++led;
}
```

This turns on all LEDs in order, but it's so quick that you can barely see anything. Add some brakes to the program, as shown in Listing 7-6.

LISTING 7-6: Slow the program down

```
int led = 2;
void setup(){
  for( int i = 2; i < 6; i++ )
    pinMode( i, OUTPUT );
}
void loop(){
  for( int i = 2; i < 7; i++ )
    digitalWrite( i, (i == led ? HIGH : LOW) );
  ++led;
  delay( 100 );
}
```

So, the program goes a fair bit more slowly, but it doesn't turn back when it has reached the last LED. Add the code from Listing 7-7 to control the direction of the pulse.

LISTING 7-7: Control the direction

```
int led = 2;
boolean dir = false;
void setup(){
  for( int i = 2; i < 6; i++ )
    pinMode( i, OUTPUT );
}
void loop(){
  for( int i = 2; i < 7; i++ )
    digitalWrite( i, (i == led ? HIGH : LOW) );
  dir ? ++led : --led;
  if( led > 6 || led < 2 )
    dir = !dir;
  delay( 100 );
}
```

We use the Knight Rider example to teach our students about iterative code and basic coding structures like if-statements and `for`-loops. It is simple enough and very safe. Let's now change from small LEDs to light bulbs. You will see that by applying the same logic you can change from controlling devices working at low voltages to some others working at much higher ones.

Controlling a Desk Lamp — The Relay

Controlling your surroundings from your Android device may be one of the more intriguing things you can do with the AOA framework. In this exercise you do something really fun, but also very dangerous, because it involves high voltage. If you're the least bit unsure how to handle high voltage, follow the basic rules as outlined in the following note. If you've never handled high voltage before, you should definitely research the area before building this example. See Figure 7-4 to see the assembled accessory that controls the desk lamp by hacking the wire

> **WARNING** *"You have to show respect for electricity." — This is probably one of the most important rules my professor would tell me during my first laboratory session ever. Just a couple of minutes before he had invited all of us to take a small 10 Ohm resistor and plug it into a very powerful power supply just to see it burn.*
>
> *Until now, you have been working with DC power sources. DC stands for* direct current *and it is the basis of digital electronics. It consists of having a source of energy where the voltage difference is constant. You also have been working with low current.*
>
> *On the other hand, AC stands for* alternating current. *In this case the power source provides an alternating voltage value.*
>
> *Many people think that AC is dangerous by default. You should change your perception on this issue. What matters are how high the voltage is and your power source's capability to provide current. As a rule of thumb, the higher the voltage and the higher the current, the higher the risk you take.*
>
> *If you are trying to switch a 12 VAC lamp using a relay, you will be in no danger. You only need to be as careful as you are when switching a bunch of LEDs working at 12 VDC. However, if you are trying to switch a 110/220 VAC light source, you need to be very careful in how you plug things in:*
>
> ➤ *First, you should never touch a naked wire with your bare hands (or any other part of your body) once the circuit is connected.*
>
> ➤ *Second, there should be no connection between the AC and DC parts of your circuit. There should be no metallic connection between the relay's outputs and the lamp.*
>
> ➤ *Third, you should try switching the relay before you even bring the AC power in; you should hear a clicking sound when it changes state.*
>
> ➤ *Fourth, you should make sure your relay allows switching the right amount of voltage because some relays cannot make it up to 220 VAC. This is written on the relay's housing.*

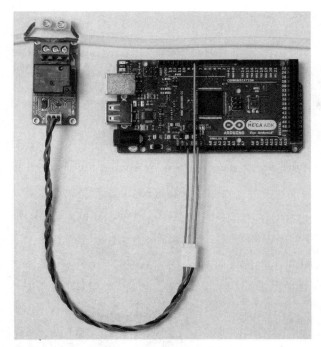

FIGURE 7-4: Accessory controlling desk lamp

Gathering Components

To build this example you need the TinkerKit relay module, an Arduino board, and a desk lamp you can use for this exercise and that you aren't very attached to. You can see all the components in the Figure 7-5.

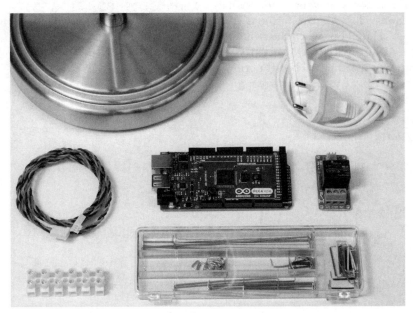

FIGURE 7-5: Components needed for the desk lamp

The following list includes all the materials you saw on Figure 7-5.

➤ An Arduino board.

➤ The TinkerKit relay module.

➤ Some wires.

➤ A desk lamp. Any lamp will do as long as the power connected to it doesn't exceed 240 V and 10 A.

➤ Wire cutters.

➤ Common terminal blocks. You'll use these to connect the two loose wires together.

Assembling the Prototype

You can think of the relay as a button capable of handling high current and that is controlled by the Arduino instead of your finger. It enables two separate circuits to interact with each other in a simple fashion; in this case, the 220 Volts or 110 Volts desk lamp circuit is controlled by the 5V Arduino circuit.

On one side, the relay is connected to a digital pin on the Arduino, and on the other side it's connected to one of the wires of the external circuit. You'll find that the TinkerKit relay module (Figure 7-6) has three connectors on the high voltage side labeled NO (normally open), NC (normally closed), and COM (common). The full description of these pins is shown in Table 7-1. You need to use only two of these connectors, depending on how you want your external circuit to act. The circuit can be closed in two fashions: either when the Arduino pin is HIGH or when the Arduino pin is LOW. You will use the NO and the COM pins for this setup. With this configuration, the lamp will be off until the Arduino board activates the relay to let the current go through.

FIGURE 7-6: TinkerKit relay module

TABLE 7-1: TinkerKit Relay Ports

NAME	DESCRIPTION	CIRCUIT CLOSED WHEN ARDUINO PIN IS
NO	Normally Open	HIGH
NC	Normally Closed	LOW
COM	Common	Always connected

Of course, you quickly realize that for this simple example, with a circuit as shown on Figure 7-7, it doesn't matter which of these you choose because the relay will only switch on and off indefinitely. For your more complex projects in the future, making the correct choice is more important.

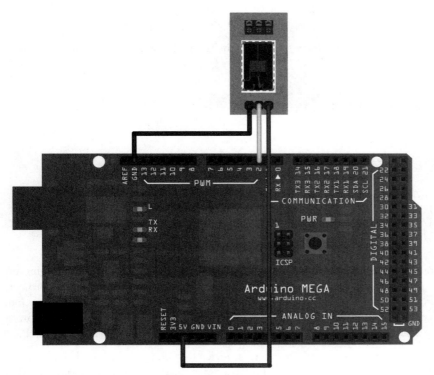

FIGURE 7-7: Circuit using the relay module

Writing the Arduino Program

As always, start with a blank canvas and add the required setup and loop functions, as shown in Listing 7-8.

LISTING 7-8: Start the relay Sketch

```
void setup(){
}
void loop(){
}
```

Declare the pin that you'll connect your relay to and set it as an OUTPUT. In Listing 7-9, it's pin number 2.

LISTING 7-9: Add the relay pin

```
int relaypin = 2;
void setup(){
  pinMode( relaypin, OUTPUT );
}
void loop(){
}
```

Let the desk lamp blink with a 5-second delay by setting the relay pin to HIGH and LOW, as shown in Listing 7-10.

LISTING 7-10: Switch the relay on and off

```
int relaypin = 2;
void setup(){
  pinMode( relaypin, OUTPUT );
}
void loop(){
  digitalWrite( relaypin, HIGH );
  delay( 5000 );
  digitalWrite( relaypin, LOW );
  delay( 5000 );
}
```

Digital electronics allow reusing the same software to control devices using little voltage values and high ones, as you saw in the previous two examples. It is now time to start building a mini project. If there is anything more fascinating than 3 LEDs blinking, it is 30 LEDs blinking. When grouping many LEDs together, there are two things that happen: First, you can use them in a clever way to represent letters, numbers and symbols; second the logic to control them gets more and more complicated.

Next you are going to experiment with an LED screen, a device that controls hundreds of LEDs thanks to the so-called LED driver chip, a dedicated microcontroller that can control many LEDs at once. You will get to control those LEDs from your Android phone/tablet.

Digital Project 1: Large SMS Display

In this example you build a large display to show the content of the SMS arriving to your phone. The scenario for this display could be your office or your home; in essence, a location where you want to be able to read text messages from a distance. If you are concerned about the possible content of the messages, you should figure out a way to filter out whatever information you don't want to be on display.

This accessory is fairly simple from a conceptual point of view: The object lays on a desk or shelf. It offers a large LED display with 64x16 multicolored dots and a USB connector. You plug in your phone or tablet with cellular connectivity and, when an SMS arrives in your Android device, the text is displayed on the screen. Because the display allows showing only two lines of text totaling 24 characters, the text will be scrolled a couple of times on the screen if the SMS is longer than that.

The arrival of a new message to the phone erases the previous message from the screen and makes it show the latest message.

Because the Arduino board doesn't have a very large storage capability, the messages themselves are not stored on the board — only the current message being displayed.

Finally, the prototype has no buttons or any other ways to interact with it. Figure 7-8 shows how we mounted both displays together and placed a piece of plexiglass in front to protect it. Its functionality is very passive. The goal behind building this project is learning how to connect a complex peripheral to an Arduino board and install the libraries to control it. However, you can do so much more beyond what we explain in this section. You could be storing several messages and loop through them, etc.

FIGURE 7-8: Large SMS display

Gathering Components

You need very few components (check Figure 7-9) to build this prototype. To start with, you need two displays, because one single display offers only a 32x16 LED matrix. This kind of LED matrix can be daisy-chained and you could potentially add as many displays as the technology allows.

The display is controlled by the HT1632c driver chip from Holtek. This chip is designed to control a whole lot of LEDs from a simple 4-pin input. You interface the chip from your Arduino board with four pins connected to the display using jumper wires.

FIGURE 7-9: Components needed for the large SMS display

The Large SMS Display (LSMSD) project requires the following bill of materials:

➤ Two units of the 32×16 RG Bicolor LED Dot Matrix manufactured by Sure Electronics. They come in two different configurations, with 5 mm or with 3 mm LEDs. One possible source for these displays is the Arduino store. You can find it at many other places as well; to help you decide whether it is the same or not, we have added the datasheet to the display to the downloads section of this chapter.

➤ One Arduino Mega ADK.

➤ One USB A-B cable and one micro USB cable to connect to your phone/tablet.

➤ A bunch of jumper wires.

Assembling the Prototype

Follow these steps to assemble the prototype:

1. Mount the LED display by connecting both displays using the flat cable. On the back of each display you'll see two connectors: one labeled INPUT and the other one labeled OUTPUT. Connect the 16-pin IDC cable from the OUTPUT from one display to the INPUT of the other. Place the displays side by side.

2. Remember to use the red and black wires provided with the displays to also transfer the power from one board to the other.

3. Take 5 Volts and GND (0 Volts) from the Arduino board to the first display.

4. Use jumper wires to connect pins 7, 6, 5, and 4 from the Arduino Mega ADK board to pins 7, 5, 2, and 1, respectively, on the 16-pin IDC cable you have left (see Figure 7-10 for a schematic and 7-11 for a close-up picture). Plug the other end of the IDC cable into the INPUT connector of the first display. Note that the wire on the flat cable marked in red corresponds to pin 1 in the connector.

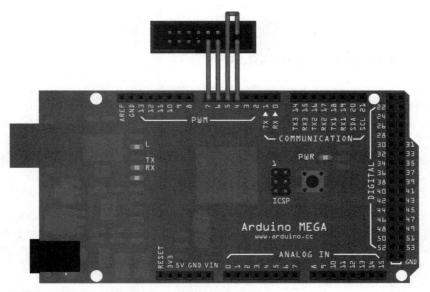

FIGURE 7-10: Circuit for the large SMS display

FIGURE 7-11: Close-up image of the IDC connector between Arduino and the large SMS display

WRITING THE ARDUINO PROGRAM

We have made a library to control the LSMSD called HT1632c. It is based on existing code by several members of the Arduino community. Whenever you are going to start a project, we recommend you check on Google whether anyone already used the parts you're about to use. Many times, if not most of them, you end up finding code that will very much speed up your process.

For the LSMSD we found different libraries but none of them were exactly what we wanted, so we created a new one reusing bits and pieces from different experiments. You can find the library we made at the downloads section on the website for this chapter. It is called HT1632c.zip.

Using this library makes all the operations of writing code to show text on the LED display very easy. The only issue you will find is how to write the interface between the display and your phone.

INSTALL THE HT1632c LIBRARY

We have uploaded the library at the official repository for this book to make easier for you to find it.

Remember that installing a library for Arduino's IDE requires uncompressing the library files inside the libraries folder within Arduino's Sketchbook. You will have to restart the IDE for the library to show under the Sketch ➪ Import Library ➪ HT1632c menu. Clicking that option in the menu adds three includes to your program, as shown in Listing 7-11.

LISTING 7-11: Import the library

```
#include <fonts.h>
#include <HT1632c.h>
#include <images.h>
```

The three header files added to your program when you include the HT1632 library take care of different blocks of code:

➤ HT1632c.h is the core library that contains all the methods to control the screen.

➤ fonts.h is a header file that describes a typeface in the form of an array. You can modify this file if you want to have a different typeface showing on your screen.

➤ images.h is a header file that includes a series of icons.

The way this library renders text and images on the screen is shown Listing 7-12.

LISTING 7-12: Scroll text on the screen

```
ht1632c.clearScreen();
ht1632c.scrollTextXColor(4,"Hola Caracola ...    ",RED,30);
```

The sentence "Hola Caracola ..." is scrolled on the screen after the ht1632c.clearScreen() method removes whatever was visible on it before.

The software structure of this project is simple. A block of the code is dedicated to communicating to the Android device and another one sends the text to the LED screen (commanded by the HT1632c library); Listing 7-13 explains this further.

LISTING 7-13: Main loop of your application

```
[...]

#define NO_PHONE 0
#define NO_PHONE_CLS 1
#define NO_SMS 2
#define NO_SMS_CLS 3
#define DISPLAY_SMS 4
#define DISPLAY_SMS_CLS 5
#define MAX_SHOW_SMS 60000    // show SMS for 1m.

char* currentSMS;  // character array to contain the SMS
int mode = NO_SMS;        // variable to store the mode
long timerShowSMS = 0;    // count for how long we showed the SMS

HT1632c LSMSD;  // object representing the display
[...]

void loop() {
  // block discriminating between modes
```

continues

LISTING 7-13 *(continued)*

```
switch (mode) {
    case NO_PHONE:
      LSMSD.showText(0,4,"NO PHONE",ORANGE);
      break;
    case NO_PHONE_CLS:
      LSMSD.cls();
      mode = NO_SMS;
      break;
    case NO_SMS:
      LSMSD.showText(0,4,"NO SMS", GREEN);
      break;
    case NO_SMS_CLS:
      LSMSD.cls();
      mode = DISPLAY_SMS;
      timerShowSMS = millis();
      break;
    case DISPLAY_SMS:
      if(millis() - timerShowSMS < MAX_SHOW_SMS) {
        Serial.println("Scroll message");
        LSMSD.scrolltextxcolor(4,currentSMS,ORANGE,30);
      } else mode = DISPLAY_SMS_CLS;
      break;
     case DISPLAY_SMS_CLS:
       LSMSD.cls();
       mode = NO_SMS;
       break;
  }
  delay(100);
}
```

An SMS is packed into a single MQTT package. In this way, once a full package has made it to the board, the content of the SMS is stored in a buffer and all the variables in the system are updated: currentSMS stores the text and the mode is updated to be DISPLAY_SMS.

The only part missing in this code, as Listing 7-14 will show you, is the block of code dedicated to creating the P2PMQTT object and handling the communication with the phone. As the Android device is our data source, the Arduino board will have to first subscribe to the phone and then check if a published message arrived containing a new SMS.

LISTING 7-14: Add the MQTT communication

```
#include <fonts.h>
#include <HT1632c.h>
#include <images.h>
#include <AndroidAccessory.h>
#include <P2PMQTT.h>

#define NO_PHONE 0
#define NO_PHONE_CLS 1
#define NO_SMS 2
#define NO_SMS_CLS 3
#define DISPLAY_SMS 4
```

```
#define DISPLAY_SMS_CLS 5
#define MAX_SHOW_SMS 60000     // show SMS for 1m.

char* currentSMS;  // character array to contain the SMS
int mode = NO_SMS;         // variable to store the mode
long timerShowSMS = 0;     // count for how long we showed the SMS

HT1632c LSMSD;  // object representing the display

P2PMQTT mqtt(true);  // add true to see debug info over the serial port
boolean subscribed = false;

void setup() {
  Serial.begin(9600);
  Serial.println("ready");
  mqtt.begin("LSMSD");
  mqtt.connect(0,60000);  // add 1min timeout
  // initialize the display
  LSMSD.setup();
}

void loop() {
  int firstByteMSB = mqtt.getType(mqtt.buffer);

  switch(firstByteMSB) {
    case CONNECT:
      Serial.println("connected");
      if(!subscribed) subscribed = mqtt.subscribe("sms");
      break;

    case PUBLISH:
      currentSMS = (char*) mqtt.getPayload(mqtt.buffer,PUBLISH);
      mode = NO_SMS_CLS;
      timerShowSMS = millis();
      break;

    default:
      // do nothing
      break;
  }
  // block discriminating between modes
  switch (mode) {
    case NO_PHONE:
      LSMSD.showText(0,4,"NO PHONE",ORANGE);
      if (mqtt.isConnected()) mode = NO_PHONE_CLS;
      break;
    case NO_PHONE_CLS:
      LSMSD.cls();
      mode = NO_SMS;
      break;
    case NO_SMS:
      LSMSD.showText(0,4,"NO SMS", GREEN);
      break;
    case NO_SMS_CLS:
      LSMSD.cls();
      mode = DISPLAY_SMS;
```

continues

LISTING 7-14 *(continued)*

```
      timerShowSMS = millis();
      break;
    case DISPLAY_SMS:
      if(millis() - timerShowSMS < MAX_SHOW_SMS) {
        Serial.println("Scroll message");
        LSMSD.scrolltextxcolor(4,currentSMS,ORANGE,30);
      } else mode = DISPLAY_SMS_CLS;
      break;
    case DISPLAY_SMS_CLS:
      LSMSD.cls();
      mode = NO_SMS;
      break;
  }
  delay(100);
}
```

This code will work by collecting the information from the SMSs arriving to the app in the LSMSD section of chapter 6. When an SMS arrives to your Android device, at the time that app is running, the text in the message is relayed to the Arduino board by means of an MQTT publish message.

This example closes the section about digital sensors and opens up the one about digital actuators. You will now explore how to sense the world, or in other words, how to read data into your programs and store it in variables.

DIGITAL SENSORS

The idea of a digital sensor is very similar to a digital actuator. A sensor is called a *digital sensor* when it can distinguish between two different states at a digital input on the microcontroller. You will either read a voltage representing logic 1 or a voltage representing logic 0.

Inside the microprocessor, you can use those readings as either boolean (TRUE, FALSE) or integer (1, 0) values as part of your programs. It is possible to use literally anything that changes voltage as a digital input.

For example, you could use a preamplified microphone plugged into a digital input on your Arduino board. You would read a series of HIGH-LOW oscillations. You will not be able to read the actual sound, but it will be possible for you to read that there is noise in the room, because the microphone will be giving values different from 0.

The most common digital sensors are buttons, switches, and tilt sensors. In the following sections you experiment with them a little.

Buttons and Switches

If not the most important sensors when building prototypes with Arduino, the button and switch are the most commonly used sensors because of their wide range of use-cases. They are really easy to build and you can build them with a plethora of different materials; however, for this example you use a normal pre-assembled pushbutton to control the state of an LED.

The pushbutton (as in Figure 7-12) doesn't work exactly like a normal light switch — it's reversed in the sense that electricity passes through when it's in the unpressed state. If you connected the LED

FIGURE 7-12: The finished button example

straight to the pushbutton instead of an Arduino pin, it would light up only when the button was not pressed. For this example, you're interested in the opposite reaction: The LED should light up when the button is pressed.

Gathering Components

The components needed to build this example are shown in Figure 7-13. There is not much to it; mainly you need some small parts around buttons for them to give readings that you can use inside your programs.

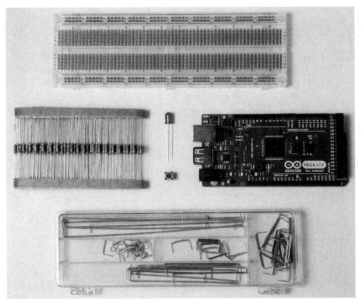

FIGURE 7-13: Components needed for the buttons

The list of parts is as follows:

➤ One Arduino board. Again, any Arduino board will work, but try to stick with the standard boards if you're new to Arduino programming.

➤ A USB cable suited for the Arduino board you're using. The most common type is the A-B cable.

➤ A breadboard.

➤ Some wires.

➤ A resistor with a fair bit more resistance than the ones used in the LED example earlier in this chapter. Usually, 10 kΩ (colored brown, black, orange) is recommended when using normal pushbuttons.

➤ Because you'll control an LED with a pushbutton, you also need a resistor for it; 220 Ω (red, red, brown) will do great.

➤ You also need a pushbutton.

➤ And, finally, an LED.

Assembling the Prototype

First of all, you'll notice that both ground (0 Volts) and 5 Volts are connected to the breadboard from the Arduino. This is because the pushbutton requires the electricity flowing through it to determine what state it is in. On the other side of the pushbutton, connect one of the legs to digital pin 2 on the Arduino.

The LED is connected to digital pin 3 on the Arduino, and to the ground through a 220 Ω resistor as shown on Figure 7-14.

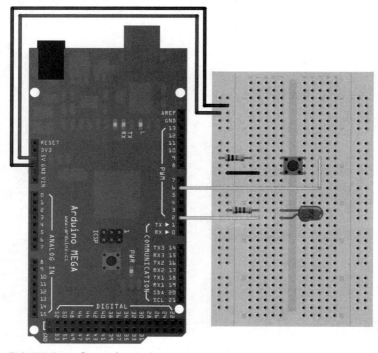

FIGURE 7-14: Circuit for the button example

Writing the Arduino Program

Create a new Arduino Sketch using the File ⇨ New menu and add the setup and loop functions as shown in Listing 7-15.

LISTING 7-15: Starting the button Sketch

```
void setup(){
}
void loop(){
}
```

You already know that you'll be using one pushbutton and one LED, so the next obvious step is to define where to connect these two components, which are the pin numbers on the Arduino. In Figure 7-12 they're connected to pins 6 and 2, respectively, but you can choose any digital pins you want. Try to avoid using pins 0 and 1, though, because those are also part of the serial communication on the Arduino. Listing 7-16 shows how to declare different pins as variables and how to configure them as inputs or outputs.

LISTING 7-16: Declare the pin variables

```
int ledpin = 2;
int buttonpin = 6;
void setup(){
  pinMode( ledpin, OUTPUT );
  pinMode( buttonpin, INPUT );
}
void loop(){
}
```

Having declared what pins you're going to use, all that's left now is to read the value coming in from the buttonpin, and writing the correct value to the ledpin. Now is a good time to remember that pushbuttons work opposite of what is commonly thought of as a light switch; you need to take this attribute into consideration when writing your program.

Start by reading the value of the buttonpin, which is an integer set to either HIGH or LOW, and then write the opposite value to the ledpin. See Listing 7-17 for details.

LISTING 7-17: Read the button and store its value

```
int ledpin = 2;
int buttonpin = 6;
int val = 0;

void setup(){
  pinMode( buttonpin, INPUT );
  pinMode( ledpin, OUTPUT );
}

void loop(){
  val = digitalRead( buttonpin );
  val == HIGH ? digitalWrite( ledpin, LOW ) : digitalWrite( ledpin, HIGH );
}
```

The pushbutton is probably the simplest sensor and therefore the easiest to understand. There are other digital sensors to explore, like for example the tilt sensor that is explained in the next section. You are going to see that you need to make little changes in both circuits and code to switch from one sensor to the other. But it is the affordances of those sensors what gives a different experience when using the different devices.

Tilt Sensor

The tilt sensor — you can see it together with the Arduino board on Figure 7-15 — is a mechanical sensor that allows current to pass through when a small metal ball connects the two pins of the sensor together. Different from a button, you have to tilt to activate instead of pressing. Just like the button it has only two states: either it allows current to pass through, or it doesn't. From a programmer's point of view, then, the two sensors are identical to each other.

Just like the pushbutton exercise, you build a circuit that lights up an LED when the sensor reaches a certain angle.

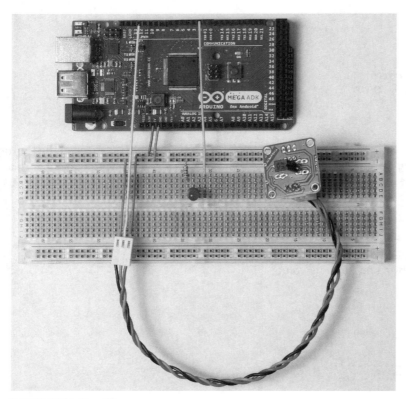

FIGURE 7-15: The tilt sensor accessory

Gathering Components

The components needed for the tilt sensor are almost identical to the ones used in the pushbutton example. As you can see in Figure 7-16, the only difference is that the 10 kΩ resistor was changed to a 1 kΩ resistor.

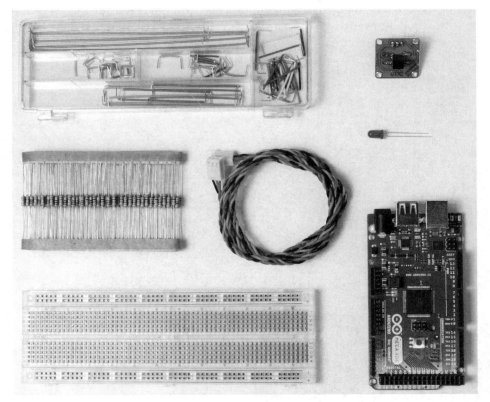

FIGURE 7-16: Components needed for tilt sensing

The parts you need to replicate this exercise are described in the following list:

➤ An Arduino board. Any type of Arduino-compatible board will work, but if you're new to Arduino it is recommended that you use a standard board like the Mega or Uno.

➤ A USB cable. The type depends on the type of board you're using; most boards use the A-B.

➤ A breadboard.

➤ Some wires.

➤ A few resistors; 220 Ω for the LED and 1 kΩ for the tilt sensor are the ones used in the example.

➤ Of course, you also need the tilt sensor and an LED.

Assembling the Prototype

Assembling the tilt sensor is very similar to the pushbutton; they work in the same way. The LED connected to pin 2 should have a 220 Ω resistor to protect it from burning out. It doesn't matter if you connect it to the cathode or the anode.

The tilt sensor shown in Figure 7-17, connected to pin 12, needs both power and ground as well as a resistor. Connect the power and ground to the tilt sensor, putting the 1 kΩ resistor where the 5 Volts connects to the sensor. Finally, connect pin 12 anywhere in between the tilt sensor and the resistor.

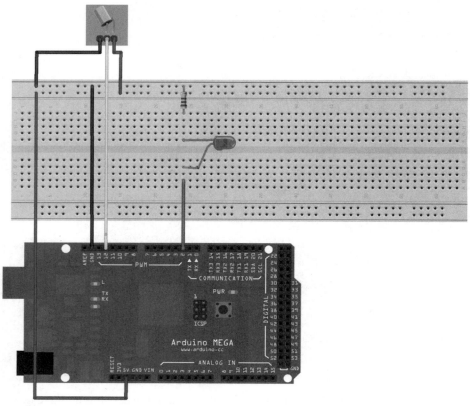

FIGURE 7-17: Circuit for the tilt sensor

Writing the Arduino Program

Because the tilt sensor and the pushbutton are so similar, you could actually reuse the code from that example. But for the sake of clarity, we take you through it step by step again. You will start by creating the program skeleton as in Listing 7-18.

LISTING 7-18: Start the Arduino Sketch

```
void setup(){
}
void loop(){
}
```

Listing 7-19 adds the pin declarations for both the sensor and the LED. It also defines how each pin will work; either as INPUT or as OUTPUT.

LISTING 7-19: Add pin declarations

```
int ledpin = 2;
int tiltpin = 12;
void setup(){
  pinMode( ledpin, OUTPUT );
  pinMode( tiltpin, INPUT );
}
void loop(){
}
```

And finally, you have to read the sensor and turn on the LED depending on the value read, as in Listing 7-20.

LISTING 7-20: Read the sensor

```
int ledpin = 2;
int tiltpin = 12;
int val = 0;
void setup(){
  pinMode( ledpin, OUTPUT );
  pinMode( tiltpin, INPUT );
}
void loop(){
  val = digitalRead( tiltpin );
  val == HIGH ? digitalWrite( ledpin, LOW ) : digitalWrite( ledpin, HIGH );
}
```

Once you started reading from one digital sensor, jumping into reading from more than one is not a big deal. The next project, where you will be building a music sampler, is going to introduce the idea of reading multiple sensors and sending their status to your Android device. The biggest difficulty you might find in this process is how to wire up the breadboard, but code-wise you will see that all the parts come together smoothly.

Digital Project 2: Small Sampler

Have you ever had the chance to play with a music sampler? The idea behind this instrument is that it can record sound in a channel and loop it. This is the way a lot of the electronic music out there is built. Musicians simply record pieces of sound and use them as a base to play back sound composing basic sound structures, rhythms, and melodies. Different types of samplers exist. Some of them just offer knobs to change some of the sound's characteristics and a button to trigger the sound, whereas some others offer full keyboards for direct sound transposition in real time.

In this case, we are going to simplify the sampler idea for this project to become a learning experience in how to combine a series of buttons to interface an app in your phone. You build an app that triggers some prerecorded sounds upon arrival of button clicks sent from an Arduino board. There will be no chance to change the sounds in real time, but it shouldn't be too complex for you to explore that possibility for a further iteration of the project.

It makes a lot of sense to build a physical interface to the sampler because you can manipulate a whole series of buttons and knobs much more easily than any virtual representation of them on a screen. For this example (check Figure 7-18), you only build the buttons part of the sampler, but once you have learned about analog sensors, it shouldn't be too hard for you to try out that part as well.

FIGURE 7-18: The finished sampler prototype

Gathering Components

This project doesn't require a huge amount of parts. It requires only using some buttons on a breadboard. We have made a picture including all the parts for you, see Figure 7-19.

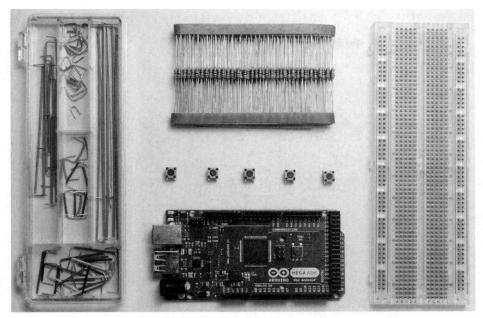

FIGURE 7-19: Components needed for the sampler

The parts integrating this project are:

➤ An Arduino Mega ADK board, because you will be connecting this project to a phone/ tablet.

➤ A USB cable. The type depends on the type of board you're using; most boards use the A-B.

➤ Micro USB cable.

➤ A breadboard.

➤ Some wires.

➤ Five resistors

➤ Five pushbuttons.

Assembling the Prototype

This project is very simple to assemble. Take a look at Figure 7-20 and you see how few jumper wires and resistors you need to implement it.

To assemble the prototype for this project, follow these steps:

1. Arrange the eight buttons along the slot in the center of the breadboard.

2. Add one wire from one end of each one of the buttons and all the way down to one of the long connections at the bottom of the breadboard. That will be common ground for all the buttons.

3. Connect the common ground from the breadboard to one of the GND pins on your Arduino Mega ADK.

4. Connect the other pin from each one of the buttons to a different digital pin on the Arduino board. If you want to make it fully compatible with the code, use pins 2 to 6.

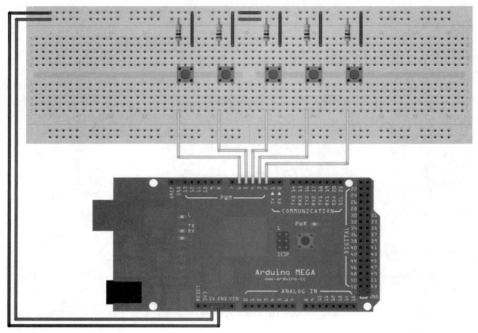

FIGURE 7-20: Circuit for the sampler

Writing the Arduino Program

The complexity in this project resides on the breadboard building side of it. For this project to work, you need to repeat the same circuit to control a button five times, read the values from those buttons, and then send those to the phone. As a way to simplify the whole communication and make it as quick as possible, you are going to pack all the five buttons as a byte. Each one of the buttons represents one bit within the byte. An active button means a 1 for the bit it represents.

You can build this project with very few lines of code, but we take you step by step through the process.

Listing 7-21 shows how to declare an array to store the numbers representing each pin to be used in your program. This enables you to move the pins easily by changing the numbers within the array.

PULL UP AND PULL DOWN

Two common terms in the electronics world are Pull Up and Pull Down. They refer to the way you connect a certain electric point in a circuit to either the power (thus Pull Up) or to ground (thus Pull Down) using another component, usually a resistor.

The Pull Up/Down resistor at the input of a logical circuit, like at the input of a pin of an Arduino board, sets a default voltage value at that point. With the default voltage value it also sets a default logical value. Typically, a Pull Up resistor will force a pin to be HIGH by default and a Pull Down one will force the pin to be Low by default.

The Atmel chips we are using on the Arduino Mega ADK board (and in most of the Arduino boards made up to 2012) have internal Pull Up resistors. This is because of how common it is having to implement a Pull Up circuit to add a digital sensor to a project. These internal resistors can be activated by using the parameter INPUT_ PULLUP when calling the function pinMode() for a certain pin.

LISTING 7-21: Declare your pin numbers in an array

```
int pins[] = {2, 3, 4, 5, 6};
[…]
```

You can then declare them as INPUT using a for loop as part of the setup, as shown in Listing 7-22.

LISTING 7-22: Make your pins INPUT_PULLUP

```
int pins[] = {2, 3, 4, 5, 6};

void setup() {
  for(int i = 0; i < 5; i++)
    pinMode(pins[i], INPUT);
}
[…]
```

By default, your buttons will read HIGH when not pressed and will read LOW when pressed. A button is active when pressed, therefore you need to read each value and invert it before composing all the five values into a single byte.

You first use the bitwise operation OR to invert the reading of the pin. After masking the result, bitwise with 0×01 gives the final result of a single bit representing a pressed button with 1 and a non-pressed button with 0. Afterward, the bit is shifted to the left and composed together with the other ones using yet again the bitwise OR. Take a look at the highlighted line in Listing 7-23, which summarizes this whole explanation in a single line.

LISTING 7-23: Read and format the values for each button

```
int pins[] = {2, 3, 4, 5, 6};
int buttons = 0;

void setup() {
  for(int i = 0; i < 5; i++)
    pinMode(pins[i], INPUT);
}

void loop() {
  buttons = 0;
  for(int i = 0; i < 5; i++)
    buttons |= (1 | digitalRead(pins[i]) & 0x01) << i;
  [...]
}
```

The only parts missing in this program are sending the data to the phone using the MQTT library and adding a small delay for the microcontroller so it doesn't saturate the communication port to the board. Check the downloads on the website for this chapter to get the full listing of the code as well as the Android code for this example.

SUMMARY

In this chapter you explored how to make use of digital inputs and outputs in microcontrollers. Beyond making some small examples, you built two projects: a display to show incoming text messages to your phone/tablet and a keyboard to trigger different sound samplers.

One of the examples required hacking a desk lamp and controlling it with Arduino. Therefore you got introduced to some basic concepts about safety. Remember that it is the product of current × voltage that can be harmful. Digital technology is usually operating at 5 Volts or less and should not represent a danger in any way. Arduino boards work at 5 Volts. When connecting to something like the desk lamp, which uses between 110 and 220 Volts AC (depending on the country you are in) you need to make sure everything is unplugged before you go on touching the circuits, wires, and so on.

When building prototypes with Arduino it's important to take proper safety measures, not only for your own sake but also for the sake of the components. Some parts are inexpensive, but some others, like accelerometers, gyroscopes, and other complex sensors, break easily. A couple of important things to remember are:

> ➤ You should remember to power your components the right way: Vin means voltage in, GND is 0 V. Some components are powered at 5 Volts, whereas some others work at 3.3 Volts.

> ➤ Respect the polarity! Some components, like LEDs, will not operate when plugged in wrong. Other components, like resistors, have no polarity.

> ➤ LEDs operate at a fixed voltage that is less than the Vin at your circuit. You will need to use a resistor to protect them from burning.

➤ There exist different protocols to control devices. For example, the LED screen used for the SMS display project uses an SPI protocol for controlling all the LEDs from a minimal set of pins. Other protocols are I2C or Serial — also known as UART.

➤ Mnemotechnic rule comparing voltage values with their binary representation and with the logical representation in code. We have only hinted at this rule throughout the text, but we needed to formulate it at once:

  ➤ HIGH = Vin = boolean TRUE = logical 1

  ➤ LOW = 0 Volts = boolean FALSE = logical 0

➤ Controlling devices running at a higher voltage than the one on your prototyping platform requires using relays to interface the logic with whatever you want to control.

➤ The different digital sensors can use the same code. For example, a tilt sensor is read the same way a pushbutton is read. The difference between them has to do with their physical affordances, thus the way the user will interact with them, the way they will hold it in their hands, or how it will react to different movements, presses, etc.

Analog Arduino

WHAT'S IN THIS CHAPTER?

➤ The real world is analog

➤ Using DACs and ADCs

➤ Pulse width modulation

➤ Sensing distance with ultrasound

➤ Understanding piezo electricity by making noise

WROX.COM CODE DOWNLOADS FOR THIS CHAPTER

The wrox.com code downloads for this chapter are found at www.wrox.com/remtitle .cgi?isbn=1118454766 on the Download Code tab. The code is in the Chapter 8 download and individually named according to the names throughout the chapter.

The physical world is not digital. The voltage between two points doesn't change only between the two levels of HIGH and LOW. It can take any value, most times it is too small to be measured in any way. However, microcontrollers cannot sense every value out there.

They can read values between 0 Volts and 5 Volts (or 3.3 Volts if you were using 3.3 Volts logic, like with the Arduino Due) through an internal peripheral. This small part of the chip is called *Analog to Digital Converter (ADC)*. In some cases, the microcontroller of your choice might not have an internal ADC, in which case you will have to add an external one to your circuit if you need it. An ADC transforms a voltage into a number of type integer that you can then read into a variable and use as part of your programs.

What characterizes an ADC is its so-called *bit depth*, or the number of bits it uses to convert analog values into numbers. The ADC inside Arduino's microcontroller has a bit depth of 10 bits. With those bits you can represent 1,024 different numbers; the chip maps 0 Volts to the integer 0 and 5 Volts to the integer 1,023. The pins on Arduino that can be used to read analog signals are grouped at a single connector. The Arduino Mega ADK has 16 analog input pins labeled A0 to A15.

Analog sensors are devices that can transform a physical property (temperature, humidity, distance, and so on) into a voltage. That voltage can, or not, accommodate the range of 0 Volts to 5 Volts. Most likely, the sensor's output will have to be amplified to fit into the microcontroller's ADC reading range; for example, a typical microphone produces very tiny voltage variations on top of a variable capacitor. The small mechanical vibrations on the microphone are translated into small variations of voltage, in the range of the tenths of a Volt. Without amplification, the signal produced by a microphone is useless in the digital realm. We need to amplify the signal to fit the 0 Volts to 5 Volts range and then map the values into numbers using an ADC.

In the same way, devices called analog actuators can affect the world by means of using an analog signal. Similar to how ADC chips work, an equivalent family of chips called *Digital to Analog Converters (DACs)* can take integer values and give back a voltage contained within a range.

DACs are, however, not needed for most cases. You might need them if you want to play high-quality audio signals from a microcontroller, or if you plan to use a super precise way to control a specific type of motor controller. A simple trick called *pulse width modulation* (PWM) is used broadly in engineering to synthesize analog signals. Not all the pins on an Arduino board can be used to push out PWM. The Arduino Mega ADK has 12 digital pins (numbered 2 to 13) that can be used with PWM.

You are now going to experiment with analog signals. You will read values from sensors and into the microcontroller and you will get to use PWM to control LEDs and motors. The following sections in this chapter will help you understand analog actuators as well as sensors. You will learn about piezo electric actuators, motors, and you will build your first robot.

ANALOG ACTUATORS

Most low-cost microcontrollers do not offer embedded DACs, which means you need to add those externally. However, for many applications DACs are not needed. The most common technique for controlling motors or dimming LEDs is based on using a digital pin that oscillates at a somewhat high frequency. Each oscillation represents a pulse that is produced when the pin goes HIGH followed by a pause when the pin settles at LOW. The amount of time the signal is HIGH expressed in a percentage is called the *duty cycle*.

The chip (the microcontroller on the Arduino board) itself has one internal register that can be programmed to set up the frequency and another one that can be programmed to control the duty cycle. As an example, imagine you want to dim the brightness of an LED. You do it by adjusting a high enough frequency so that the eye cannot register the light flickering. In Arduino, the default PWM frequency is 1 KHz; that is, the signal oscillates 1,000 times per second. The duty cycle determines how long you keep the LED on: 50 percent means half the time, 100 percent means all the time. The light flickers, but it does it so quickly that your eye can't distinguish it. The retina contains two types of photoreceptors: rods and cones. The perception of shapes and color depends on firing these types of nerve cells. Once a cell is active, it takes some time until it resets, even if there is no more light stimulating the cell. Therefore, the cells in our eyes are somehow making an average of the amount of light arriving to them. The bigger the duty cycle, the more light reaches your eye, and the higher the average, the stronger the light you perceive.

If instead of using an LED, you used a direct current motor (DC motor), the inertia in the motor would keep the motor moving. But the PWM signal would just be turning the motor on and off. The bigger the duty cycle, the more energy would be transmitted to the motor, and the faster it would move.

The Arduino function that takes care of writing PWM to a certain pin is called `analogWrite(pin,duty_cycle)`, where `pin` is the pin number and `duty_cycle` represents the time the signal will be on expressed as a byte (in other words, 255 means 100 percent of the duty cycle, 127 means 50 percent, and so on).

The Piezo Element

Piezo electricity is a property of some materials that makes them change their physical shape when a small current passes through them. This has been used from the beginning of electronics for the production of speakers and microphones. Piezo elements, also known as contact microphones, are robust and you can find them either contained inside a plastic housing or as a circular metal plate with two terminals. The metal produces a click both when the current is applied and when it is taken away. That clicking sound at a high enough frequency will modulate into a tone.

The following example illustrates how the sound modulates the piezo element when the duty cycle changes. Figure 8-1 shows how to connect a piezo element to your Arduino board to play sound through it.

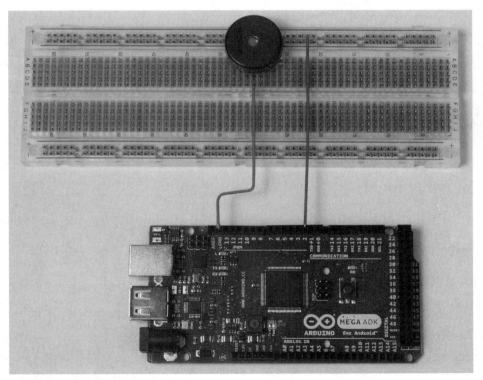

FIGURE 8-1: Finished example

Gathering Components

To build this example you need just a few parts, as you can see in Figure 8-2 and described in the list that follows.

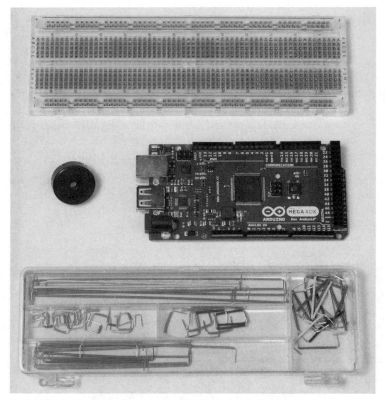

FIGURE 8-2: Components needed for the piezo element

➤ An Arduino board
➤ A piezo element
➤ Some wires
➤ A USB cable
➤ A breadboard

Assembling the Prototype

You can connect the piezo element straight to any Arduino pin of your liking. What's important to remember is that the piezo element needs to be connected to a PWM active pin on the board; otherwise, the sound that will be played won't be modulated. On the Arduino Mega ADK all the pins in the ranges 2 to 13 and 44 to 46 can provide the possibility of writing PWM signals using the function `analogWrite`. Figure 8-3 is an example on how to assemble the parts.

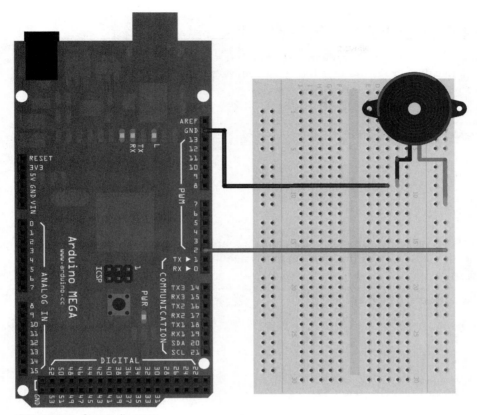

FIGURE 8-3: Circuit diagram

Writing the Arduino Program

Start a new, clean Arduino sketch and add the required `setup` and `loop` functions as shown in Listing 8-1.

LISTING 8-1: Start a new Arduino Sketch

```
void setup(){
}
void loop(){
}
```

Add the pin where you'll connect your piezo element; in Figure 8-3 you'll notice that we're using pin 2 and Listing 8-2 declares the variable `piezopin` to store the pin number. This may change depending on the Arduino board you're using; the Arduino UNO, for example, doesn't support PWM on pin 2.

> ### PINMODE FOR PINS USING ANALOGWRITE
>
> The `analogWrite` function configures the pins internally. In other words, you will not need to call the `pinMode` function when you want to use PWM on a pin.

LISTING 8-2: Declare the piezo pin

```
int piezoPin = 2;
void setup(){
}
void loop(){
}
```

Listing 8-3 makes the piezo element fade in by adding a simple `for-loop` with a short delay to play the current tone; the `analogWrite` function can take values between 0 and 255.

LISTING 8-3: Fade the piezo element

```
int piezoPin = 2;
void setup()  {
}
void loop()  {
  for(int i = 0 ; i <= 255; i++) {
    analogWrite(piezoPin, i);
    delay(50);
  }
}
```

Finally, Listing 8-4 shows how to turn the piezo element off for a few seconds before it starts playing again.

LISTING 8-4: Turn the piezo element off

```
int piezoPin = 2;
void setup()  {
}
void loop()  {
  for(int i = 0 ; i <= 255; i ++) {
    analogWrite(piezoPin, i);
    delay(50);
  }
  analogWrite(piezoPin, 0);
  delay( 5000 );
}
```

As we hinted earlier, there is not a big difference between turning a light on and off and moving a motor. Piezo elements are, in a way, flat motors that can perform minimal movements. To increase the complexity of the new things being introduced through the book, in the next section you are going to see how servo motors work.

Motors

You've probably noticed that many of the actuators function in a similar manner; in this example, you control the speed and direction of a small continuous rotation servo motor. Servo motors are controlled using a PWM signal at a specific frequency, and the width of the duty cycle determines the motor's behavior.

Two types of servo motors exist: standard and continuous rotation. The standard type uses the duty cycle to fix the motor's angle, whereas the continuous rotation type uses the duty cycle to determine the direction of rotation as well as the speed.

FIGURE 8-4: A servo connected to Arduino

MOTORS

Many types of motors exist; however, we use three main types for prototyping: servo motors, steppers, and DC motors.

Servo motors are used when you need precision and speed in reaching a certain position. A typical use for them is radio-controlled vehicles like model cars and airplanes. Servos are really easy to control because they just need a PWM pulse, and the duty cycle controls either the angle or the rotation speed/direction of them. Arduino comes with a library that handles all the low-level operations with the servos. You can read more about the library while building this example.

Stepper motors turn in small jumps, also called steps. These motors are defined by their resolution in terms of degrees for each step. They are controlled by sending pulses through the inputs of the motors. One pulse represents a turn of X degrees. The smaller the turn per pulse, the better the motor. They are used in machines that require high precision in the movement in terms of speed, such as scanners or printers that require constant speed to assure proper functionality.

Finally, DC (as in direct current) motors are the cheapest ones you can find. They are simple coils where you can control the direction of turn by playing with the polarity of the signal you send to the motor, and you can control the speed by adjusting the PWM signal. These motors are mostly useless without gear boxes, because they turn too quickly and have no torque by themselves. You can find them inside almost any cheap toy with moving parts.

Gathering Components

This example requires the components you can see in Figure 8-5.

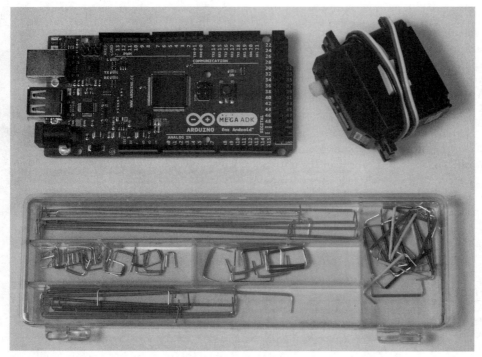

FIGURE 8-5: Components needed for the servo motor

The list of materials is as follows:

➤ An Arduino board

➤ A servo motor

➤ Wires

➤ A USB cable

Assembling the Prototype

The servo has three wires, and it's important to connect them properly. It has one ground wire that is usually black, a red wire that should be connected to either 5 Volts or 3.3 Volts on your Arduino depending on the motor you're using, and a control wire that can vary in color. The control wire should be connected to digital pin 2 on the Arduino Mega. See the circuit diagram in Figure 8-6 for more details.

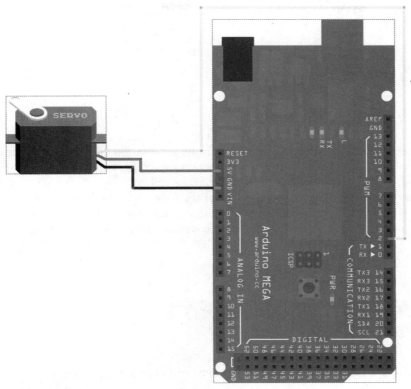

FIGURE 8-6: Circuit for the servo example

Writing the Arduino Program

Start by creating a fresh Arduino sketch, and add the `setup` and `loop` functions. Because you'll be using a built-in Arduino library for controlling servo motors, go ahead and add the `include` statement for that too.

LISTING 8-5: Create the fresh new Arduino sketch

```
#include <Servo.h>
void setup(){
}
void loop(){
}
```

As in Listing 8-6, you have to declare the `Servo` object and attach it to pin 2. You can use another pin if you'd like as long as it is PWM enabled.

LISTING 8-6: Declare the Servo object

```
#include <Servo.h>
Servo myservo;
void setup(){
  myservo.attach(2);
}
void loop(){
}
```

The library is written to control standard servos, and not continuous rotation ones, but it happens to work for both. The servo in this example is of a continuous rotation type, which means that you can't set an angle; instead, you control the speed of the rotation by adding to or subtracting from 90 degrees. The further away from 90 degrees you get, the faster the rotation is. Table 8-1 shows how continuous-rotation servo motors behave in comparison to the standard servos. Using this trick, with the same library you control standard servo motors; you will be capable of moving those with continuous rotation.

TABLE 8-1: Continuous-Rotation Servo Angles

0–90 DEGREES	90 DEGREES	90–180 DEGREES
Backward	Stopped	Forward

Let the servo pause by setting it to 90 degrees and set the delay for one second, as shown in Listing 8-7.

LISTING 8-7: Set the angle to 90 degrees to stop the motor

```
#include <Servo.h>
Servo myservo;
void setup(){
  myservo.attach(2);
}
void loop(){
  myservo.write(90);
  delay(500);
}
```

Let the servo motor move forward by setting it to 110 degrees for five seconds. See Listing 8-8.

LISTING 8-8: Set the angle to 110 degrees to move forward

```
#include <Servo.h>
Servo myservo;
void setup(){
  myservo.attach(2);
}
void loop(){
  myservo.write(90);
  delay(500);
  myservo.write(110);
  delay(5000);
}
```

Finally, stop the servo by setting the angle back to 90 degrees and letting it rest for a couple of seconds, as shown in Listing 8-9.

LISTING 8-9: Reset the angle

```
#include <Servo.h>
Servo myservo;
void setup(){
  myservo.attach(2);
}
void loop(){
  myservo.write(90);
  delay(500);
  myservo.write(110);
  delay(5000);
  myservo.write(90);
  delay(5000);
}
```

Once you are managing one motor, what about controlling two? And what about mounting those two together to make your first robot? Let's continue exploring how to make an inexpensive robot out of cardboard using servo motors and 9 Volt batteries, like the ones you can find at any store close to you.

Analog Project 1: The Basic Robot

In this mini project you build a small robot, like the one we modelled on Figure 8-7, with very little material, most of which you can find in your home or office. The robot will be capable of moving forward, backward, left, and right. To avoid traffic accidents, you should also add some way of stopping this monster.

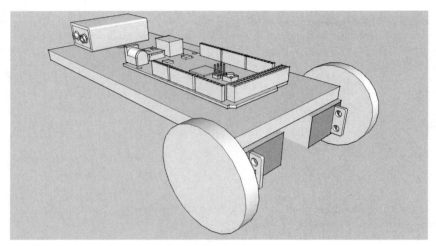

FIGURE 8-7: The 3-D model of the Basic Robot

Gathering Components

You will mount the Basic Robot on a piece of 1.4 mm-thick corrugated cardboard (we just found a box in our office; the thickness is not so important as long as if doesn't bend); it will have two wheels, also made of the same cardboard, attached to one continuous servo motor each. To increase the grip of the robot, you'll also add a rubber band around the wheels. The whole set of parts can be seen on Figure 8-8.

Often in this kind of robot you'll see two active wheels and a third free-turning passive wheel. However, we've noticed that in this small size the third wheel doesn't really function as intended, so instead of this third free-turning wheel, you'll use a Ping-Pong ball firmly attached to the robot. It's light and it can easily slide over most surfaces.

FIGURE 8-8: Components needed for the Basic Robot

Put together the following list of materials to build your robot:

➤ An Arduino board.

➤ A USB cable for programming the Arduino.

➤ Some wires.

➤ Two continuous-rotation servo motors.

➤ One 9 Volt battery; because the two servo motors in this example are draining quite a bit of amperes, you should take care to use a high-quality battery.

➤ A battery connector for the 9 V battery.

➤ A Ping-Pong ball.

➤ Two rubber bands; it's important that these fit well around the wheels.

➤ Some cardboard to build the frame and wheels of the robot.

➤ Scissors or a cutting knife; or, if you're lucky enough to have access to one, a laser cutter is really helpful.

➤ Some tape; try to avoid using glue or other permanent adhesives because you might want to use the more expensive components in later projects.

Use the schematic in Figure 8-9 to build the frame and wheels of your robot, or create your own imaginative construction and share it with your friends.

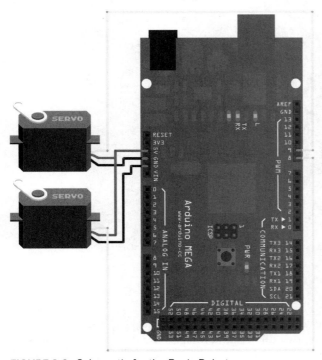

FIGURE 8-9: Schematic for the Basic Robot

Assembling the Prototype

The motors are very simple to attach to the Arduino Mega. They each require 5 Volts of power, a ground connection, and a PWM-enabled pin to control the speed and direction. However, there is a small problem in that the Arduino has only one pin pushing 5 Volts out. To work around this, you can either use a breadboard or you can solder the two 5 Volt wires together as we have chosen to do.

Attach the two motors under the main cardboard plate. This will make the motors rotate in opposite directions, but you'll solve that when you program the robot later. Glue the Ping-Pong ball to the small hole at the rear of the robot. The ball won't be rolling as you might expect it to; instead it will be dragged across the surface, but don't worry because the material of the ball makes it work well on most surfaces.

Put the rubber bands around the wheels as shown in Figure 8-10. This will give the robot good traction on most surfaces, but make sure to use rubber bands that fit well with your wheels.

Finally, attach the electronics to the top. You can play around with the placement of them; a good idea would be to align the USB Host port to the rear end of the robot to make it easy to attach to both the computer when programming the robot and the Android device when controlling it.

FIGURE 8-10: The assembled Basic Robot

Writing the Arduino Program

The code to command this robot is simple conceptually, but it requires keeping track of the communication from the phone and moving two different motors. As usual, you need to focus on separating the state machine that controls the motors and the state machine that handles communication.

When it comes to the communication, the board will subscribe to the phone and then use the data coming from any publish requests to control the direction that the motors turn.

VOLTAGE AND CURRENT ON THE ARDUINO BOARDS

Servo motors are not very demanding in terms of current. In this project you use a 9 Volt battery because it is both easy to find and has a nice form factor to be mounted on the robot.

The amount of current a battery can provide is measured in milliamperes per hour (mAh). The higher this value, the better response the battery will give to the power demands from the motors.

As it turns out, sudden movement changes on the motors make them demand high values of current at once. You have three ways around this issue:

➤ You can use better batteries, with higher mAh values. The ones for RC cars are optimal for any of your robotics projects, but will increase your project's budget.

➤ Implement, via software, a way for the speed to change in a smooth fashion.

➤ Use different powering lines for the intelligence in your system (the Arduino board) and the moving parts. You can separate the two power supplies by using different batteries and voltage regulators; one for the arduino, and the other for the moving parts, but most likely having different power circuitry and using a single battery will suffice.

The main issue you will be facing if the current demands are too high is that your board will reset itself, rendering the whole program unusable.

The following code listings are examples of how to implement the second method. This is a trick you can always rely on when working with motors.

Listing 8-8 showed how to control a single motor, but this robot has two servo motors. Using the Servo library for Arduino it is possible to declare many more. Simply connect two motors: one to pin 8 and one to pin 9. Listing 8-9 shows how you can instantiate more than one object from the same Servo class.

LISTING 8-9: Configure Arduino to use two servo motors

```
#include <Servo.h>
// create servo objects
Servo myservoL;
Servo myservoR;
void setup() {
```

continues

LISTING 8-9 *(continued)*

```
    // attach servos to pins 8 and 9
    myservoL.attach(8);
    myservoR.attach(9);
}
[…]
```

Next, because you are going to implement the trick of changing the speed on the motors in a smooth fashion, you need some constants in your code to take care of the maximum and minimum speeds, a value with which to increment/decrement the speed, and so on.

Upon arrival of a publish message from the phone, the robot gets a command that determines the next speed for each motor. You store those in the servoL_Next and servoR_Next variables. The current speed for each motor is stored in the servoL and servoR variables.

LISTING 8-10: Add limits to the motor movement

```
#include <Servo.h>
// motor limits
#define MOTOR_STOP   90
#define MOTOR_MAX    120
#define MOTOR_MIN    60
#define INCREMENT    5     // speed for changing speed
// create servo objects
Servo myservoL;
Servo myservoR;
// variables to store current and next state of servos
byte servoL_Next = MOTOR_STOP;
byte servoR_Next = MOTOR_STOP;
byte servoL = MOTOR_STOP;
byte servoR = MOTOR_STOP;
void setup() {
  // attach servos to pins 8 and 9
  myservoL.attach(8);
  myservoR.attach(9);
}
[…]
```

A clean way for storing the next state for each one of the motors consists of creating a function to handle this, like the one shown in Listing 8-11.

LISTING 8-11: Function to determine the next state of the motors

```
[…]
// decide for motors' next state based on the
// command arriving from the phone
void nextMotorState(int command) {
  switch (command) {
    // stop motors
```

```
      case 0:
        servoL_Next = MOTOR_STOP;
        servoR_Next = MOTOR_STOP;
        break;
      // move forwards
      case 1:
        servoL_Next = MOTOR_MAX;
        servoR_Next = MOTOR_MIN;
        break;
      // turn right
      case 2:
        servoL_Next = MOTOR_MAX;
        servoR_Next = MOTOR_MAX;
        break;
      // move backwards
      case 3:
        servoL_Next = MOTOR_MIN;
        servoR_Next = MOTOR_MAX;
        break;
      // turn left
      case 4:
        servoL_Next = MOTOR_MIN;
        servoR_Next = MOTOR_MIN;
        break;
      // do nothing
      default:
        break;
    }
  }
```

At this point you should add the P2PMQTT object to handle the communication between Arduino and your Android phone. You will have to instantiate the object and initialize the communication inside the setup function. Don't forget to include the AndroidAccessory library as well as the P2PMQTT one. Also, just to be able to monitor what is going on in your phone, you should activate the serial port. See Listing 8-12 for details.

LISTING 8-12: Initialize the communication object

```
#include <AndroidAccessory.h>
#include <P2PMQTT.h>
#include <Servo.h>
[…]
byte servoR = MOTOR_STOP;
P2PMQTT mqtt(true); // add parameter true for debugging
void setup() {
  // use the serial port to monitor that things work
  Serial.begin(9600);
  Serial.println("ready");

  // initiate the communication to the phone
  mqtt.begin("Basic Robot");
```

continues

LISTING 8-12 *(continued)*

```
    mqtt.connect(0,60000); // add 1min timeout

    // attach servos to pins 8 and 9
    myservoL.attach(8);
    myservoR.attach(9);
  }
  [...]
```

You read the data arriving inside the loop and call the previously defined `nextMotorState` function using the payload of the publish message as a parameter. You should define a global variable to store that payload. Listing 8-13 starts by declaring the payload variable and initializes it as -1, which is a value we should never get from the communication. It reads the payload later on and uses it to control the motors' movements.

LISTING 8-13: Read the payload

```
  [...]
  // to store the data
  int payload = -1;
  [...]
  void loop() {
    // get a P2PMQTT package and extract the type
    int type = mqtt.getType(mqtt.buffer);
    // depending on the package type do different things
    switch(type) {
      case CONNECT:
        Serial.println("connected");
        break;
      case PUBLISH:
        payload = mqtt.getPayload(mqtt.buffer, type)[0];
        Serial.print("command: ");
        Serial.println(payload);
        nextMotorState(payload);
        break;
      default:
        // do nothing
        break;
    }
  [...]
  }
```

The only bit missing in this project is to implement the counter within the `loop` that increments and decrements the motors speeds. This block of code executes directly inside the `loop` after it checks for the arrival of a message from the phone. It also requires using a global timer to execute the increments at a certain pace. Listing 8-14 is pushing changes to the motors at a slow pace, instead of forcing a sudden change of directions on the motors; it makes the speeds change slowly. This avoids the problem of the motors demanding too much current from the batteries at once.

LISTING 8-14: Control speed changes with a timer

```
[…]
// timer
long timer = millis();
[…]
void loop() {
[…]
  // if we are connected and we are getting data
  // we will keep on updating the motor's position
  // in a smooth fashion, but if there is no connection
  // we will stop the motors as a safety measure
  if (mqtt.isConnected()) {
    if( millis() - timer > 20 ) {
      if(servoL < servoL_Next) {
        servoL += INCREMENT;
        if(servoL > MOTOR_MAX) servoL = MOTOR_MAX;
      }
      if(servoR < servoR_Next) {
        servoR += INCREMENT;
        if(servoR > MOTOR_MAX) servoR = MOTOR_MAX;
      }
      if(servoL > servoL_Next) {
        servoL -= INCREMENT;
        if(servoL < MOTOR_MIN) servoL = MOTOR_MIN;
      }
      if(servoR > servoR_Next) {
        servoR -= INCREMENT;
        if(servoR < MOTOR_MIN) servoR = MOTOR_MIN;
      }
      myservoL.write(servoL);
      myservoR.write(servoR);
      timer = millis();
    }
  } else {
    // turn off the motors, we want no problem!!
    myservoL.write(MOTOR_STOP);
    myservoR.write(MOTOR_STOP);
  }
}
```

Get the full listing for this example at the downloads section on the website of the book, and upload it to your Arduino Mega ADK board. You will then be ready to control two servo motors from your Android device in any context! You will need to install the proper Android code on your phone as shown on chapter 6 in the section titled "Basic Robot."

ANALOG SENSORS

Plenty of different transducers can translate different physical measurements into electrical signals: microphones, light sensors, infrared temperature sensors, and so on. As long as their output is contained in the range of 0 Volts to 5 Volts, it will be possible for you to bring that signal into one of the 16 available analog pins of the Arduino Mega ADK.

From then on, everything gets very simple. A function called `analogRead`, taking as a parameter the pin number, reads the voltage at that pin and translates it into an integer number in the range 0 to 1,023 that you can use in your programs.

Potentiometers

You can think of the potentiometer as a resistor that can change its resistance. When passing voltage over the potentiometer, the output depends on the current resistance; you can then read the voltage using the `analogRead` function.

In this example you use the potentiometer to control the delay of a blinking LED.

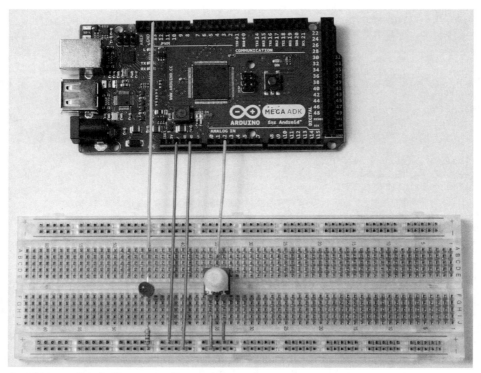

FIGURE 8-11: The finished potentiometer example

Gathering Components

Beyond the common materials — Arduino, wires, and breadboard — you need a potentiometer, a 220 Ω resistor, and an LED to build this example. Figure 8-12 shows all the materials at once.

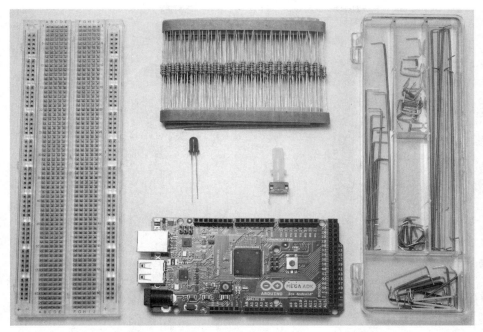

FIGURE 8-12: Components needed for the potentiometer

The list of materials goes as follows:

➤ An Arduino board

➤ A 10K potentiometer

➤ A 220 Ω resistor

➤ A 5 mm LED

➤ A breadboard

➤ Wires

➤ USB cable

Assembling the Prototype

The potentiometer has three connectors. Two of these connectors are used to pass a voltage over the resistor, so connect one of them to 5 Volts and one of them to GND (0 Volts); it doesn't matter which of these two you connect to 5 Volts or GND because the potentiometer doesn't have polarity. However, it's important not to connect 5 Volts or GND to the middle pin (the pin that you'll use to read the variable resistance), because that may create a short circuit and damage your components. See the circuit in Figure 8-13 for details.

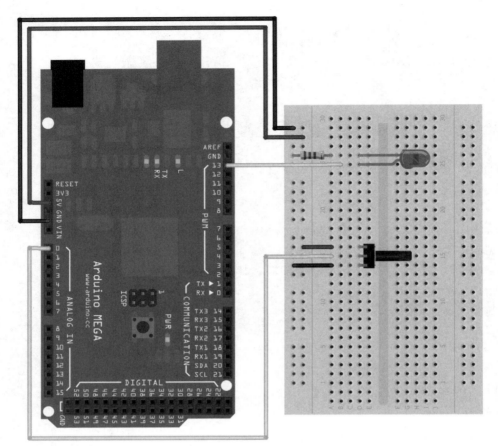

FIGURE 8-13: Circuit for the potentiometer example

Writing the Arduino Program

Start a clean sketch and add the required `setup` and `loop` functions, as shown in Listing 8-15.

LISTING 8-15: Create a new Sketch

```
void setup(){
}
void loop(){
}
```

Declare the pins you're going to use; in this example, you're using the potentiometer as a sensor and the LED as the actuator for that sensor. Don't forget that although the potentiometer pin doesn't require any `pinMode` declarations, the LED pin does. See Listing 8-16 for details.

LISTING 8-16: Declare the pins

```
int potentiometerPin = A2;
int ledPin = 13;
void setup() {
  pinMode(ledPin, OUTPUT);
}
void loop() {
}
```

As in Listing 8-17, read the value from the potentiometer; by default, the value you get from this function is an integer in the range of 0 to 1,023. Store it in a new variable called `value`.

LISTING 8-17: Read the sensor value

```
int potentiometerPin = A2;
int ledPin = 13;
int value = 0;
void setup() {
  pinMode(ledPin, OUTPUT);
}
void loop() {
  value = analogRead(potentiometerPin);
}
```

You can either use the value you read directly, or you can apply some mapping or otherwise alter the value to suit your needs. In this example, you just use it straight away because the range is quite appropriate.

Add the code to blink the LED on and off, letting the sensor value represent the delay between the blinks.

LISTING 8-18: Use the sensor value

```
int potentiometerPin = A2;
int ledPin = 13;
int val = 0;
void setup() {
  pinMode(ledPin, OUTPUT);
}
void loop() {
  val = analogRead(potentiometerPin);
  digitalWrite(ledPin, HIGH);
  delay(val);
  digitalWrite(ledPin, LOW);
  delay(val);
}
```

Ultrasound Sensors

This example deals with an ultrasound transceiver, which is a sensor that both sends and receives ultrasound tones and answers back with a voltage in the range 0 Volts to 5 Volts mapping the distance to objects in front of it. This sensor detects objects from 0 meters to 6 meters. The farther away the object, the bigger the voltage. Figure 8-14 shows how to use the ultrasound sensor connected to an Arduino board.

FIGURE 8-14: The assembled ultrasound example

Gathering Components

Because the sensor comes pre-attached on its own circuit board, you don't need much material at all (see Figure 8-15).

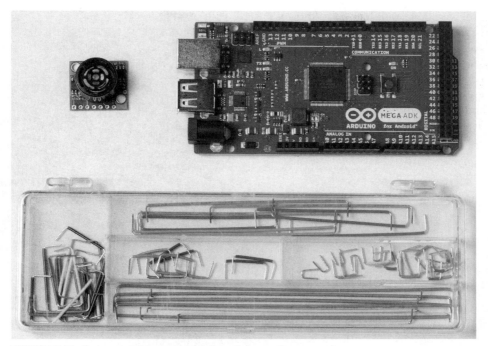

FIGURE 8-15: Components needed for the ultrasound sensor

The following list shows what you need to reproduce the experiment shown in Figure 8-15:

➤ An Arduino board

➤ Wires

➤ MaxSonar Ultrasound sensor

➤ A breadboard

➤ A USB cable

Assembling the Prototype

Most often, the ultrasound sensors come delivered without any pins or cables attached (see Figure 8-16). Your first task, then, is to attach either cables or male pins to the sensor; use a soldering iron, but if you've never used one you should definitely read a tutorial online how to solder in a safe, and proper, way. In chapter 10, in the Kitchen Lamp project, we provide a note on where to find information on soldering. Alternatively you could just wrap some wires in the holes; if you did so, please be careful with short circuiting different pins with each other.

Because this sensor allows multiple ways of reading the sensor data, it's important that you first familiarize yourself with the layout of the pins. Fortunately, on the MaxSonar sensor, the pins are all labeled according to their specific purpose. If you're interested you can also read more about this sensor and the pins in the datasheet available online at www.maxbotix.com/documents/ MB1010_Datasheet.pdf.

FIGURE 8-16: The ultrasound sensor pin labels

FIGURE 8-17: The ultrasound sensor, with soldered wires

The sensor is now ready to be used in projects. Reading the analog values of this sensor is identical to reading values from other analog sensors; it has one 5 Volt connector, one GND connector, and a sensor pin. See the diagram in Figure 8-18 for details.

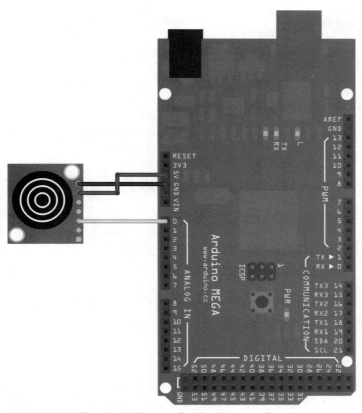

FIGURE 8-18: The circuit diagram for the ultrasound sensor

Writing the Arduino Program

Start with a brand new Arduino sketch, and add the setup and loop functions as shown in Listing 8-19.

LISTING 8-19: Create a new Arduino sketch

```
void setup(){
}
void loop(){
}
```

Declare the pin where you'll connect the ultrasound sensor; in this example you're using analog in 0, which is A0 in code.

LISTING 8-20: Declare the ultrasound sensor pin

```
int ultrasoundPin = A0;
void setup(){
}
void loop(){
}
```

Read the sensor values by calling `analogRead`; these values correspond to the range of the sensor. For the MaxSonar sensor the maximum range at 5 Volts is 6.45 meters, with a resolution of approximately 1 inch.

Listing 8-21 also adds a short delay; the sensor will only deliver readings at most every 50 milliseconds.

LISTING 8-21: Get the sensor readings

```
int ultrasoundPin = A0;
int val = 0;
void setup(){
}
void loop(){
  val = analogRead(ultrasoundPin);
  delay(50);
}
```

Finally, print the value to the serial port of the Arduino to get an idea of what values this sensor produces. You need to remember that the ultrasound sensor has a fairly wide beam, so keep the nozzle clear when working with this sensor. Since the maximum distance the sensor can cover is 6 meters, you should expect reading 1,023 at that distance, approximately half of it (512) at 3 meters, and so on.

LISTING 8-22: Print the sensor readings to the serial port

```
int ultrasoundPin = A0;
int val = 0;
void setup(){
  Serial.begin(9600);
}
void loop(){
  val = analogRead(ultrasoundPin);
  Serial.println(val);
  delay(50);
}
```

THE SERIAL PORT

You have used the serial port before. However, it is time to look at how it works in a little more depth. The Serial library comes with Arduino. It is used so often that the IDE already includes it by default. The way you instantiate it is by calling the method `Serial.begin(baudrate)`. You should make sure your board is configured to use the same baud rate as the device it connects to.

The baud rate is measured in bits per second. Different speeds at the emitting and receiving side would mean that the devices trying to communicate wouldn't "understand" each other.

The `Serial` class includes a whole series of methods to send bytes, arrays, and strings through the port. For sending a single byte you could use `Serial.write(val)`, which would send it as a raw value, or `Serial.print(val)`, which would parse it into a string and send the different cyphers in the number as ASCII symbols.

The Arduino Mega ADK has four serial ports available. By default, one uses the Serial to USB converter on the board to send data to or get data from the computer. The other three are exposed on a connector on your board and labeled as TX#/RX# for you to use. Many sensors and actuators are available that use the serial protocol as a communication method. And many of those work at a baud rate of 9600 bps. Therefore, you will see how in most examples using the Serial library, people use 9,600 as a parameter.

Analog Project 2: The Parking Assistant

In this project you build an application that helps you park by detecting objects up to six meters behind your car. The application will, apart from playing a short beeping sound, also have a simple visual representation of the distance displayed on the screen.

To protect the sensor and the Arduino board, you should build casings for them. You can download the schematics shown in Figures 8-19 and 8-20 to build the casings later in this exercise. We built them using a laser engraver, but you could use any kind of box to protect your electronics, they do not need to be built specifically for this project.

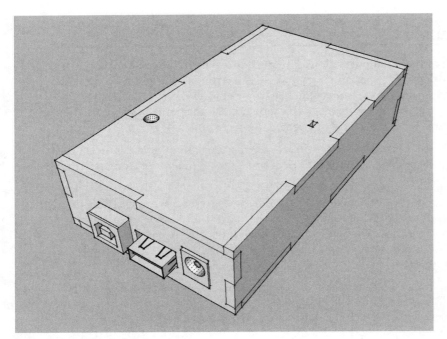

FIGURE 8-19: The Arduino casing

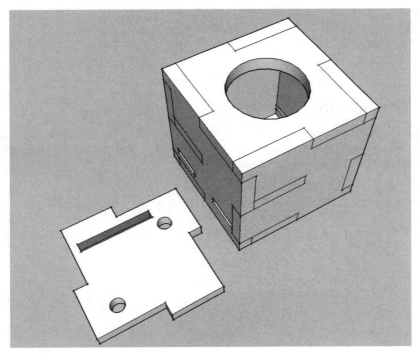

FIGURE 8-20: The sensor casing

Gathering Components

Hopefully, you'll have a car to attach the final prototype to; of course, you can go creative too and put it on a bike or other means of transportation. Figure 8-21 shows the materials we used to build this project.

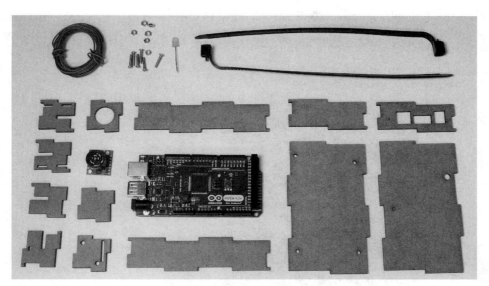

FIGURE 8-21: Components needed for the Parking Assistant

The list of materials you should use to build this prototype is as follows:

➤ An Arduino board.

➤ A micro USB cable.

➤ Wires; these needs to be quite long because the sensor is placed outside the car and the Arduino is placed inside.

➤ Wood, plastic, or cardboard to build the two enclosures used for the sensor and the Arduino board.

➤ Screws to firmly attach the sensor and Arduino board to their respective casing.

➤ A green LED to use as an indicator.

➤ Plastic straps to attach the sensor to the registration sign on the back of the car.

➤ Glue to assemble the casings.

➤ A 9 Volt battery and a battery connector or a USB cable and a car-charger for 5 Volt devices (one of those converters that can be plugged into the car's lighter and that have a USB connector as an output to plug in your board).

If you choose to build your own casings, you can use the blueprints we provide in the downloads section on the website of the book. You can find both PDF and Corel Draw versions of the files for you to use, as well as SketchUp models.

Assembling the Prototype

Mounting this is really simple; the circuit is almost identical to the one from the previous ultrasound example, with one small difference — we added an indicator LED to let us know that the system is working. See the circuit diagram in Figure 8-22 for details.

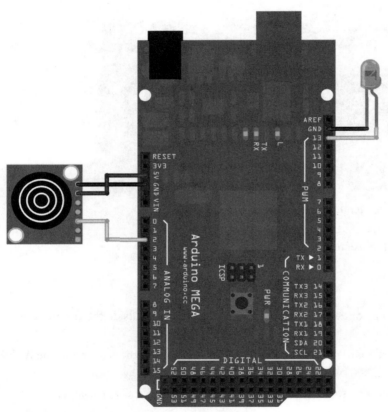

FIGURE 8-22: Circuit for the Parking Assistant

When you mount the prototype, you should have two protective casings with a long wire between them.

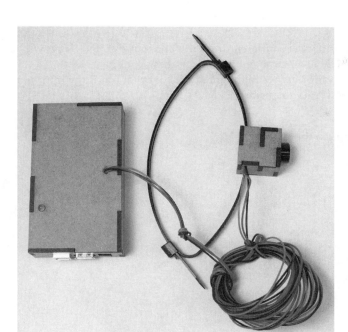

FIGURE 8-23: The finished Parking Assistant

The Parking Assistant should look something like Figure 8-24 when you mount it on the car.

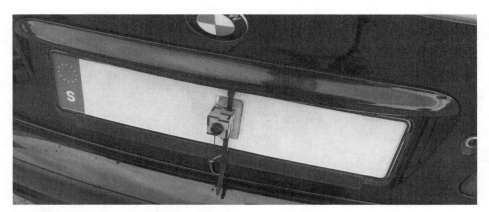

FIGURE 8-24: The mounted Parking Assistant

Writing the Arduino Program

The program to implement this project is not very different from the previous example. You will have to wait until the phone subscribes to the board before publishing anything back to it. Listing 8-23 is the full program that you need for this project. We highlighted the part that sends the information back to the phone after packaging the information using P2PMQTT.

LISTING 8-23: Send the sensor readings to the phone

```
#include <AndroidAccessory.h>
#include <P2PMQTT.h>
// are we subscribed?
boolean subscribed = false;
// store the sensor reading
int val = 0;
int ledPin = 13;
P2PMQTT mqtt(true); // add parameter true for debugging
P2PMQTTpublish pub;
void setup() {
  // use the serial port to monitor that things work
  Serial.begin(9600);
  Serial.println("ready");
  // initiate the communication to the phone
  mqtt.begin("Parking Assistant");
  mqtt.connect(0,60000);  // add 1min timeout
  // turn the LED on to show things are working
  pinMode(ledPin, OUTPUT);
  digitalWrite(ledPin, HIGH);
}
void loop() {
  // get a P2PMQTT package and extract the type
  int type = mqtt.getType(mqtt.buffer);
  // depending on the package type do different things
  switch(type) {
    case SUBSCRIBE:
      subscribed = mqtt.checkTopic(mqtt.buffer, type, "us");
      if (subscribed) {
        Serial.println("subscribed");
      }
      break;
    default:
      // do nothing
      break;
  }
  // if we are connected and subscribed, then we can
  // send data
  if (mqtt.isConnected() && subscribed) {
    val = analogRead(A2);
    pub.fixedHeader = 48;
    pub.length = 5;
    pub.lengthTopicMSB = 0;
    pub.lengthTopicLSB = 2;
    pub.topic = (byte*) "us";
```

```
        pub.payload = (byte*) val;
        mqtt.publish(pub);
    }
}
```

This example has an Android counterpart that you can find in chapter 6, in the Parking Assistant section.

SUMMARY

You can now read information coming from analog sensors and send it to a phone. At the same time, you can control actuators using PWM as a way to dim lights or control the speed of motors.

Analog sensors read values from the physical world and map them into voltages that can then be read through Analog to Digital Converters into microcontrollers. The voltages are translated into integer numbers that can easily be manipulated inside variables from within your programs.

Piezo elements can read vibrations or sound, but they also produce sound when they are stimulated with signals oscillating within the audible range. You can find piezo speakers just about everywhere in consumer electronics. Sometimes they are called buzzers, and they might be contained inside some sort of plastic housing both to protect them mechanically from other parts and to act as resonance box.

Ultrasound sensors are very precise tools to measure distance. They emit tones and get the echo from those tones. They then calculate the time difference between the tone and the echo, which gives a measurement of the distance between the sensor and the object reflecting the ultrasound burst. You can find other systems to detect distance, but ultrasound is the most precise at long distances for a reasonable price. It is used broadly in robotics.

PART II
Projects

Bike Ride Recorder

➤ Understanding bike computers

➤ A look at the Design Brief

➤ Understanding the Arduino side

➤ Constructing the Android app

Bike computers tell you about your performance when you are racing on the road. They store information about the speed of your wheels, the distance of your trip, or the time you have been riding. Bike computers are available that connect to your phone and enable you to log your performance to later compare it with other trips via graphs.

The project in this chapter brings you a little further into making your own bike computer using your Android device and a little help from embedded electronics. We think it is interesting to compare the turn of the wheel with the turn of the pedals. If you are racing downhill, the amount of effort you make on the bike is much less than when you are on a flat road. You can measure that effort by comparing the data of two identical sensors: one on a wheel and one on a pedal.

This is a challenging project for which you are going to make use of low-level code on the Arduino side (in the form of hardware interrupts) and represent data on top of video on the Android side. Because we don't want you to run any kind of risk by taking your attention away from riding, the app will record your trip in a video file that you can play back later. At the end of this project, you will have a video recording of your races with information about your speed as well as a representation of your real effort generated by correlating the wheel's turns with how much you moved your legs while pedaling.

THE CONCEPT BEHIND BIKE COMPUTERS

The very essence of this project is creating a device to help you improve the kind of information you get from contemporary bike computers. Usually you receive information about speed and distance. The most recent computers enable you to enter personal information, such as your weight or body mass, to estimate the effort (measured in kilocalories) you made during your exercise.

> **NOTE** *Something to remember about this project. Effort is measured in terms of the data acquired from the amount of pedaling you do during your exercise in comparison to the distance you traveled. For example, if most of your path is downhill, you might travel a long distance without moving your legs, thus exerting minimal effort. Riding the same path but in the opposite direction would result in completely different data.*

At the same time, we want to offer you tools to explore alternative ways to represent the information obtained from the bike. The use of the camera, when installed properly on the bike's handle, offers a view of your trip from your own viewpoint and allows you to add more information as a layer on top of the video.

Most cyclists have preferred routes for their training. This tool can help you learn about the way you exercise; for example it can show when you might be pushing to the limit.

Figure 9-1 shows the bicycle before anything is installed on it. As you can see, it is a standard racer bike that we acquired for the purpose of making this project. You are not going to modify the bicycle, so you do not need any knowledge of mechanics to build this project.

FIGURE 9-1: View of the bike

RIDE SAFE, USE A HELMET, AND DON'T LOOK AT THE SCREEN!

Before you start building this project, please note that we have designed it to work in the following way:

➤ Data gathering is done without direct interaction with the screen.

➤ Data visualization is done after stopping the recording process, ideally once you have stepped down from the bike.

All the information visualization could be done in real time, but we don't want you to divert your attention from riding, which is the reason why you take your bike in the first place.

It should also be possible to give auditory feedback over headphones, but you would need to purchase some sort of wireless headset. Because all those options are possible, we have chosen a slightly more low-tech approach and we suggest augmenting the bike computer with two LEDs and two buttons. In this way it's possible for you to start/stop the recording, and get clear feedback about it through a simple light.

THE DESIGN BRIEF

The following lists the requirements for this project. They are a mix of mechanics, hardware, and software. You will need to:

➤ Design a circuit that reads information from two sensors, one attached to a wheel and one attached to the bike's pedals.

➤ House the circuit inside a box mounted on the bike's handle.

➤ Build the box to have enough room to carry the phone (or tablet, but we provide you with blueprints for a box with room for a phone only).

➤ Design a box to carry a battery pack.

➤ Because you will be experimenting with improving the software, leave the connectors to the Arduino board visible, so that you can improve its firmware as you go.

➤ Use some LEDs to provide visual feedback without using the screen.

➤ Use single command buttons to interact with the Android device without touching the screen.

➤ Create software to record a video sequence of the trip as well as the instant rotation speeds from the pedals and the wheels.

➤ Create software that plays back the video with a layer of information on top.

➤ Make everything run on batteries.

Figure 9-2 shows the control mounted on the bike's handle including the phone in its dock.

FIGURE 9-2: Prototype on the bike's handle

WORKING WITH THE ARDUINO SIDE

This time, the electronics involved in this project aren't complex. You will be using two new things, though: magnetic switches — triggered when a magnet passes by the mechanism by which the sensors work on the bike wheels — and hardware interrupts.

INTERRUPTS: HARDWARE VERSUS SOFTWARE

You can use two types of interrupts in processors, and if you are familiar with the subject of computer architecture, you will know about those for sure. However, we think it is important to mention them, because working with embedded electronics at a low level becomes difficult without knowing something about them.

Interrupts are hooks in the processor's hardware with the power to stop whatever the processor is doing at that time to make it operate a predefined callback function. In other words, you can tell the processor something along the lines of "if A happens, then do B." What is interesting is that you can trigger these callback functions either from a timer (software interrupt) or from a change at one of the processor's pins (hardware interrupt).

When programming for Arduino boards, you will always find yourself thinking about doing sequential programs in which each line of code is executed after the previous one. You can use interrupts to add event-based programming to embedded electronics on top of the sequential code. You do not really need to use interrupts to read a button, because polling the different inputs and outputs at the right speed is enough for the processor to respond. However, dealing with the turns of the wheel or turns of the pedals is a different story. Those happen at really high speeds and, therefore, you will have to use interrupts to capture the arrival of the events.

Creating the Hardware and Mechanics

The mechanics of this project are solved by making a box that can be mounted on top of the bike's handle (see Figure 9-2). We first modeled it in 3-D and cut it using a laser-engraver on 4 mm MDF (synthetic wood). You could use other materials — we provide the Sketchup models to the box, and you are welcome to modify them to fit your needs. Each bike handle is a little different, so you might need to adjust the dimensions. However, it is possible to install the whole device within a much less elaborate housing (for example, using a plastic lunch box) on a bike basket or similar.

Figure 9-3 shows all the parts to use on the bike except for the magnet sensors that you'll mount on the wheels and pedals. You can find those at a bike store. We bought two cheap bike computers and got rid of all the electronics to keep the sensors for our own use.

BIKE COMPUTERS AND MAGNETIC SWITCHES

Bike computers are usually a plastic enclosure with an LCD and an external sensor. That sensor hangs from a long wire (something in the range of 1 to 1.5 meters). At the other end of the wire, there is a plastic holder for you to mount the computer on the bike handle. The sensor is a magnetic switch that is activated by a magnet instead of pushing it mechanically (like in a pushbutton) or shaking it (like in a tilt sensor).

It is possible to buy magnetic sensors in many different forms. They are also used on top of doors for security systems to detect when a door is open or closed. The sensing component is kind of fragile (it is actually made of glass) and therefore it comes casted into a plastic box. The magnetic sensors used for doors are too bulky for mounting them on a bike. At the same time the "raw" sensor is too fragile and hard to use for a project like this.

Therefore we decided to take off-the-shelf bike computers, that can cost as little as 4 EUR new, and take the sensor from them to implement the project. When taking the sensor from the bike computer you have to cut the wire close to the LCD screen, the actual computer. You will not be using the computer itself, only the sensor with the wire that you will be connecting to Arduino.

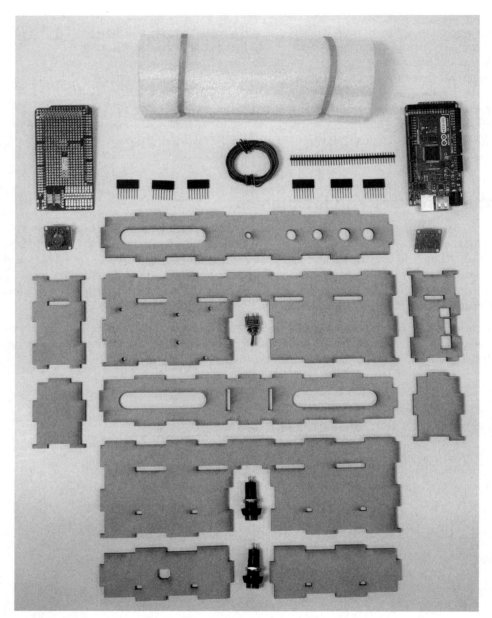

FIGURE 9-3: Parts needed in the Bike Computer project

The final list of parts for this project is as follows:

➤ Arduino Mega ADK + micro USB cable for your processor

➤ Arduino prototyping shield for Arduino Mega

➤ Pin headers, both male-only and female with long pins

➤ Pushbuttons to be mounted on the box

➤ Multithreaded wire for power and ground

➤ Sugarcubes to join the wires

➤ Two bike computers (we bought them for 4 EUR each)

➤ LEDs (we used TinkerKit LEDs to avoid having to solder resistors and so on, but you could solder resistors on the prototyping shield and use whatever LEDs you have in your toolbox)

➤ Our home-brew laser-cut box (see Figure 9-4 for the model)

The schematic for the shield is shown in Figure 9-5. Note that the inputs for the magnet sensors are located at very specific pins. Not all the pins on the microcontroller can handle interrupts. For this project to work you should make sure you do not change those. When it comes to the LEDs or the pushbuttons, you are welcome to move them around as you need; just remember to configure them properly in the software.

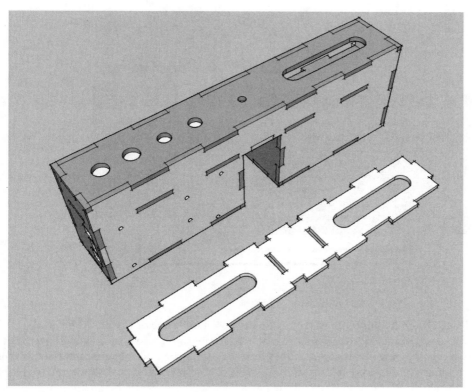

FIGURE 9-4: 3-D model of the prototype's box

The power for the whole system comes from a battery. We simply added a cable to the Vin pin of the shield to power up the Arduino board directly. The voltage regulator on the board takes care of providing voltage to the whole installation, Android device included. We housed the battery at a different part of the bike's frame to allow exchanging batteries in a much easier way. We could have placed the battery inside the same box as the Arduino Mega ADK and the phone, but it would make the box much bigger and you also make the system harder to maintain. Therefore we went for placing the batteries using plastic cable ties on the frame leaving two wires to connect them to the Arduino board.

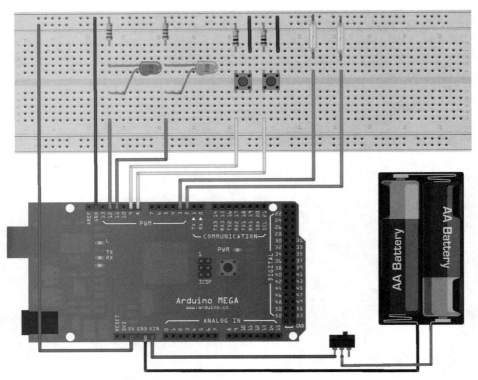

FIGURE 9-5: Schematic for the bike project

We decided to leave all the Arduino board connectors exposed on a side of the box. This is a prototype at a very early stage and you want to be able to reprogram the system as you experiment further. The disadvantage of this is that you cannot use the prototype under bad weather conditions because the electronics are not protected from rain, snow, and so on. Figure 9-6 shows the soldering work we did on the shield to accommodate all the parts.

To connect the TinkerKit LEDs to the shield, we cut one of the TinkerKit cables in two and soldered the cut ends to the shield. The cables of the buttons are soldered directly to the shield. Finally, we added a power switch to turn the whole system on and off at will.

FIGURE 9-6: View of the shield on top of Arduino once soldered

We have designed the box with holes to pass cable ties through (Figure 9-7). The idea is to have a system that you can move onto other bikes, but at the same time be able to stress-test it without fearing the system will fall apart on the road. Stripes are cheap enough that having to cut them when removing the prototype from the bike isn't an issue.

Programming the Bike Computer

The software to command this project is simple. It can be explained in three lines:

FIGURE 9-7: Detail of the cable ties

➤ Wait until an Android device connects; do nothing while waiting.

➤ Upon connection, start listening to the buttons. When the user presses the "start" button, inform the phone and start sending the speed for the wheel and the pedal at periodic intervals.

➤ Continue until the user presses the "stop" button (or until the user disconnects the phone). Report to the phone.

You might think we are forgetting about the way to estimate the speed of the turning wheel and pedal, but no, we aren't! That information is going to be computed in parallel.

The interrupts trigger callback functions in parallel to the transmissions to the phone/tablet. At the moment of transmitting the data, you must to disable the interrupts to avoid any problems with communication. As explained earlier, interrupts can stop any process.

You must attach interrupts in the program's setup function and enable them from the moment the user presses the start button. You will use two C commands to disable and enable interrupts. It hasn't been mentioned until this moment in the book, but the Arduino programming language is an abstraction of the C language. Please note the difference between attach/detach and enable/disable:

➤ **Attaching an interrupt:** Means configuring the processor to be ready to jump to the callback function when the interrupt arrives.

➤ **Detaching an interrupt:** Means configuring the processor not to do so.

➤ **Enabling interrupts:** Means telling the processor to accept any interrupts, both software and hardware ones.

➤ **Disabling interrupts:** Implies telling the processor to ignore any interrupt.

THE ARDUINO CORE AND INTERRUPTS

The Arduino core implements software interrupts to count time and run PWM. Therefore, disabling interrupts implies stopping all the internal counters used in functions like `delay()` or `analogWrite()`. You should be careful in the way you handle these functions. Nothing will break, but things will not work as you expect. We ask you to follow our instructions carefully.

Creating the Program's Skeleton

The program's skeleton (Listing 9-1) shows different blocks as at the beginning of this section. However, do not copy this code into your IDE, because it will not work. We include this listing here to make clear to you what you will have to code from a more abstract point of view.

LISTING 9-1: Program's skeleton

```
#include <libraries_Communication>
int declareSomeVariables;
libComm mqtt = mqttConstructor();
long timer = 0; // used to count time
void setup() {
  initSerialComm(); // to debug that things are going ok
  mqtt.initMqttComm(); // to establish the communication towards the Android device
  // determine which function will act for each interrupt arrival
  attachInterrupt(Wheel, callBackWheel);
```

```
    attachInterrupt(Pedal, callBackPedal);
}
void loop() {
  if(!connected) turnOffGreenLED();
  if(connected && !subscribed) {
    subscribed = mqtt.checkSubscription();
    turnOnGreenLED();
  }
  if(connected && subscribed) {
    if(buttonStart()) {
      mqtt.publish(start);
      turnOnRedLED();
    }
    if(buttonStop())  {
      mqtt.publish(start);
      turnOffRedLED();
    }
  }
  if(aSecondPassed(timer)) {
    disableInterrupts();
    mqtt.publish(counterWheel);
    reset(counterWheel);
    mqtt.publish(counterPedal);
    reset(counterPedal);
    reset(timer);
    enableInterrupts();
  }
}
void callBackWheel() {
  counterWheel++;
}
void callBackPedal() {
  counterPedal++;
```

Creating the Interrupt Callback Functions

The core of your project when it comes to your accessory is making a robust program capable of counting turns of the wheel and pedal. You add the communication block of the program at the very end, because it is as simple as using a timer to decide when you should be sending data back to the phone. Listing 9-2 shows how to declare two different callback functions, and how to attach the interrupts to get those to wake up.

> **NOTE** *We have declared the variables used inside the callback functions as* volatile. *This is required for the program to prioritize performing operations on those. We leave as an exercise to the reader to declare the variables as plain integers and see if the program behaves as expected.*

LISTING 9-2: Callback functions and interrupt declarations

```
volatile int counterWheel = 0;
volatile int counterPedal = 0;
void setup() {
  // make sure the interrupt pins have pull-ups active
  pinMode(2, INPUT_PULLUP);
  pinMode(3, INPUT_PULLUP);
  // attach interrupts
  attachInterrupt(0, countWheel, FALLING); // wheel sensor on pin 2
  attachInterrupt(1, countPedal, FALLING); // pedal sensor on pin 3
}
void loop() {
[…]
}
// declare the wheel's interrupt callback function
void countWheel() {
  counterWheel++;
}
// declare the pedal's interrupt callback function
void countPedal() {
  counterPedal++;
}
```

INTERRUPTS' MODES

When monitoring a pin of a microcontroller, the hardware can detect four different states:

➤ LOW: Triggers the interrupt whenever the pin is low

➤ CHANGE: Triggers the interrupt whenever the pin changes value

➤ RISING: Triggers when the pin goes from low to high

➤ FALLING: For when the pin goes from high to low

You are interested in detecting an edge, or a change in the signal from LOW to HIGH or vice versa. The magnet switch is configured to use the internal pull-up inside the microcontroller. This means that, when the magnet is not present, the pin will be read as HIGH. When the magnet activates the switch, the sensor value read inside Arduino will be LOW instead.

Monitoring the instant in time when the change happens is a very precise way of knowing that either the pedal or the wheel completed a full turn.

The two modes reflecting this change are RISING and FALLING. For the current application it doesn't really matter which one you choose. The mode is the third parameter of the attachInterrupt function. The other two, LOW and CHANGE, are the number representing the interrupt in the interrupt vector and the name of the callback function.

A final word about the interrupt-vector number and the pins — there is a correspondence between the pin numbers and the first parameter of the `attachInterrupt` function. Table 9-1 shows which pins can handle hardware interrupts and their positions inside the interrupt vector.

TABLE 9-1: Correspondence between Pins and Interrupt Numbers

Pin #	2	3	21	20	19	18
Interrupt #	0	1	2	3	4	5

Using the Serial Port to Debug Your Code

You need to test that things work properly. As you have been doing in other projects, you use the serial port to print out whatever you are interested in monitoring at each occasion. In this case in Listing 9-3, you add a serial port at 9600 bauds.

This code also adds a timer that sends data back over the serial port every 30 seconds just to test that the counters are working properly. You could use a couple of buttons on a breadboard connected to pins 2 and 3 to check the proper functionality of the code.

LISTING 9-3: Add serial for debugging the code

```
#define PERIOD 30000  // seconds between data transfers over serial
volatile int counterWheel = 0;
volatile int counterPedal = 0;
long timer = 0;  // time counter
void setup() {
  // init the Serial port
  Serial.begin(9600);
  Serial.println("ready");
  // make sure the interrupt pins have pull-ups active
  pinMode(2, INPUT_PULLUP);
  pinMode(3, INPUT_PULLUP);
  // attach interrupts
  attachInterrupt(0, countWheel, FALLING); // wheel sensor on pin 2
  attachInterrupt(1, countPedal, FALLING); // pedal sensor on pin 3
  // initialize the timer
  timer = millis();
}
void loop() {
  if(millis() - timer >= PERIOD) {
    noInterrupts();  // disable interrupts
    Serial.print("Wheel: "); Serial.println(counterWheel);
    counterWheel = 0;
    Serial.print("Pedal: "); Serial.println(counterPedal);
    counterPedal = 0;
    timer = millis();
    interrupts();  // enable interrupts
  }
}
// declare the wheel's interrupt callback function
```

continues

LISTING 9-3 *(continued)*

```
void countWheel() {
  counterWheel++;
}
// declare the pedal's interrupt callback function
void countPedal() {
  counterPedal++;
}
```

Configuring the Communication to the Phone

Setting up the P2PMQTT library and opening the communication to the phone requires including the library and calling a constructor for the mqtt object handling the data transfers. As part of the loop you have to first detect when the phone gets connected and again when it subscribes to the Arduino board's sensor data. Listing 9-4 highlights this.

You will notice how we have packed the turns of both wheel and pedal as a single byte each. We are counting on sending data to the phone once every couple of seconds. It is highly improbable that anyone will get the wheels on a bike to turn over 10 times per second! The payload is made of three bytes:

➤   Byte 0 carries the control information: START recording, STOP, and SEND data.
      (Listing 9-5 shows them as define commands at the beginning of the code.)

➤   Byte 1 carries the number of turns for the wheel.

➤   Byte 2 carries the number of turns for the pedal.

LISTING 9-4: Add the MQTT communication block

```
#include <AndroidAccessory.h>
#include <P2PMQTT.h>
#define PERIOD 30000  // seconds between data transfers over serial
// are we subscribed?
boolean subscribed = false;
volatile int counterWheel = 0;
volatile int counterPedal = 0;
long timer = 0;  // time counter
P2PMQTT mqtt(); // add parameter true for debugging
P2PMQTTpublish pub;
void setup() {
  [...]
  // initiate the communication to the phone
  mqtt.begin("Bike Computer");
  mqtt.connect(0,60000);  // add 1min timeout
}
void loop() {
  if(!mqtt.isConnected()) {
    [...]
  } else {
    // get a P2PMQTT package and extract the type
    int type = mqtt.getType(mqtt.buffer);
```

```
        // depending on the package type do different things
        switch(type) {
          case SUBSCRIBE:
            subscribed = mqtt.checkTopic(mqtt.buffer, type, "bc");
            if (subscribed) {
              Serial.println("subscribed");
            }
            break;
          default:
            // do nothing
            break;
        }
        // if we are connected and subscribed, then we can
        // send data periodically
        if (mqtt.isConnected() && subscribed)
          if(millis() - timer >= PERIOD) {
            noInterrupts();  // disable interrupts
            pub.fixedHeader = 48;
            pub.length = 7;
            pub.lengthTopicMSB = 0;
            pub.lengthTopicLSB = 2;
            pub.topic = (byte*) "bc";
            pub.payload[0] = 0x03;
            pub.payload[1] = counterWheel & 0xFF;
            pub.payload[2] = counterPedal & 0xFF;
            mqtt.publish(pub);
            Serial.print("Wheel: "); Serial.println(counterWheel);
            counterWheel = 0;
            Serial.print("Pedal: "); Serial.print(counterPedal);
            counterPedal = 0;
            timer = millis();
            interrupts();  // enable interrupts
          }
      }
    }
    [...]
```

Adding the Buttons and the LEDs to the Mix

Now you're only missing the use of the buttons and LEDs in the code. The code is getting long and, therefore, we do not present all the code here at once. Please refer to the downloads section on the website for this chapter to get the whole sketch. Listing 9-5 shows how we configured the different pins for buttons and LEDs, as well as the way those trigger different parts in the code. If you are about to detect when a button state changes from HIGH to LOW, you will need to declare variables to store the current and the previous state of the button. In Listing 9-5 we have declared them as greenButton and greenButtonOld. When one is HIGH and the other is LOW at the same time, it means that the button was pressed just now.

Note how we have moved the code for sending data to the phone into a function. This allows making the code inside loop a little cleaner, easier to understand and reusing the code to inform the phone about the moments when we start and stop recording.

LISTING 9-5: Buttons and LEDs

```
[…]
#define RED_LED 12
#define RED_BUTTON 9
#define GREEN_LED 11
#define GREEN_BUTTON 8
// encode the command sent to the phone for the current topic
#define START    1
#define STOP     2
#define SEND     3
// button status
int greenButton = HIGH;
int greenButtonOld = HIGH;
int redButton = HIGH;
int redButtonOld = HIGH;

// are we subscribed?
boolean subscribed = false;

// are we recording?
boolean recording = false;
[…]
void setup() {
  // init the Serial port
  […]
  // configure the pins for the LEDs and buttons
  pinMode(RED_LED, OUTPUT);
  pinMode(GREEN_LED, OUTPUT);
  pinMode(RED_BUTTON, INPUT_PULLUP);
  pinMode(GREEN_BUTTON, INPUT_PULLUP);
}
void loop() {
  if(!mqtt.isConnected()) {
    // no connection = no light
    digitalWrite(RED_LED, LOW);
    digitalWrite(GREEN_LED, LOW);
  } else {
    // connection = Green LED on
    digitalWrite(GREEN_LED, HIGH);
    // get a P2PMQTT package and extract the type
    […]
    // if we are connected and subscribed, then we can
    // send data periodically
    if (mqtt.isConnected() && subscribed) {
      greenButton = digitalRead(GREEN_BUTTON);
      redButton = digitalRead(GREEN_BUTTON);
      if (!greenButton && greenButtonOld) {
        recording = true;
        publishToPhone(START);
      }
      if (!redButton && redButtonOld) {
        recording = false;
        publishToPhone(STOP);
```

```
      }
      if(millis() - timer >= PERIOD && recording) {
        publishToPhone(SEND);
      }
      greenButtonOld = greenButton;
      redButtonOld = redButton;
    }
  }
}

// publish data back to the phone
void publishToPhone(byte control) {
  noInterrupts();  // disable interrupts
  pub.fixedHeader = 48;
  pub.length = 6;
  pub.lengthTopicMSB = 0;
  pub.lengthTopicLSB = 2;
  pub.topic = (byte*) "bc";
  pub.payload[0] = control & 0xFF;
  pub.payload[1] = counterWheel & 0xFF;
  pub.payload[2] = counterPedal & 0xFF;
  mqtt.publish(pub);
  Serial.print("Wheel: ");
  Serial.println(counterWheel);
  counterWheel = 0;
  Serial.print("Pedal: ");
  Serial.print(counterPedal);
  counterPedal = 0;
  timer = millis();
  interrupts();  // enable interrupts
}
[...]
```

BUILDING THE ANDROID APP

This application consists of multiple parts that you need to implement before you can actually start testing your prototype on a bike. First of all, the app should be able to record the video, and it should also be able to play this video back to you while displaying the collected data on a user interface on top of the video.

THE CAMERA

The camera in Android enables you to capture both still images and video; however, the camera won't work unless you have a preview display set. You have ways around this requirement; for example, hiding the preview display under other components or setting its visibility to hidden.

If you don't set a preview display the camera will generate an error when you start recording, and you won't get a video output.

To build this app, then, you need to create three different activities for the user interface and one service to run the communication that will be available from all of the activities. Figure 9-8 shows a sketch of the components your project will contain.

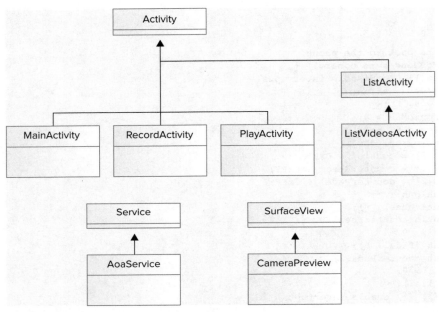

FIGURE 9-8: UML sketch of the Bike Ride Recorder project

Building a `Service` for the communication, as shown here, simplifies the setup and communication with the accessory and potentially enables you to add more components later that can communicate with the service simply by letting them bind to it.

Creating the Bike Ride Recorder Project

The first thing you need to do is create the project. Follow these steps to create a project in Eclipse:

1. Create your new Android project by opening the File menu and selecting New ➪ Android Application Project.

2. Enter `Bike Ride Recorder` as the Application Name.

3. Enter `Bike Ride Recorder` again as the Project Name.

4. Enter `com.wiley.aoa.bike_ride_recorder` as the Package Name.

5. Set the minimum required SDK to 12; you could also build the project with the `USBAccessory` introduced in Android 2.3.4. If you do pick the backported version you should remember to pick the Google libraries.

6. Click Next.

7. Choose a launcher icon image or clipart that matches your preferences.

8. Select Next and allow Eclipse to create a `BlankActivity`.

9. Set the title of the `MainActivity` to `Bike Trip Recorder`.

Creating the User Interface

Although your app has three different user interfaces, one of them is created for you automatically within a `ListActivity`. The first of this section shows how to create the other two.

Creating the First View

Starting with the first view, your user will see the `activity_main.xml`. This view contains only two buttons, letting the user select to either start a new recording or view an already available recording. To center the buttons in the middle of the screen, create a container for them with the attributes `layout_centerHorizontal` and `layout_centerVertical` set to true. A vertically oriented `Linear Layout` will do the trick nicely. Open your `activity_main.xml` file and add the buttons as shown in Listing 9-6.

LISTING 9-6: Create the main menu for your app

```xml
<RelativeLayout xmlns:android="http://schemas.android.com/apk/res/android"
  xmlns:tools="http://schemas.android.com/tools"
  android:layout_width="match_parent"
  android:layout_height="match_parent" >
<LinearLayout
  android:layout_width="match_parent"
  android:layout_height="wrap_content"
  android:layout_centerHorizontal="true"
  android:layout_centerVertical="true"
  android:layout_margin="20dp"
  android:orientation="vertical" >
  <Button
    android:id="@+id/button_new"
    android:layout_width="match_parent"
    android:layout_height="wrap_content"
    android:onClick="menu_new"
    android:text="Start New Ride" />
  <Button
    android:id="@+id/button_load"
    android:layout_width="match_parent"
    android:layout_height="wrap_content"
    android:onClick="menu_load"
    android:text="Load Previous Ride" />
</LinearLayout>
</RelativeLayout>
```

Your main menu should look something like Figure 9-9.

Creating the Second View

The second view of your application is the view where you record your videos and data. Because you won't really interact with the application as you ride your bike, the interface should be really simple; add a `Button` to the top of the view and let a `FrameLayout` which will act as the container for the camera preview. But first, create your new layout file:

1. Open the File menu and select New ⇨ Other.

2. In the dialog box that appears, select Android XML Layout File and click Next.

3. In the File field, enter the name `activity_record`.

4. Select `RelativeLayout` as the Root Element and click Finish.

FIGURE 9-9: The main menu of your Bike Ride Recorder

Open your brand new layout file and add the `FrameLayout` and the `Button` as shown in Listing 9-7. Remember that about half the phone will be "submerged" in the physical object, so you should avoid placing UI widgets at the bottom half of the screen in this view.

LISTING 9-7: Add Button and FrameLayout to activity_record.xml

```xml
<?xml version="1.0" encoding="utf-8"?>
<RelativeLayout xmlns:android="http://schemas.android.com/apk/res/android"
  android:layout_width="match_parent"
  android:layout_height="match_parent" >
  <FrameLayout
    android:id="@+id/videoframe"
    android:layout_width="match_parent"
    android:layout_height="match_parent"
    android:layout_alignParentLeft="true"
    android:layout_alignParentTop="true" >
  </FrameLayout>
  <Button
    android:id="@+id/button_record"
    android:layout_width="match_parent"
    android:layout_height="wrap_content"
    android:onClick="record"
    android:text="Start Recording" />
</RelativeLayout>
```

The record view should look something like Figure 9-10.

Creating the Play View

The third, and last, user interface that you have to build yourself is the play view, consisting of a `VideoView` to display the video and a couple of `TextViews` where the data will be displayed. You'll use a `SlidingDrawer` to allow the user to hide the `TextViews`. Create the third, and last, layout file:

FIGURE 9-10: The record view for the Bike Ride Recorder

1. Open the File menu and select New ➪ Other.

2. In the dialog box that appears, select Android XML Layout File and click Next.

3. In the File field, enter the name `activity_play`.

4. Select `RelativeLayout` as the Root Element and click Finish.

Begin by adding the `VideoView`. Let it take up the entire screen by setting both width and height to `match_parent`. Because of some issues with video recording, you may get a frame around the video. To make this extra frame as unnoticeable as possible, set the background of the root container to the color black. See Listing 9-8 for details.

LISTING 9-8: Add Button and FrameLayout to activity_record.xml

```xml
<?xml version="1.0" encoding="utf-8"?>
<RelativeLayout xmlns:android="http://schemas.android.com/apk/res/android"
  android:layout_width="match_parent"
  android:layout_height="match_parent"
  android:background="#000000" >
  <VideoView
    android:id="@+id/video_playback"
    android:layout_width="match_parent"
    android:layout_height="match_parent"
    android:layout_centerInParent="true" />
</RelativeLayout>
```

Add the `SlidingDrawer` to the layout and let it take up the whole space above the `VideoView`. This creates an expandable and retractable user interface to display the data gathered during the bike ride. The `SlidingDrawer` widget has two children: the handle to slide the drawer in and out, and the content, which can be any of the other layout containers. The standard choice is always the `LinearLayout`, but in this project you use a `RelativeLayout` because that offers some more freedom to organize the contents. See Listing 9-9 for details on how to use the `SlidingDrawer`.

LISTING 9-9: Add the SlidingDrawer to the activity_record.xml

```xml
<?xml version="1.0" encoding="utf-8"?>
<RelativeLayout xmlns:android="http://schemas.android.com/apk/res/android"
  android:layout_width="match_parent"
  android:layout_height="match_parent"
  android:background="#000000" >
  <VideoView
    android:id="@+id/videoView1"
    android:layout_width="match_parent"
    android:layout_height="match_parent"
    android:layout_alignParentLeft="true"
    android:layout_alignParentTop="true"
    android:layout_alignParentBottom="true"
    android:layout_alignParentRight="true" />
  <SlidingDrawer
    android:id="@+id/slidingDrawer1"
    android:layout_width="match_parent"
```

continues

LISTING 9-9 *(continued)*

```
      android:layout_height="match_parent"
      android:layout_alignParentBottom="true"
      android:layout_alignParentLeft="true"
      android:content="@+id/content"
      android:handle="@+id/handle">
      <Button
        android:id="@+id/handle"
        android:layout_width="wrap_content"
        android:layout_height="wrap_content"
        android:text="Stats" />
      <RelativeLayout
        android:id="@+id/content"
        android:layout_width="wrap_content"
        android:layout_height="wrap_content"
        android:background="#aa000000" >
      </RelativeLayout>
    </SlidingDrawer>
  </RelativeLayout>
```

The `SlidingDrawer` contains four `TextViews`, each displaying its own data source, and you should organize them in some fashion. Add the `TextViews` shown in Listing 9-10.

LISTING 9-10: Add the TextViews to activity_play.xml

```
<?xml version="1.0" encoding="utf-8"?>
<RelativeLayout xmlns:android="http://schemas.android.com/apk/res/android"
  android:layout_width="match_parent"
  android:layout_height="match_parent"
  android:background="#000" >
  <VideoView
    android:id="@+id/videoView1"
    android:layout_width="match_parent"
    android:layout_height="match_parent"
    android:layout_alignParentLeft="true"
    android:layout_alignParentTop="true"
    android:layout_alignParentBottom="true"
    android:layout_alignParentRight="true" />
  <SlidingDrawer
    android:id="@+id/slidingDrawer1"
    android:layout_width="match_parent"
    android:layout_height="match_parent"
    android:layout_alignParentBottom="true"
    android:layout_alignParentLeft="true"
    android:content="@+id/content"
    android:handle="@+id/handle">
    <Button
      android:id="@+id/handle"
      android:layout_width="wrap_content"
      android:layout_height="wrap_content"
      android:text="Stats" />
    <RelativeLayout
```

```
        android:id="@+id/content"
        android:layout_width="wrap_content"
        android:layout_height="wrap_content"
        android:background="#aa000000" >
        <LinearLayout
          android:layout_width="wrap_content"
          android:layout_height="wrap_content"
          android:layout_alignParentLeft="true"
          android:layout_alignParentTop="true"
          android:orientation="vertical" >
          <TextView
            android:id="@+id/wheel_rpm"
            android:layout_width="wrap_content"
            android:layout_height="wrap_content"
            android:layout_margin="5dp"
            android:text="Large Text"
            android:textAppearance="?android:attr/textAppearanceLarge"
            android:textColor="#ccc" />
          <TextView
            android:id="@+id/wheel_speed"
            android:layout_width="wrap_content"
            android:layout_height="wrap_content"
            android:layout_margin="5dp"
            android:text="Large Text"
            android:textAppearance="?android:attr/textAppearanceLarge"
            android:textColor="#ccc" />
        </LinearLayout>
        <LinearLayout

          android:layout_width="wrap_content"
          android:layout_height="wrap_content"
          android:layout_alignParentRight="true"
          android:layout_alignParentTop="true"
          android:orientation="vertical" >
          <TextView
            android:id="@+id/pedal_rpm"
            android:layout_width="wrap_content"
            android:layout_height="wrap_content"
            android:layout_margin="5dp"
            android:text="Large Text"
            android:textAppearance="?android:attr/textAppearanceLarge"
            android:textColor="#ccc" />
          <TextView
            android:id="@+id/pedal_speed"
            android:layout_width="wrap_content"
            android:layout_height="wrap_content"
            android:layout_margin="5dp"
            android:text="Large Text"
            android:textAppearance="?android:attr/textAppearanceLarge"
            android:textColor="#ccc" />
        </LinearLayout>
      </RelativeLayout>
    </SlidingDrawer>
  </RelativeLayout>
```

The finished playback view should look something like Figure 9-11.

Before you build your Activities for your user interfaces you should create the service that handles the accessory connection, which the activities will connect to.

Setting up the AoaService

All the accessory communication for the Bike Ride Recorder is handled by a service, because this makes it easier on your end to access the information stream and communicate with the accessory from multiple activities and dialog boxes. Create the `AoaService.java` class, and let it extend `android.app.Service`.

FIGURE 9-11: The playback view

1.   Open the File menu and select New ⇨ Class.

2.   As the Package Name, enter `com.wiley.aoa` `.bike_ride_recorder`.

3.   Enter `AoaService` as the Name.

4.   As the Superclass, enter `android.app.Service`.

5.   Select the "Inherited abstract methods" checkbox to let Eclipse create all the required methods for the service, which is really just one method called `onBind`.

6.   Click Finish to create the class.

Your new `AoaService` class should look something like Listing 9-11.

LISTING 9-11: Add the TextViews to activity_play.xml

```
package com.wiley.aoa.bike_ride_recorder;
import android.app.Service;
import android.content.Intent;
import android.os.IBinder;
public class AoaService2 extends Service {
  @Override
  public IBinder onBind(Intent intent) {
    return null;
  }
}
```

Returning null in the `onBind` method means that no other components can connect to and communicate directly with the service. This is not what you're after because the service is the component that will contain the `WroxAccessory` connection. The `onBind` method then needs to return an instance of a special `Binder` class; the `Binder` is part of the asynchronous communication interface between a service and any other application component (for example, `Activity` or `BroadcastReceiver`).

Add an inner class to your new `AoaService.java` class, and call it `AoaBinder`. This binder class will be the interface to your `AoaService`, and should return the current instance of the `AoaService` to whoever binds to it. See Listing 9-12.

LISTING 9-12: Add the local binder

```
package com.wiley.aoa.bike_ride_recorder;
import android.app.Service;
import android.content.Intent;
import android.os.Binder;
import android.os.IBinder;
public class AoaService extends Service {
  private final IBinder mBinder = new AoaBinder();
  public class AoaBinder extends Binder {
    AoaService getService() {
      return AoaService.this;
    }
  }
  @Override
  public IBinder onBind(Intent intent) {
    return mBinder;
  }
}
```

Because your service runs both in the background waiting for clients to connect and with clients already bound to it, you should override all the life-cycle methods in your AoaService.java class. Let the onStartCommand return the constant START_STICKY; this means the service will continue running until explicitly stopped. See Listing 9-13.

LISTING 9-13: Override the life-cycle methods

```
package com.wiley.aoa.bike_ride_recorder;
import android.app.Service;
import android.content.Intent;
import android.os.Binder;
import android.os.IBinder;
public class AoaService extends Service {
  private final IBinder mBinder = new AoaBinder();
  public class AoaBinder extends Binder {
    AoaService getService() {
      return AoaService.this;
    }
  }
  @Override
  public void onCreate() {
    super.onCreate();
  }
  @Override
  public int onStartCommand(Intent intent, int flags, int startId) {
    return START_STICKY
  }
  @Override
  public IBinder onBind(Intent intent) {
    return mBinder;
  }
```

continues

LISTING 9-13 *(continued)*

```
  @Override
  public boolean onUnbind(Intent intent) {
    return super.onUnbind(intent);
  }
  @Override
  public void onDestroy() {
    super.onDestroy();
  }
}
```

THE LIFE CYCLE OF A SERVICE

You can run a Service on Android in two different ways: you can let it run by itself in the background without any clients connected to it, or you can bind clients to it. The first way requires you to stop the service yourself when the service is done with the task it is supposed to complete. If you decide to bind to a service, however, you don't necessarily need to keep track of the life of the service; it is recycled automatically by the system when the service is done with its task or when no more clients are connected to it.

There is a catch, though. If the life-cycle method onStartCommand() was executed, that means that the service won't be recycled automatically and you still need to stop the service manually when appropriate. The onStartCommand() method gets called whenever you start a service using the startService() method. If you only call bindService(), you're safe!

Add the WroxAccessory-specific code using UsbConnection12. (You can use UsbConnection10 or BTConnection too, but be aware that some of the code in the examples will change. See Chapter 6 for details on the different connection types.)

See Listing 9-14 for details on the added WroxAccessory code for your AoaService.

LISTING 9-14: Add the WroxAccessory code

```
package com.wiley.aoa.bike_ride_recorder;
import java.io.IOException;
import android.app.Service;
import android.content.Context;
import android.content.Intent;
import android.hardware.usb.UsbManager;
import android.os.Binder;
```

```
import android.os.IBinder;
import com.wiley.wroxaccessories.UsbConnection12;
import com.wiley.wroxaccessories.WroxAccessory;
public class AoaService extends Service {
  private WroxAccessory mAccessory;
  private UsbManager mUsbManager;
  private UsbConnection12 connection;
  private final IBinder mBinder = new AoaBinder();
  public class AoaBinder extends Binder {
    AoaService getService() {
      return AoaService.this;
    }
  }
  @Override
  public void onCreate() {
    super.onCreate();
    mUsbManager = (UsbManager) getSystemService(USB_SERVICE);
    connection = new UsbConnection12(this, mUsbManager);
    mAccessory = new WroxAccessory(this);
    try {
      mAccessory.connect(WroxAccessory.USB_ACCESSORY_12, connection);
    } catch (IOException e) {
      e.printStackTrace();
    }
  }
  @Override
  public void onDestroy() {
    super.onDestroy();
    try {
      mAccessory.disconnect();
    } catch (IOException e) {
      e.printStackTrace();
    }
  }
  @Override
  public int onStartCommand(Intent intent, int flags, int startId) {
    return START_STICKY;
  }
  @Override
  public IBinder onBind(Intent intent) {
    return mBinder;
  }
  @Override
  public boolean onUnbind(Intent intent) {
    return super.onUnbind(intent);
  }
}
```

Add a public method for your client to subscribe to the "bc" topic. See Listing 9-15.

LISTING 9-15: Create a method in the service to allow clients to subscribe to topics

```java
package com.wiley.aoa.bike_ride_recorder;
import android.content.BroadcastReceiver;
[...]
public class AoaService extends Service {
  private WroxAccessory mAccessory;
  private UsbManager mUsbManager;
  private UsbConnection12 connection;
  private int id;
  private final IBinder mBinder = new AoaBinder();
  public class AoaBinder extends Binder {
    AoaService getService() {
      return AoaService.this;
    }
  }
  [...]
  public String subscribe(BroadcastReceiver receiver, String topic) {
    String sub = null;
    try {
      sub = mAccessory.subscribe(receiver, topic, id++);
    } catch (IOException e) {
      e.printStackTrace();
    }
    return sub;
  }
}
```

Add the service tag to your `AndroidManifest` file, as shown in Listing 9-16.

LISTING 9-16: Add the service tag to your manifest

```xml
<manifest xmlns:android="http://schemas.android.com/apk/res/android"
  package="com.wiley.aoa.bike_trip_recorder"
  android:versionCode="1"
  android:versionName="1.0" >
  <uses-sdk
    android:minSdkVersion="12"
    android:targetSdkVersion="15" />
  <application
    android:icon="@drawable/ic_launcher"
    android:label="@string/app_name"
    android:theme="@style/AppTheme" >
    <activity
      android:name=".MainActivity"
      android:label="@string/title_activity_main" >
      <intent-filter>
        <action android:name="android.intent.action.MAIN" />
        <category android:name="android.intent.category.LAUNCHER" />
      </intent-filter>
    </activity>
    <service android:name="AoaService"></service>
  </application>
</manifest>
```

Building the Main Menu Activity

Recall from the activity_main.xml file that you added two Button widgets, each with its own onClick attribute. In MainActivity.java, then, you need to add these two methods. See the following code snippet:

```
public void menuNew(View v){
}
public void menuLoad(View v){
}
```

You also need to start the AoaService in this activity because it's the one that marks the start and end of your application. In the onCreate life-cycle method you should start the service by calling startService, and then in onDestroy you can stop the service with stopService. See Listing 9-17.

LISTING 9-17: Start, and stop, the AoaService

```
package com.wiley.aoa.bike_ride_recorder;
import android.app.Activity;
import android.os.Bundle;
import android.view.Menu;
import android.view.View;
public class MainActivity extends Activity {
  @Override
  public void onCreate(Bundle savedInstanceState) {
    super.onCreate(savedInstanceState);
    setContentView(R.layout.activity_main);
    startService(new Intent(MainActivity.this, AoaService.class));
  }
  @Override
  protected void onDestroy() {
    super.onDestroy();
    stopService(new Intent(MainActivity.this, AoaService.class));
  }
  @Override
  public boolean onCreateOptionsMenu(Menu menu) {
    getMenuInflater().inflate(R.menu.activity_main, menu);
    return true;
  }
  public void buttonNew(View v){
  }
  public void buttonLoad(View v){
  }
}
```

You'll fill in the button_new and button_load methods when you've created the corresponding activities, but for now you're done with the MainActivity.java file.

Building the Recording Activity

For simplicity's sake, you build this activity using a class developed by Google and available in the Android SDK Samples; the class you'll use is called CameraPreview.java and is available in the APIDemos project, inside the com.example.android.apis.graphics package.

1. To install the `APIDemos` project, open the File menu and select New ⇨ Other.

2. Expand the Android category and select Android Sample Project. Click Next.

3. Select Android 4.1 (SDK16) as the Build Target, and click Next.

4. Find the Sample called APIDemos and click Finish.

You should now have a new project in your Eclipse workspace called `ApiDemos`; find the class called `CameraPreview` located inside the `com.example.android.apis.graphics` package and copy it to your own project.

1. Select the `CameraPreview` class.

2. From the Edit menu, select Copy.

3. Expand your Bike Ride Recorder project.

4. Select the `com.wiley.aoa.bike_ride_recorder` package.

5. From the Edit menu, select Paste.

Now that you have the `CameraPreview` activity in your own project it's time to trim it; delete the methods called `onCreateOptionsMenu` and `onOptionsItemSelected`. Also remove the import statement `import com.example.android.apis.R`.

Let the `CameraPreview` use your previously built layout by modifying the `onCreate` method. Remove the following line:

```
setContentView(mPreview);
```

Replace it with the highlighted code from Listing 9-18.

LISTING 9-18: The modified onCreate method

```
[...]
@Override
protected void onCreate(Bundle savedInstanceState) {
  super.onCreate(savedInstanceState);
  requestWindowFeature(Window.FEATURE_NO_TITLE);
  getWindow().addFlags(WindowManager.LayoutParams.FLAG_FULLSCREEN);
  mPreview = new Preview(this);
  // setContentView(mPreview);
  setContentView(R.layout.activity_record);
  FrameLayout frame = (FrameLayout) findViewById(R.id.videoframe);
  frame.addView(mPreview);
  numberOfCameras = Camera.getNumberOfCameras();
  CameraInfo cameraInfo = new CameraInfo();
  for (int i = 0; i < numberOfCameras; i++) {
    Camera.getCameraInfo(i, cameraInfo);
    if (cameraInfo.facing == CameraInfo.CAMERA_FACING_BACK) {
      defaultCameraId = i;
    }
  }
}
[...]
```

In the `MainActivity` class, call `startActivity()` in the `button_new()` method, as shown in the following code snippet:

```
public void button_new(View v) {
   startActivity(new Intent(MainActivity.this, CameraPreview.class));
}
```

To get the camera preview to show in full-screen portrait mode, you need to edit a few more lines in the `Preview` inner class. Find the method called `onLayout`, and remove the following lines:

```
if (mPreviewSize != null) {
  previewWidth = mPreviewSize.width;
  previewHeight = mPreviewSize.height;
}
```

The method should then look like Listing 9-19.

LISTING 9-19: The modified onLayout method

```
[...]
@Override
protected void onLayout(boolean changed, int l, int t, int r, int b) {
   if (changed && getChildCount() > 0) {
     final View child = getChildAt(0);
     final int width = r - l;
     final int height = b - t;
     int previewWidth = width;
     int previewHeight = height;
     // if (mPreviewSize != null) {
     //    previewWidth = mPreviewSize.width;
     //    previewHeight = mPreviewSize.height;
     // }
     if (width * previewHeight > height * previewWidth) {
       final int scaledChildWidth = previewWidth * height / previewHeight;
       child.layout((width - scaledChildWidth) / 2, 0,
         (width + scaledChildWidth) / 2, height);
     } else {
       final int scaledChildHeight = previewHeight * width / previewWidth;
       child.layout(0, (height - scaledChildHeight) / 2, width,
         (height + scaledChildHeight) / 2);
     }
   }
}
[...]
```

This makes the camera preview display full screen even in portrait mode; however, the image will be rotated and distorted. To fix this there's a small hack you can use; find the `surfaceChanged` method and add the following line:

```
mCamera.setDisplayOrientation(90);
```

Place it just before the call to `startPreview`. This should rotate the camera preview back to normal and non-distorted. See Listing 9-20.

LISTING 9-20: The modified surfaceChanged method

```
public void surfaceChanged(SurfaceHolder holder, int format, int w, int h) {
  Camera.Parameters parameters = mCamera.getParameters();
  parameters.setPreviewSize(mPreviewSize.width, mPreviewSize.height);
  requestLayout();
  mCamera.setParameters(parameters);
  mCamera.setDisplayOrientation(90);
  mCamera.startPreview();
}
```

This class only shows the preview of the camera. To record video you need to add some more methods to it. Start by adding the prepareRecorder method; make sure to place it inside the CameraPreview activity, and not the inner class called Preview. See Listing 9-21.

LISTING 9-21: Add the prepareRecorder method

```
[...]
private MediaRecorder mMediaRecorder;
private boolean isRecording;
private String lastfilename;
@Override
protected void onCreate(Bundle savedInstanceState) {
  [...]
}
[...]
public void record(View v){
}
private boolean prepareRecorder() {
  mRecorder = new MediaRecorder();
  mCamera.unlock();
  mRecorder.setCamera(mCamera);
  mRecorder.setAudioSource(MediaRecorder.AudioSource.MIC);
  mRecorder.setVideoSource(MediaRecorder.VideoSource.CAMERA);
  mRecorder.setProfile(CamcorderProfile.get(CamcorderProfile.QUALITY_1080P));
  mRecorder.setOrientationHint(90);
  Date now = new Date();
  lastfilename = "brr_" + now.getTime();
  String path = getOutputFile(lastfilename + ".mp4");
  mRecorder.setOutputFile(path);
  mRecorder.setPreviewDisplay(mPreview.mHolder.getSurface());
  try {
    mRecorder.prepare();
  } catch (IllegalStateException e) {
    mRecorder.release();
    return false;
  } catch (IOException e) {
    mRecorder.release();
    return false;
  }
  return true;
}
}
class Preview extends ViewGroup implements SurfaceHolder.Callback[
[...]
```

The `prepareRecorder` method requires another method, though; a method that creates a new file for you in the public Movies directory, which is where you'll save all the media in this application. Add the `getOutputFile` method as shown in Listing 9-22.

LISTING 9-22: Add the getOutputFile method

```
[...]
private MediaRecorder mMediaRecorder;
private boolean isRecording;
private String lastfilename;
@Override
protected void onCreate(Bundle savedInstanceState) {
  [...]
}
[...]
public void record(View v) {
}
private boolean prepareRecorder() {
  mRecorder = new MediaRecorder();
  mCamera.unlock();
  mRecorder.setCamera(mCamera);
  mRecorder.setAudioSource(MediaRecorder.AudioSource.MIC);
  mRecorder.setVideoSource(MediaRecorder.VideoSource.CAMERA);
  mRecorder.setProfile(CamcorderProfile.get(CamcorderProfile.QUALITY_1080P));
  mRecorder.setOrientationHint(90);
  Date now = new Date();
  lastfilename = "brr_" + now.getTime();
  String path = getOutputFile(lastfilename + ".mp4");
  mRecorder.setOutputFile(path);
  mRecorder.setPreviewDisplay(mPreview.mHolder.getSurface());
  try {
    mRecorder.prepare();
  } catch (IllegalStateException e) {
    mRecorder.release();
    return false;
  } catch (IOException e) {
    mRecorder.release();
    return false;
  }
  return true;
}
  private String getOutputFile(String filename) {
    File mediaStorageDir =
      Environment.getExternalStoragePublicDirectory(Environment.DIRECTORY_MOVIES);
    File mediaFile = new File(mediaStorageDir, filename);
    if (!mediaStorageDir.exists())
      if (!mediaStorageDir.mkdirs())
        return null;
    return mediaFile.getAbsolutePath();
  }
}
class Preview extends ViewGroup implements SurfaceHolder.Callback {
[...]
```

Together, these two methods will handle the preparation of the `MediaRecorder` by setting all the required parameters to record in portrait mode, and by creating the unique filename starting with "brr_" and ending with the current time in milliseconds, which will always create a unique filename for you.

When saving a video or image from the camera to a place on the filesystem, it's important to pick the correct place. Saving the media to the public External Storage means that the file is accessible to any application on the device, which is unsafe. If you're recording sensitive media you should consider using the Internal Storage, which is accessible only to your application.

Add the code to start the recording inside your `record` method, as shown in Listing 9-23.

LISTING 9-23: Start and stop the recording inside record

```java
public void record(View v) {
  if (isRecording) {
    mMediaRecorder.stop();
    mMediaRecorder.release();
    mCamera.lock();
    isRecording = false;
    File dir =
      Environment.getExternalStoragePublicDirectory(Environment.DIRECTORY_MOVIES);
    File movie = new File(dir, lastfilename + ".mp4");
    File data = new File(dir, lastfilename + ".txt");
    MediaScannerConnection.scanFile(CameraPreview.this,
      new String[] { movie.getAbsolutePath(), data.getAbsolutePath() }, null,
        new MediaScannerConnection.OnScanCompletedListener() {
        public void onScanCompleted(String path, Uri uri) {
        }
      });
  } else {
    if (prepareRecorder()) {
      mMediaRecorder.start();
      isRecording = true;
    } else {
      mMediaRecorder.release();
    }
  }
}
```

The `MediaScannerConnection` in the above listing will make your recorded files available to other applications which might be good if you want to view your movies in your normal gallery application.

You need to do one more thing when starting the recording; subscribe to the sensor input values from the accessory. You'll do this by first binding the `AoaService` and then subscribing to the "bc" topic.

To bind to the service you first need the `ServiceConnection` object; add it to your `CameraPreview` `.java` class as seen in Listing 9-24.

LISTING 9-24: Add the ServiceConnection

```
public class CameraPreview extends Activity {
  [...]
  private AoaService mService;
  boolean isBound;
  @Override
  protected void onCreate(Bundle savedInstanceState) {
    super.onCreate(savedInstanceState);
    [...]
  }
  private ServiceConnection connection = new ServiceConnection() {
    @Override
    public void onServiceConnected(ComponentName name, IBinder service) {
      AoaService.AoaBinder binder = (AoaService.AoaBinder) service;
      mService = binder.getService();
      isBound = true;
    }
    @Override
    public void onServiceDisconnected(ComponentName name) {
      isBound = false;
    }
  };
}
```

This will only create the facilities needed to bind to the service however. You'll need to call the methods bindService and unbindService to actually bind and unbind to it. See Listing 9-25.

LISTING 9-25: Bind to the AoaService

```
public class CameraPreview extends Activity {
  private AoaService mService;
  boolean isBound;
  @Override
  protected void onCreate(Bundle savedInstanceState) {
    super.onCreate(savedInstanceState);
    [...]
  }
  @Override
  protected void onStart() {
    super.onStart();
    Intent service = new Intent(CameraPreview.this, AoaService.class);
    bindService(service, connection, BIND_AUTO_CREATE);
  }
  @Override
  protected void onStop() {
    super.onStop();
    if( isBound )
      unbindService(connection);
  }
  private ServiceConnection connection = new ServiceConnection() {
    @Override
    public void onServiceConnected(ComponentName name, IBinder service) {
```

continues

LISTING 9-25 *(continued)*

```
      AoaService.AoaBinder binder = (AoaService.AoaBinder) service;
      mService = binder.getService();
      isBound = true;
    }
    @Override
    public void onServiceDisconnected(ComponentName name) {
      isBound = false;
    }
  };
}
```

Having bound to the `AoaService` you're now free to start listening for updates from the accessory, and in particular updates for the sensor values. Add the `BroadcastReceiver` and call `subscribe` from within the `record` method to start listening for values. See Listing 9-26.

LISTING 9-26: Subscribe to updates from the accessory

```
public class CameraPreview extends Activity {
  [...]
  String subscription;
  public void record(View v) {
    if (isRecording) {
      mMediaRecorder.stop();
      mMediaRecorder.release();
      mCamera.lock();
      isRecording = false;
      File dir = Environment
          .getExternalStoragePublicDirectory(Environment.DIRECTORY_MOVIES);
      File movie = new File(dir, lastfilename + ".mp4");
      File data = new File(dir, lastfilename + ".txt");
      MediaScannerConnection.scanFile(CameraPreview.this, new String[] {
          movie.getAbsolutePath(), data.getAbsolutePath() }, null,
          new MediaScannerConnection.OnScanCompletedListener() {
            public void onScanCompleted(String path, Uri uri) {
            }
          });
    } else {
      if (prepareRecorder()) {
        mMediaRecorder.start();
        subscription = mService.subscribe(mReceiver, "bc");
        isRecording = true;
      } else {
        mMediaRecorder.release();
      }
    }
  }
  private BroadcastReceiver mReceiver = new BroadcastReceiver() {
    @Override
    public void onReceive(Context context, Intent intent) {
      byte[] payload = intent.getByteArrayExtra(subscription + ".payload");
    }
  };
}
```

This will give you the whole list of bytes with the values read by the sensors; all you need to do now is the store them temporarily in JavaScript Object Notation (JSON) arrays, which will later be saved to a file when the movie is done recording. When you play this movie back the text file will also be opened and the correct values will be read as the movie is being played. Add the JSON specific code as shown in Listing 9-27.

LISTING 9-27: Add the JSON specific code

```
public class CameraPreview extends Activity {
  [...]
  private JSONObject recording;
  private JSONArray wheel_speed, wheel_rpm;
  private JSONArray pedal_speed, pedal_rpm;
  [...]
  BroadcastReceiver receiver = new BroadcastReceiver() {
    @Override
    public void onReceive(Context context, Intent intent) {
      if (intent.getAction().equals(subscription)) {
        byte[] payload = intent.getByteArrayExtra(subscription
            + ".payload");
        wheel_speed.put(payload[0]);
        wheel_rpm.put(payload[1]);
        pedal_speed.put(payload[2]);
        pedal_rpm.put(payload[3]);
      }
    }
  };
  [...]
  public void record(View v) {
    if (isRecording) {
      mMediaRecorder.stop();
      mMediaRecorder.release();
      mCamera.lock();
      isRecording = false;
      File dir = Environment
          .getExternalStoragePublicDirectory(Environment.DIRECTORY_MOVIES);
      File movie = new File(dir, lastfilename + ".mp4");
      File data = new File(dir, lastfilename + ".txt");
      MediaScannerConnection.scanFile(CameraPreview.this, new String[] {
          movie.getAbsolutePath(), data.getAbsolutePath() }, null,
          new MediaScannerConnection.OnScanCompletedListener() {
            public void onScanCompleted(String path, Uri uri) {
            }
          });
    } else {
      if (prepareRecorder()) {
        wheel_rpm = new JSONArray();
        wheel_speed = new JSONArray();
        pedal_rpm = new JSONArray();
        pedal_speed = new JSONArray();
        mMediaRecorder.start();
        subscription = mService.subscribe(receiver, "bc");
        isRecording = true;
```

continues

LISTING 9-27 *(continued)*

```
            } else {
              mMediaRecorder.release();
            }
          }
        }
      }
```

When the recording has stopped you also need to write all the extra sensor data which now only exists in the temporary JSONArrays. Add the writeToTextFile method and call it from within the record method — just before you release the MediaRecorder object. See Listing 9-28 below.

LISTING 9-28: Add the writeToTextFile method

```
public class CameraPreview extends Activity {
  […]
  public void record(View v) {
    if (isRecording) {
      mMediaRecorder.stop();
      mMediaRecorder.release();
      mCamera.lock();
      isRecording = false;
      File dir = Environment
          .getExternalStoragePublicDirectory(Environment.DIRECTORY_MOVIES);
      File movie = new File(dir, lastfilename + ".mp4");
      File data = new File(dir, lastfilename + ".txt");
      MediaScannerConnection.scanFile(CameraPreview.this, new String[] {
          movie.getAbsolutePath(), data.getAbsolutePath() }, null,
          new MediaScannerConnection.OnScanCompletedListener() {
            public void onScanCompleted(String path, Uri uri) {
            }
          });
    } else {
      if (prepareRecorder()) {
        // JSON Code
        wheel_rpm = new JSONArray();
        wheel_speed = new JSONArray();
        pedal_rpm = new JSONArray();
        pedal_speed = new JSONArray();
        mMediaRecorder.start();
        subscription = mService.subscribe(receiver, "bc");
        isRecording = true;
      } else {
        writeToTextFile();
        mMediaRecorder.release();
      }
    }
  }
  private void writeToTextFile(){
    String json_path = getOutputFile(lastfilename + ".txt");
    recording = new JSONObject();
    try {
      recording.put("wheel_speed", wheel_speed);
```

```
        recording.put("wheel_rpm", wheel_rpm);
        recording.put("pedal_speed", pedal_speed);
        recording.put("pedal_rpm", pedal_rpm);
        FileWriter fwriter = new FileWriter(json_path);
        fwriter.append(recording.toString());
        fwriter.flush();
        fwriter.close();
      } catch (JSONException je) {
        je.printStackTrace();
      } catch (IOException e) {
        e.printStackTrace();
      }
    }
  }
}
```

Add the `CameraPreview` activity to your `AndroidManifest` file. Because this activity also uses the camera, you need to add a few camera-specific permissions and features to the manifest. Because you're recording to the external filesystem (the SD card in many phones), you also need permission to read and write to it. See Listing 9-29 for details.

LISTING 9-29: Add the CameraPreview activity

```
<manifest xmlns:android="http://schemas.android.com/apk/res/android"
  package="com.wiley.aoa.bike_trip_recorder"
  android:versionCode="1"
  android:versionName="1.0" >
  <uses-sdk
    android:minSdkVersion="12"
    android:targetSdkVersion="15" />
  <uses-permission android:name="android.permission.CAMERA" />
  <uses-feature
    android:name="android.hardware.camera"
    android:required="true" />
  <uses-permission android:name="android.permission.WRITE_EXTERNAL_STORAGE" />
  <uses-permission android:name="android.permission.READ_EXTERNAL_STORAGE" />
  <uses-permission android:name="android.permission.RECORD_AUDIO" />
  <application
    android:icon="@drawable/ic_launcher"
    android:label="@string/app_name"
    android:theme="@style/AppTheme" >
    <activity
      android:name=".MainActivity"
      android:label="@string/title_activity_main" >
      <intent-filter>
        <action android:name="android.intent.action.MAIN" />
        <category android:name="android.intent.category.LAUNCHER" />
      </intent-filter>
    </activity>
    <service android:name="AoaService"></service>
    <activity android:name="CameraPreview"
      android:screenOrientation="portrait">
    </activity>
  </application>
</manifest>
```

Building the List Recordings View

Create a new `Activity`, call it `ListRecordingsActivity`, and let it extend the `ListActivity` class:

1. From the File menu, select New ⇨ Class.

2. Enter `com.wiley.aoa.bike_ride_recorder` as the Package Name.

3. As the Name, enter `ListRecordingsActivity`.

4. As the Superclass, enter `android.app.ListActivity`.

5. Click Finish to create the class.

The only thing this class will do is create a list of all past recordings, and then allow the user to select to play one by clicking it. To list all movies you first need to find them all, so create a method that generates a String array of all movie files inside the public Movie folder whose names start with "brr_" (see Listing 9-30).

LISTING 9-30: Create the getAllMovies method

```
package com.wiley.aoa.bike_ride_recorder;
import java.io.File;
import java.io.FilenameFilter;
import android.app.ListActivity;
import android.os.Environment;
public class ListRecordingsActivity extends ListActivity {
  private String[] getAllMovies() {
    File mediaStorageDir =
      Environment.getExternalStoragePublicDirectory(Environment.DIRECTORY_MOVIES);
    FilenameFilter filter = new FilenameFilter() {
      @Override
      public boolean accept(File dir, String filename) {
        return (filename.endsWith(".mp4") && filename.contains("brr_"));
      }
    };
    return mediaStorageDir.list(filter);
  }
}
```

Initialize the built-in `ListView` of the `ListRecordingsActivity` and populate it using your new method. See Listing 9-31.

LISTING 9-31: Initialize the ListView

```
package com.wiley.aoa.bike_trip_recorder;
import java.io.File;
import java.io.FilenameFilter;
import android.app.ListActivity;
import android.os.Bundle;
import android.os.Environment;
import android.widget.ArrayAdapter;
public class ListRecordingsActivity extends ListActivity {
  String[] files;
  @Override
```

```
protected void onCreate(Bundle savedInstanceState) {
  super.onCreate(savedInstanceState);
  files = getAllMovies();
  ArrayAdapter<String> adapter = new ArrayAdapter<String>(this,
    android.R.layout.simple_list_item_1, files);
  setListAdapter(adapter);
}
private String[] getAllMovies() {
  File mediaStorageDir =
    Environment.getExternalStoragePublicDirectory(Environment.DIRECTORY_MOVIES);
  FilenameFilter filter = new FilenameFilter() {
    @Override
    public boolean accept(File dir, String filename) {
      return (filename.endsWith(".mp4") && filename.contains("brr_"));
    }
  };
  return mediaStorageDir.list(filter);
}
}
```

Let `ListRecordingsActivity` implement the interface `onItemClickListener`. This allows it to listen for clicks on each row of the `ListView` and to load the selected movie, as shown in Listing 9-32.

LISTING 9-32: Implement the onItemClickListener

```
package com.wiley.aoa.bike_trip_recorder;
import java.io.File;
import java.io.FilenameFilter;
import android.app.ListActivity;
import android.content.Intent;
import android.os.Bundle;
import android.os.Environment;
import android.view.View;
import android.widget.AdapterView;
import android.widget.AdapterView.OnItemClickListener;
import android.widget.ArrayAdapter;
public class ListRecordingsActivity extends ListActivity implements
    OnItemClickListener {
  String[] files;
  @Override
  protected void onCreate(Bundle savedInstanceState) {
    super.onCreate(savedInstanceState);
    files = getAllMovies();
    ArrayAdapter<String> adapter = new ArrayAdapter<String>(this,
        android.R.layout.simple_list_item_1, files);
    setListAdapter(adapter);
    getListView().setOnItemClickListener(this);
  }
  private String[] getAllMovies() {
    File mediaStorageDir =
      Environment.getExternalStoragePublicDirectory(Environment.DIRECTORY_MOVIES);
    FilenameFilter filter = new FilenameFilter() {
      @Override
      public boolean accept(File dir, String filename) {
```

continues

LISTING 9-32 *(continued)*

```
            return (filename.endsWith(".mp4") && filename.contains("brr_"));
        }
    };
    return mediaStorageDir.list(filter);
}
@Override
public void onItemClick(AdapterView<?> parent, View v, int position, long id) {
    Intent playmovie = new Intent(ListMoviesActivity.this, PlayActivity.class);
    playmovie.putExtra("filename", files[position]);
    startActivity(playmovie);
}
}
```

Notice that the intent you're creating here has an extra field that contains the filename of the
selected recording. Add the `ListRecordingsActivity` to the `AndroidManifest.xml` file, as shown
in Listing 9-33.

LISTING 9-33: Add the ListRecordingsActivity to the AndroidManifest.xml file

```
<manifest xmlns:android="http://schemas.android.com/apk/res/android"
  package="com.wiley.aoa.bike_trip_recorder"
  android:versionCode="1"
  android:versionName="1.0" >
  <uses-sdk
    android:minSdkVersion="12"
    android:targetSdkVersion="15" />
  <uses-permission android:name="android.permission.CAMERA" />
  <uses-feature
    android:name="android.hardware.camera"
    android:required="true" />
  <uses-permission android:name="android.permission.WRITE_EXTERNAL_STORAGE" />
  <uses-permission android:name="android.permission.READ_EXTERNAL_STORAGE" />
  <uses-permission android:name="android.permission.RECORD_AUDIO" />
  <application
    android:icon="@drawable/ic_launcher"
    android:label="@string/app_name"
    android:theme="@style/AppTheme" >
    <activity
      android:name=".MainActivity"
      android:label="@string/title_activity_main" >
      <intent-filter>
        <action android:name="android.intent.action.MAIN" />
        <category android:name="android.intent.category.LAUNCHER" />
      </intent-filter>
    </activity>
    <service android:name="AoaService"></service>
    <activity android:name=".CameraPreview" android:screenOrientation="portrait">
    </activity>
    <activity android:name="ListMoviesActivity" >
    </activity>
  </application>
</manifest>
```

Building the Playback View Activity

The `PlayActivity` contains the `VideoView` where you'll play the recorded movie. It also contains some `TextViews` where you'll update the data recorded by the accessory. Create the `PlayActivity` `.java` class:

1. From the File menu, select New ⇨ Class.

2. Enter `com.wiley.aoa.bike_ride_recorder` as the Package Name.

3. As the Name, enter `PlayActivity`.

4. Enter `android.app.Activity` as the Superclass.

5. Click Finish to create the class.

Start by loading the entire user interface which consists of the four `TextViews` and the `VideoView`. See Listing 9-34.

LISTING 9-34: Load the user interface of the PlayActivity

```java
package com.wiley.aoa.bike_ride_recorder;
import android.app.Activity;
import android.os.Bundle;
import android.view.Window;
import android.widget.TextView;
import android.widget.VideoView;
public class PlayActivity extends Activity {
  TextView wheel_speed, wheel_rpm, pedal_speed, pedal_rpm;
  VideoView videoview;
  @Override
  protected void onCreate(Bundle savedInstanceState) {
    super.onCreate(savedInstanceState);
    getWindow().requestFeature(Window.FEATURE_NO_TITLE);
    setContentView(R.layout.activity_play);
    wheel_speed = (TextView) findViewById(R.id.wheel_speed);
    wheel_rpm = (TextView) findViewById(R.id.wheel_rpm);
    pedal_speed = (TextView) findViewById(R.id.pedal_speed);
    pedal_rpm = (TextView) findViewById(R.id.pedal_rpm);
    videoview = (VideoView) findViewById(R.id.videoView1);
  }
}
```

If you want to avoid displaying the title bar when viewing videos, go ahead and request the specific window feature as shown here:

```java
getWindow().requestFeature(Window.FEATURE_NO_TITLE);
```

To load the correct file, get the filename from the intent (passed from the `ListRecordingsActivity`) and call the method `setVideoUri`, as shown in Listing 9-35.

LISTING 9-35: Add the readFile method

```
package com.wiley.aoa.bike_trip_recorder;
import java.io.File;
import android.app.Activity;
import android.net.Uri;
import android.os.Bundle;
import android.os.Environment;
import android.view.Window;
import android.widget.TextView;
import android.widget.VideoView;
public class PlayActivity extends Activity {
  TextView wheel_speed, wheel_rpm, pedal_speed, pedal_rpm;
  VideoView videoview;
  @Override
  protected void onCreate(Bundle savedInstanceState) {
    super.onCreate(savedInstanceState);
    getWindow().requestFeature(Window.FEATURE_NO_TITLE);
    setContentView(R.layout.activity_play);
    wheel_speed = (TextView) findViewById(R.id.wheel_speed);
    wheel_rpm = (TextView) findViewById(R.id.wheel_rpm);
    pedal_speed = (TextView) findViewById(R.id.pedal_speed);
    pedal_rpm = (TextView) findViewById(R.id.pedal_rpm);
    videoview = (VideoView) findViewById(R.id.videoView1);
    String filename = getIntent().getStringExtra("filename");
    File mediaDir = Environment
        .getExternalStoragePublicDirectory(Environment.DIRECTORY_MOVIES);
    File mediaFile = new File(mediaDir, filename);
    videoview.setVideoURI(Uri.parse(mediaFile.getAbsolutePath()));
    videoview.requestFocus();
  }
}
```

Add the buttonPlay method, which is connected to the onClick attribute of the Button inside the SlidingDrawer that you built earlier in this chapter. See Listing 9-36.

LISTING 9-36: Start the playback from the buttonPlay method

```
package com.wiley.aoa.bike_trip_recorder;
import java.io.File;
import android.app.Activity;
import android.net.Uri;
import android.os.Bundle;
import android.os.Environment;
import android.view.View;
import android.view.Window;
import android.widget.TextView;
import android.widget.VideoView;
public class PlayActivity extends Activity {
  TextView wheel_speed, wheel_rpm, pedal_speed, pedal_rpm;
  VideoView videoview;
  @Override
  protected void onCreate(Bundle savedInstanceState) {
```

```
      super.onCreate(savedInstanceState);
      getWindow().requestFeature(Window.FEATURE_NO_TITLE);
      setContentView(R.layout.activity_play);
      wheel_speed = (TextView) findViewById(R.id.wheel_speed);
      wheel_rpm = (TextView) findViewById(R.id.wheel_rpm);
      pedal_speed = (TextView) findViewById(R.id.pedal_speed);
      pedal_rpm = (TextView) findViewById(R.id.pedal_rpm);
      videoview = (VideoView) findViewById(R.id.videoView1);
      String filename = getIntent().getStringExtra("filename");
      File mediaDir = Environment
          .getExternalStoragePublicDirectory(Environment.DIRECTORY_MOVIES);
      File mediaFile = new File(mediaDir, filename);
      videoview.setVideoURI(Uri.parse(mediaFile.getAbsolutePath()));
      videoview.requestFocus();
    }
    public void buttonPlay(View v){
      videoview.start();
    }
  }
```

The last thing you need for the PlayView is to load and display the recorded sensor data for your bike trip. As you recall, the recording is stored in a text file which is encoded according to the JSON format. You'll need a way to open the file contents and read them into a JSON object which you'll then read values from and display on screen through TextViews.

Start by reading the file contents; add the readFile method as shown in Listing 9-37.

LISTING 9-37: Add the readFile method

```
package com.wiley.aoa.bike_trip_recorder;
import java.io.BufferedReader;
import java.io.DataInputStream;
import java.io.File;
import java.io.FileInputStream;
import java.io.IOException;
import java.io.InputStreamReader;
import android.app.Activity;
import android.net.Uri;
import android.os.AsyncTask;
import android.os.Bundle;
import android.os.Environment;
import android.view.View;
import android.view.Window;
import android.widget.TextView;
import android.widget.VideoView;
public class PlayActivity extends Activity {
  TextView wheel_speed, wheel_rpm, pedal_speed, pedal_rpm;
  VideoView videoview;
  @Override
  protected void onCreate(Bundle savedInstanceState) {
    super.onCreate(savedInstanceState);
    getWindow().requestFeature(Window.FEATURE_NO_TITLE);
    setContentView(R.layout.activity_play);
```

continues

LISTING 9-37 *(continued)*

```
      wheel_speed = (TextView) findViewById(R.id.wheel_speed);
      wheel_rpm = (TextView) findViewById(R.id.wheel_rpm);
      pedal_speed = (TextView) findViewById(R.id.pedal_speed);
      pedal_rpm = (TextView) findViewById(R.id.pedal_rpm);
      videoview = (VideoView) findViewById(R.id.videoView1);
      String filename = getIntent().getStringExtra("filename");
      File mediaDir = Environment
          .getExternalStoragePublicDirectory(Environment.DIRECTORY_MOVIES);
      File mediaFile = new File(mediaDir, filename);
      File dataFile = new File(mediaDir, filename.replace("mp4", "txt"));
      String file = null;
      try {
        file = readFile(dataFile);
      } catch (IOException e) {
        e.printStackTrace();
      }
      videoview.setVideoURI(Uri.parse(mediaFile.getAbsolutePath()));
      videoview.requestFocus();
    }
    public void button_play(View v) {
      videoview.start();
    }
    private String readFile(File dataFile) throws IOException {
      FileInputStream fstream = new FileInputStream(dataFile);
      DataInputStream in = new DataInputStream(fstream);
      BufferedReader reader = new BufferedReader(new InputStreamReader(in));
      StringBuffer sb = new StringBuffer();
      String line;
      while ((line = reader.readLine()) != null)
        sb.append(line);
      return sb.toString();
    }
  }
```

The readFile method returns a single string with all the contents of the text file. This string can then be used to create a JSONObject which contains all the recorded data; you don't want to display all of this data instantly so you should create a thread to only update the UI when appropriate — a good choice for this would be an AsyncTask since those also include a nice method to post updates to the UI. Add the DisplayTask to your PlayActivity, seen in Listing 9-38.

LISTING 9-38: Update the TextViews with the DisplayTask

```
package com.wiley.aoa.bike_trip_recorder;
[…]
import org.json.JSONArray;
import org.json.JSONException;
import org.json.JSONObject;
public class PlayActivity extends Activity {
  TextView wheel_speed, wheel_rpm, pedal_speed, pedal_rpm;
  VideoView videoview;
```

```
private DisplayTask displaytask;
@Override
protected void onCreate(Bundle savedInstanceState) {
  [...]
  displaytask = new DisplayTask(file);
}
public void button_play(View v) {
  videoview.start();
  displaytask.execute();
}
private class DisplayTask extends AsyncTask<String, Integer, Void> {
  JSONArray data_wheel_speed, data_wheel_rpm;
  JSONArray data_pedal_speed, data_pedal_rpm;
  String json;
  public DisplayTask(String json) {
    this.json = json;
  }
  @Override
  protected Void doInBackground(String... params) {
    try {
      JSONObject root = new JSONObject(json);
      data_wheel_speed = root.getJSONArray("wheel_speed");
      data_wheel_rpm = root.getJSONArray("wheel_rpm");
      data_pedal_speed = root.getJSONArray("pedal_speed");
      data_pedal_rpm = root.getJSONArray("pedal_rpm");
    } catch (JSONException e) {
      e.printStackTrace();
    }
    int length = wheel_speed.length();
    for (int i = 0; i < length; i++) {
      this.publishProgress(i);
      try {
        Thread.sleep(100);
      } catch (InterruptedException e) {
        e.printStackTrace();
      }
    }
    return null;
  }
  @Override
  protected void onProgressUpdate(Integer... vals) {
    for (int i = 0; i < vals.length; i++) {
      try {
        wheel_speed.setText(Integer.toString(data_wheel_speed.getInt(vals[i])));
        wheel_rpm.setText(Integer.toString(data_wheel_rpm.getInt(vals[i])));
        pedal_speed.setText(Integer.toString(data_pedal_speed.getInt(vals[i])));
        pedal_rpm.setText(Integer.toString(data_pedal_rpm.getInt(vals[i])));
      } catch (JSONException e) {
        e.printStackTrace();
      }
    }
  }
}
}
```

Making Further Improvements

This section gives some suggestions on what you might consider doing to take the chapter project to the next level. We, therefore, offer tweaks and improvements you might consider both to the project's mechanics, sensors and to the app itself.

Mechanics

The current box for the project is just the first iteration of what it could become. Once the code is clean enough, the first thing to take into account is hiding all metallic contacts. This means the box will take a completely different shape. It would also be clever to make a design that completely covers the phone (except for the camera) to protect it from adverse weather conditions. For this reason, you should consider using transparent acrylic at least for part of the box.

More Sensors

As mentioned in the beginning of the chapter, this project is an invitation to make better measurements of the effort expended while exercising. Other interesting sensors that could provide information about your physical condition could be:

➤ A pulse sensor implemented on the handle by exposing a couple of metallic contacts. It will help measuring your heart condition while exercising.

➤ A gyroscope to measure the bike's angle in respect to the ground.

➤ A pressure sensor under the seat because cycling while you stand requires a greater effort than when you sit.

The question is not so much to map all this data, but how it can be translated into effort or energy consumption. In other words, you should figure a way to map all that information into kilocalories to understand whether or not you are allowed to eat that pizza for dinner!

Making a Better App

You could make many improvements to the Android app in this project; most of them are related to the Android design principles and making the user interface more attractive and accessible. Some of the most obvious improvements are:

➤ In the `CameraPreview` class, you can have the Start Recording button change appearance depending on the state of the `MediaRecorder`. When you're recording it should, at minimum, change the text to Stop Recording. Preferably you should even change the visual appearance of it using images.

➤ You can apply the previous tip to the button in the `PlayActivity` too, letting it change appearance depending on the state of the `VideoView`.

➤ Create a new activity that displays the overall stats for all of your bike rides and your last bike ride, and then visually compare them in a graph.

➤   You can develop a SQLite database to store everything instead of writing it to common text files; this protects the data from accidental deletion by other apps. If you wanted to open the data up to other apps later on, you could add a `ContentProvider`.

➤   The SlidingDrawer used in the `PlayView` activity can be designed in a better fashion; for example making it only occupy the lower part of the user interface.

SUMMARY

The process of creating a reliable data gathering platform is now shorter than ever thanks to off-the-shelf cell phones (and tablets) together with embedded electronics. The Bike Rider Recorder project is an example of how to integrate electronics, mechanical design, and software.

For projects made using Arduino boards as an embedded platform, you can use hardware interrupts when you interface any kind of digital input device requiring a high-speed response. Interrupts refer to callback functions when attached. In that way, when the interrupt condition is met, the program stops whatever it is doing and executes the callback function instead. Arduino's core uses software interrupts, also known as timers, to measure time and operate PWM pins as well as the delay function. Disabling interrupts prevents those (PWM and delay) from working.

There is a difference between attaching/detaching interrupts and enabling/disabling them. Attaching implies configuring the processor to start using interrupts; enabling implies getting the processor to start listening to interrupts.

Using the camera in Android requires you to attach a `SurfaceView` class to show the preview; the camera won't record images or videos without this preview. You also need to add the `uses-permission` element to your `AndroidManifest.xml` when using the camera; and to follow standard procedure when using any hardware features, you should declare a `uses-feature` element for the camera.

When you're done with the camera you should always return possession of it to the system by calling `release()` on it, otherwise other applications wanting to use the camera will fail.

10

Kitchen Lamp

WHAT'S IN THIS CHAPTER?

➤ Using extremely long LED strips

➤ Using high-current power supplies

➤ Sending notifications to accessories

➤ Housing your boards

➤ Bit-banging versus SPI

In this chapter you build a kitchen lamp as an accessory to your Android device. It will be augmenting notifications from your phone (call or SMS arrivals, or the status of a timer) by means of using the light coming from a stripe with 144 full-color LEDs.

This chapter takes you through the process of building a real-life accessory, one that people use every day. We opted for a kitchen lamp, because the kitchen is an environment where it makes a lot of sense to have some sort of hands-free interaction with some of the existing appliances. We also chose a lamp because kitchens are noisy and light seems the most effective way to get feedback from the phone/tablet. We could as well connect the phone's audio jack to a sound amplifier to listen to any kind of notifications. However, in this case you are going to explore the possibilities offered by light, its intensity and color.

We are positive you have at least one lamp in your kitchen. We hope that looking at how we brought this project to life will trigger your imagination and push you into building something that you will use. You learn the most when you try to fit the device's behavior to your personal needs.

THE CONCEPT

We did some research looking for possible materials, and we came to the conclusion that it would be interesting to use an RGB (as in full-color) addressable LED strip, because it would enable us to make small animations to trigger different events that happen while in the kitchen.

The Android device doesn't detect whether there is anyone in the kitchen, neither does the Arduino board used in this project. It will trigger events happening in the phone/tablet like the arrival of an SMS or reaching the timeout of a timer, but if the user is not there to see them, it will be as if they hadn't happened.

Kitchens are noisy. The air extractor might be running, or the microwave might be on, or you might be using the blender; you might be listening to louder-than-necessary music just for those reasons. How can you then notice the arrival of a certain notification on your phone? This is when the idea crossed our minds: we had to connect the RGB-LED kitchen lamp to our Android device. In that way, the phone/tablet would be triggering the events and reporting back to the LEDs.

Because this was going to be part of a real kitchen (see Figure 10-1), and a serious investment in terms of time and money had to be made, we had to put a lot of focus on creating a really high finish of the lamp. The lamp had to be aesthetically pleasant. This should not be a prototype, but a real lamp to be installed in my kitchen for the next 15 or 20 years. The lamp itself consists of a line of 114 RGB LEDs and is almost 3 m long. It is covered by a 5 mm-thick layer of translucent acrylic. The tiles on the wall are of a white that nicely matches the color of the plastic.

FIGURE 10-1: View of the kitchen mentioned in the project

Making this project required us to think in a slightly different way in comparison to the other projects included in this book. Here the object was (and is) going to be part of the everyday life of everyday people. This is a design challenge, but also an interesting opportunity and a great excuse to get hands-on with electronics and software.

THE DESIGN BRIEF

When building a project like this lamp, where we involved a furniture designer and carpenter in the process, it is convenient to have a framework that allows everyone to be on the same page. It's not only important to budget time, but also to make sure that those building the actual objects are aware of not just the function but also the aesthetic you expect of your installation. My co-author and I were the ones deciding what materials (LEDs and power supply in this case) we were going to use. But it had to be the carpenter who figured out how to embed that into the kitchen. A 3 m-long lamp is not something you can easily get rid of.

The brief to the project allows building a framework for the different stakeholders to discuss. The following list outlines the goals of this project:

➤ Create a lamp to illuminate the stove and sink area of a kitchen.

➤ Make sure the lamp operates as a lamp (using white light) by default, requiring no further interaction from a user than pressing the on/off switch.

➤ Make the lamp act as an Android accessory offering the possibility of augmenting parts of the notification system of the phone by means of using light.

➤ Make the lamp respond to the arrival of SMS and phone calls with different light animations.

➤ Enable the lamp to be used as a cooking timer showing the amount of time left as a VU-meter (all the lights on is 100 percent of the time, half the lights is 50 percent of the time, and so on). Figure 10-2 is an example of this functionality.

FIGURE 10-2: Lamp acting as VU-meter

THE ARDUINO SIDE

This project's bill of materials does not include many parts (see Figure 10-3). Essentially, you need the Arduino Mega ADK, some small parts, and an LED strip. The key to having a lamp you really want to use and that will make your kitchen time more enjoyable (and even playful) is choosing the right LED strip. You need to find one that is easy to control from your software with a minimal set of commands.

Many types of LED strips are available, and they differ depending on which drivers they use to control the LEDs. The drivers are chips that can control both the amount and color of light projected by each LED, and the communication to/from the microcontroller board.

The LED lamp, which we had designed for the kitchen, had to be placed on top of the area where we cook. The furniture designer suggested making a lamp as long as the kitchen's bench. A nice way of making a lamp that long (3 meters in this case) is using LED strips.

What allows having very long LED strips is the fact that those drivers can be daisy-chained. They have a serial-in pin and a serial-out pin. The data comes in through the input and, one instant later, it is pushed out through the output. Yet another pin on the chip, called a latch, tells the chips whether they should load the data in their internal memory, thus pushing different RGB values to the LEDs, or if they (the chips) should just do nothing about that data.

This brings a certain complexity in the software. If you want to change the color of a certain LED, you will need to send data for all the LEDs at once. You can do this via software by keeping a buffer in memory to store the color information for all the LEDs and pushing out the whole buffer toward the strip every time you want to change the color of one or many of the LEDs.

But you are lucky this time! Because this type of strip has been around for quite a while, you can find a whole series of different libraries to gracefully handle the strip. You just need to find the one that best accommodates your needs.

AVOID USING SPI TO RUN YOUR STRIP … SOMETIMES

If you want to explore the different libraries that exist, keep in mind that the Arduino Mega ADK and compatible boards use a chip to handle the USB Host functionality. The communication between Arduino's main processor and that chip happens through the internal SPI peripheral.

Some implementations of libraries use SPI as a way to communicate with the strip, whereas some others use the bit-banging technique. Bit-banging means writing your code to implement — via software — an algorithm to communicate between chips using one or several pins. That functionality could be existing at an internal peripheral inside the processor. Usually internal peripherals operate much faster than the bit-banging version of the same technique.

An analogy for the bit-banging vs. internal peripheral discussion would be an MP3 player. You can have a software MP3 player, made as a program running in your computer (like WinAmp, Rhythmbox or iTunes). At the same time, you can have a dedicated chip to do MP3 decompression. While the same software can run on multiple computers, the dedicated chip is much more efficient. In this analogy, bit-banging is like the software decompressing MP3, while the internal peripheral is represented by the decoding chip.

Using the internal SPI allows for faster interaction with the strip, which leads to less CPU time, on the embedded side, to handle the strip. On the other hand, it will make it very hard to keep communicating with the USB Host chip, as both the USB Host library and the LED strip need to use the SPI peripheral to communicate. It is not impossible getting this to work; it just has not been tested at the time of writing.

From a user's perspective, controlling the 114 LEDs of the kitchen lamp featured in this chapter gives the same results whether it is controlled via bit-banging or SPI. Therefore, we decided to go for the first technique. But if you wanted to control a much larger number of LEDs (in the order of eight times as many, or about 900), you should consider using SPI. The slower the communication and the bigger the number of LEDs, the longer time it takes to update the whole strip. If you want to have smooth fades in the light and nice-looking visual effects, you will need at least 10 updates per second.

The project in this chapter builds upon the work of others and uses a modified version of the library originally offered by Limor Fried (owner of Adafruit Industries), which was based on a library created by Synoptic Labs. The latter took code from John Cohn and Xander Hudson, the people who originally cracked the code to drive the easy-to-find LED strips used in this chapter.

You can find our revision of the library in the downloads section on the website for this book (www.wrox.com), but if you are interested in exploring the other implementations and some documentation about those libraries, check the following list of references:

➤ Adafruit's library (you will need to make a small modification to make it compatible with Arduino 1.0.1 or later; the library in the downloads section on the website of this book is based on this one and fixes any issues. However, we added this library here for reference): `https://github.com/adafruit/HL1606-LED-Strip`

➤ Synoptic Labs' library: `http://code.google.com/p/ledstrip/`

➤ The fastSPI library: `http://code.google.com/p/fastspi/`

Please note that, if you are using Arduino Due or another Google ADK2-compatible board, you can use the SPI port to drive your LED strip. The processors on those boards have an internal peripheral that supports both USB Host functionality and SPI simultaneously. However, at the time of writing, no library had been tested to drive LED strips for these kinds of boards.

In short, SPI is more efficient but hasn't been tested on the Arduino Mega ADK in parallel to the USB Host functionality, so use the bit-banging approach unless you have lots of more than 900 LEDs.

Hardware

If, like in this project, you are going to deploy a prototype in a real setting, you have to consider things like the box you'll use to host the device and a power supply that can provide enough current to run everything. LEDs are very power-hungry; in particular, the 114 RGB ones running this lamp have empirically been shown to need 2.3 Amps as measured at our laboratory.

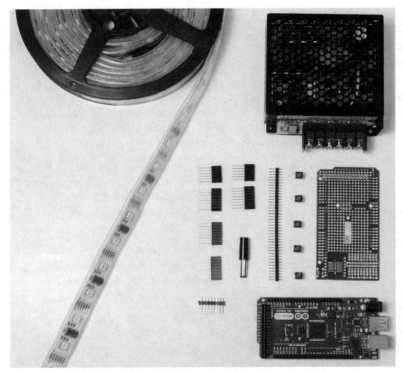

FIGURE 10-3: Parts needed in the kitchen lamp project

The final list of parts for this project is as follows:

➤ Arduino Mega ADK + micro USB cable for your processor.

➤ Arduino prototyping shield for Arduino Mega.

➤ Pin headers, both male-only and female, with long pins.

➤ Pushbuttons (these are optional, but they are handy for troubleshooting your installation when you do not have a computer).

➤ Multithreaded wire. Because it will be carrying a significant amount of current, you should use multithreaded wire for power and ground.

➤ H-U Terminal Block connectors to join the wires.

➤ Switched 5 V power supply. We used one with metallic housing to make sure it would be safe to use in a demanding environment like the kitchen. You cannot put a power supply providing 3 or 4 Amps in a tiny wooden box. You can hide your power supply in a locker, but make sure there is enough air in the box for the supply to cool down (a kitchen locker sized 35 × 40 × 60 cms will be enough). Ours is capable of providing 8 Amps, even though this project needs a maximum of only 2.3 Amps.

➤ An LED strip. We used one with HL1606 drivers, but many different ones are available. Just find one with good documentation so that you can write a basic communication library if one doesn't already exist. The strip we used is shielded in a transparent silicon case, which makes it suitable for the kitchen environment because the electronics are protected from steam and possibly food that could short-circuit any of the wires.

➤ A plastic box for the Arduino + Shield combo as they don't heat up at all. We used the standard plastic box for Arduino projects provided by the Arduino store, but anything will suffice.

The schematic for the shield is shown in Figure 10-4. It shows that we have connected a male pin header on the shield for providing the data, clock, and latch signals to the strip. We have also added a bunch of buttons to test that the different light patterns work in the project.

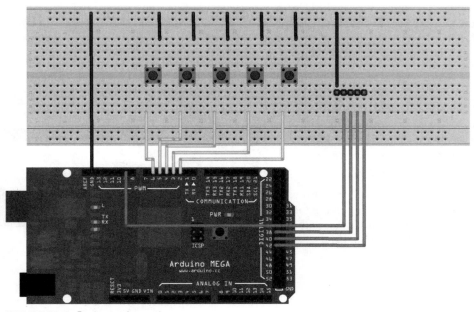

FIGURE 10-4: Project schematic

The power for the whole system comes from the 5 V power supply. We simply added a wire to the 5 V pin on the shield (and another to the GND pin) to draw power from the same supply feeding the LED strip.

In our case, the strip came with a connector exposing the different pins. It might be different for you. In that case, you should solder wires from the different anchor points in the strip. As mentioned earlier, the LED driver we are using is called HL1606 and it exposes the following pins (in order):

➤   **GND** — Ground or 0 Volts.

➤   **SI/SO** — Strobe. This is not used in the code, but we chose to wire it up anyway for future development. The strobe at SI is transferred directly to SO on the chip.

➤   **DI/DO** — Data pin carrying the information bit by bit. The current bit is passed out to DO at the arrival of the next clock edge.

➤   **CI/CO** — Clock. At the arrival of a rising edge on the clock signal, the HL1606 loads the voltage value on the DI pin into memory.

➤   **LI/LO** — Latch. Tells the driver to load the values inside memory onto the LEDs.

➤   **5 V** — Power to the strip, it has to be exactly 5 Volts and will need enough current to make all the LEDs shine. In our case, 114 LEDs need 2.3 Amps of current at 5 Volts.

Figure 10-5 shows one segment of the LED strip with two LEDs and the driver chip in between. On the left side you can see the inputs to the segment, and on the right side you see the outputs. This particular strip comes as a series of these segments tied up to each other. Some of them will be casted in silicon (like the one we are showing), but some of them won't.

It is possible to solder wires directly on the metallic contacts at the input of the strip segment and connect it directly to a microcontroller. It is also possible to feed the 5 V needed for the strip directly from the 5 V output coming from your Arduino, as long as you do not have many LEDs hanging from that pin. The 114 LEDs used in this project are far too many, so we needed the external power supply.

As Figure 10-6 shows, we soldered everything together onto a prototyping shield, making it very easy to push the project into a box and embed the whole thing into the kitchen.

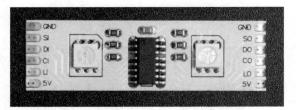

FIGURE 10-5: Segment of the strip

FIGURE 10-6: View of the shield on top of Arduino once soldered

---

LEARNING HOW TO SOLDER

If you have never soldered before, you should not be afraid of trying. There are plenty of places where you can see how to do it and learn by yourself. The one we recommend to our students is the comic book titled *Soldering is Easy* by Mitch Altman, Andie Nordgren, and Jeff Keyzer that can be found at: http://mightyohm.com/soldercomic.

Software

You are already familiar with creating basic Arduino programs, so we will jump over the very basic steps. Just keep in mind that you want to write a program that:

➤ Checks whether or not an Android device is connected

➤ Provides a constant white light if no Android device is connected

➤ Subscribes to the information feed and listens to data published by the Android device if connected

➤ Discriminates between three types of events: calls, SMS arrival, and kitchen timer

➤ Renders different light animations depending on the event

Create the Program's Skeleton

The program's skeleton contains different blocks that you have to check periodically, as well as some room for adding different light effects by means of writing your own functions on top of the HL1606 library (remember it is the driver used to control each pair of LEDs).

Listing 10-1 shows an idea of the whole program you need to produce. Note that this is pseudo code and not real code!

LISTING 10-1: Program's skeleton

```
#include <libraries_LEDs>
#include <libraries_Communication>
int declareSomeVariables;
libLEds strip = stripConstructor();
libComm mqtt = mqttConstructor();
void setup() {
  initSerialComm(); // to debug that things are going ok
  mqtt.initMqttComm(); // to establish the communication towards the Android device
}
void loop() {
  if(!connected) strip.turnOnWhiteLight();
  if(connected && !subscribed) subscribed = mqtt.subscribe();
  if(subscribed) {
    if(mqtt.publishArrived()) executeCommand(mqtt.getPayload());
  }
}
void executeCommand(int com) {
  switch (com) {
    case CALL:
      lightAnimationCall();
      break;
    case SMS:
      lightAnimationSMS();
      break;
    case TIMER:
      barGraph(mqtt.getPayload()[1]); // check the second byte
      break;
  }
}
[... here you should add the different animations to be performed on the LEDs ...]
```

Add the Libraries to Control the LEDs

If you understand the basic skeleton for the program, it then becomes fairly easy to translate it into real code. You just need to go step by step. As for the LEDs, we used the HL1606 library. It is not the latest code, but it is properly documented because a whole lot of people have been using it.

SOME BASICS ABOUT THE HL1606 LIBRARY

This library sends data to the LEDs through bit-banging. You need to remember a couple of functions in order to create your own animations out of code:

➤ HL1606strip (data, latch, clock, LEDs) — This is the constructor. You have to specify the pins you used to connect the data, latch, clock, and the total amount of LEDs in the strip.

➤ HL1606strip::setLEDcolor(i, color) — This function changes the color of one of the LEDs on the strip, but only on the buffer. The change is not executed until you call HL1606::writeStrip().

➤ HL1606::writeStrip() — This function sends the buffer containing the light data down to the whole strip.

➤ There are a series of predefined colors for you to choose, the library defines them as constants: BLACK, WHITE, TEAL, BLUE, RED, GREEN, YELLOW and VIOLET.

Using the library's basic function set and color definitions, we created the functions doubleDipping(), vuMeter(), and knightRider() to inform about the arrival of different notifications. These functions are introduced in Listing 10-2.

LISTING 10-2: Libraries, constructors, and functions for the strip

```
#include <HL1606strip.h>

#define STRIP_D 36
#define STRIP_C 38
#define STRIP_L 40
#define NUM_LEDS 114

HL1606strip strip = HL1606strip(STRIP_D, STRIP_L, STRIP_C, NUM_LEDS);

void setup() {
}
void loop() {
  // cycle trough the different examples
  knightRider(5);
  doubleDipping(WHITE);
  for(int i = 0; i < 100; i++) {
    vuMeter(i);
    delay(100);
  }
}

// the parameter fixes the amount of LEDs that
```

continues

LISTING 10-2 *(continued)*

```
    // will be moving back and forth
    void knightRider(int width) {
      for (int i=0; i< strip.numLEDs() - width; i++) {
        for (int j = 0; j < width; j++)
          strip.setLEDcolor(i+j, RED);
        if (i != 0)
          strip.setLEDcolor(i-1, BLACK);
        strip.writeStrip();
      }
      for (int i=strip.numLEDs() - width; i > 0; i--) {
        for (int j = 0; j < width; j++)
          strip.setLEDcolor(i+j, RED);
        if (i != 0)
          strip.setLEDcolor(i+width, BLACK);
        strip.writeStrip();
      }
    }

    // doubleDipping takes the color we will use to light up
    // the LEDs
    void doubleDipping(int color) {
      for (int i=0; i< int(strip.numLEDs()/2); i++) {
        strip.setLEDcolor(i, color);
        strip.setLEDcolor(strip.numLEDs() - i, color);
        strip.writeStrip();
      }
    }

    // the parameter determines in percentage how many
    // LEDs will be on
    void vuMeter(int percent) {
      for (int i=0; i< int(strip.numLEDs()*percent/100); i++) {
        strip.setLEDcolor(i, BLUE);
      }
      for (int i=int(strip.numLEDs()*percent/100); i < strip.numLEDs(); i++) {
        strip.setLEDcolor(i, BLACK);
      }
      strip.writeStrip();
    }
```

Add the Libraries to Control Communication

Next you add the code to control the communication from the phone. Note that we named the initialization method after the application running on the phone/tablet.

To make the code a little easier to read, in Listing 10-3 we separated the execution of the different animations into a different function called executeCommand().

LISTING 10-3: Communication libraries and payload analysis

```
#include <AndroidAccessory.h>
#include <P2PMQTT.h>
#include <HL1606strip.h>

#define STRIP_D 36
#define STRIP_C 38
#define STRIP_L 40
#define NUM_LEDS 114

#define VUMETER 0
#define SMS 1
#define CALL 2

HL1606strip strip = HL1606strip(STRIP_D, STRIP_L, STRIP_C, NUM_LEDS);

P2PMQTT mqtt(true);  // add true to see debug info over the serial port
boolean subscribed = false;

void setup() {
  Serial.begin(9600);
  Serial.println("ready");
  mqtt.begin("Kitchen Lamp");
}
void loop() {
  int firstByteMSB = mqtt.getType(mqtt.buffer);
  int payload = 0;

  switch(firstByteMSB) {
    case CONNECT:
      Serial.println("connected");
      if(!subscribed) subscribed = mqtt.subscribe("kl");
      break;

    case PUBLISH:
      payload = mqtt.getPayload(mqtt.buffer,PUBLISH)[0];
      executeCommand(payload);
      break;

    default:
      // do nothing
      break;
  }
}
void executeCommand(int c) {
  int val = 0;
  switch (c) {
    case VUMETER:
      // VU meter sends the value in the second byte
      // of the payload
      val = mqtt.getPayload(mqtt.buffer,PUBLISH)[1];
```

continues

LISTING 10-3 *(continued)*

```
        vuMeter(val);
        break;

    case SMS:
        doubleDipping(WHITE);
        break;

    case CALL:
        knightRider(5);
        break;
    default:
        // do nothing
        break;
    }
  }
  [...]
```

Periodically Check Whether or Not the Android Device Is Connected

The final part of the code (Listing 10-4) for getting this project to work is analyzing whether there is a connection to the phone/tablet. If nothing is connected, the lamp should just be on. You will do a periodic check to make sure devices can be connected to or disconnected from the lamp at any time.

You have to add a boolean variable to monitor whether it is the first time the program's main loop runs. If it is the case, the lamp should simply go on. There is also a timer to check from time to time if the Android device is connected.

You also need the function that turns all the LEDs on: `lightsON()`. It takes the color as a parameter.

LISTING 10-4: Ensuring the "lamp as such" functionality

```
#include <AndroidAccessory.h>
#include <P2PMQTT.h>
#include <HL1606strip.h>

[...]

boolean firstTime = true;
long timer = 0;

void setup() {
  Serial.begin(9600);
  Serial.println("ready");
  mqtt.begin("Kitchen Lamp");
}
void loop() {
  if(firstTime || (millis() - timer > 1000 && !mqtt.isConnected())) {
```

```
        lightsON(WHITE);
        timer = millis();
        firstTime = false;
    }
    int firstByteMSB = mqtt.getType(mqtt.buffer);
    int payload = 0;

    switch(firstByteMSB) {
      [...]
    }
}

// turn the all the LEDs on taking color as a parameter
void lightsON(int color) {
    for (uint8_t i=0; i < strip.numLEDs(); i++) {
      strip.setLEDcolor(i, color);
    }
    strip.writeStrip();
}
[...]
```

Embedded Code Done, What is Next?

You now have a lamp up and running. When plugged to the power socket, it will get lit and shine with all the LEDs at once. Next step is producing the Android app to command your lamp. The following section will guide you in creating an Android program capable of responding to events like SMS messages or calls by sending commands to the kitchen lamp.

BUILDING THE ANDROID APP

In this project your Android application acts as the P2PMQTT server, meaning it distributes all the data to the Arduino microcontroller (the accessory) and controls the current status of the lamp. You need to add at least the following three data sources to your app, but you can add more if you want:

➤ Act as a kitchen timer

➤ Catch incoming phone calls

➤ Catch incoming text messages

This might seem like a very large application just by viewing these sources, but remember that Android has most of these capabilities built into the very core of the system; the resulting project will be fairly simple to build.

Sketching the Application Layout

This first version of the accessory application consists of only two classes: the Activity and a class for constants. Of course, you can expand the project later on; for example, you can add an AsyncTask to get information from Yahoo! Weather and displaying it through the kitchen lamp.

Create the Kitchen Lamp Project

Start by creating the Eclipse project. In this example it's called Kitchen Lamp and will have the package `com.wiley.aoa.kitchen_lamp`. These are just suggested values; you can select any names you want, but make sure to remember them throughout the chapter.

1. Create your new Android project by opening the File menu and choosing New ⇨ Android Application Project.

2. Enter **Kitchen Lamp** as the Application Name.

3. Enter **Kitchen Lamp** as the Project Name.

4. For the Package Name, enter **com.wiley.aoa.kitchen_lamp**.

5. Set the minimum required SDK to 12; you'll be using the NumberPicker, a UI widget introduced for the first time in API 11. This means that you cannot install this particular example on a device with the backported version of the Accessory library. You can get around this using other UI widgets or custom libraries.

6. Click Next.

7. Choose a launcher icon image or clipart that matches your preferences.

8. Select Next and allow Eclipse to create a BlankActivity.

9. Set the title of the MainActivity to **Kitchen Lamp**.

Create the User Interface

The user interface for the Kitchen Lamp application consists of a timer section and a set of checkboxes used to enable or disable event listeners. You'll build this interface using something called a `ViewFlipper`, which is a container that can animate transitions between multiple views without causing the lifecycle events to be called.

Add the `ViewFlipper` tag as shown in Listing 10-5. This allows the user to swipe between the two different views without using multiple activities and dealing with lifecycle events; the views will then also share the same accessory connection.

LISTING 10-5: Add the ViewFlipper root

```
<?xml version="1.0" encoding="utf-8"?>
<LinearLayout xmlns:android="http://schemas.android.com/apk/res/android"
  android:layout_width="match_parent"
  android:layout_height="match_parent"
  android:orientation="vertical" >
  <ViewFlipper
```

```
      android:id="@+id/viewFlipper1"
      android:layout_width="match_parent"
      android:layout_height="match_parent" >
    </ViewFlipper>
  </LinearLayout>
```

The `ViewFlipper` contains two views. The first allows control over the timer, and the second lets the user select what events to listen for. When you notice that a layout file may grow fairly large, it's always a good idea to consider using the tools available to simplify the code; in this case you'll use the include tag rather than adding the two views directly to the `activity_main.xml` layout.

You'll also need some way to switch between the views in the `ViewFlipper`; often you'd probably want to react to a swipe gesture, but in this example you'll use a simple `Button`. Add the two `include` tags and the `button` as shown in Listing 10-6.

LISTING 10-6: Add two include tags

```xml
<?xml version="1.0" encoding="utf-8"?>
<?xml version="1.0" encoding="utf-8"?>
<LinearLayout xmlns:android="http://schemas.android.com/apk/res/android"
  android:layout_width="match_parent"
  android:layout_height="match_parent"
  android:orientation="vertical" >
  <ViewFlipper
    android:id="@+id/viewFlipper1"
    android:layout_width="match_parent"
    android:layout_height="wrap_content" >
    <include
      android:layout_width="match_parent"
      android:layout_height="match_parent"
      layout="@layout/timer_view" />
    <include
      android:layout_width="match_parent"
      android:layout_height="match_parent"
      layout="@layout/event_view" />
  </ViewFlipper>
  <Button
    android:id="@+id/button1"
    android:layout_width="wrap_content"
    android:layout_height="wrap_content"
    android:layout_gravity="center_horizontal"
    android:text="Switch View"
    android:onClick="switchView" />
</LinearLayout>
```

Before you continue on to building the rest of the user interface make sure to add the `switchView` method to your `MainActivity`, as shown in Listing 10-7.

LISTING 10-7: Add the switchView method

```
package com.wiley.aoa.kitchen_lamp;
import android.app.Activity;
import android.os.Bundle;
import android.view.View;
import android.widget.ViewFlipper;
public class MainActivity extends Activity {
  private ViewFlipper mViewFlipper;
  @Override
  public void onCreate(Bundle savedInstanceState) {
    super.onCreate(savedInstanceState);
    setContentView(R.layout.activity_main);
    mViewFlipper = (ViewFlipper) findViewById(R.id.viewFlipper1);
  }
  public void switchView(View v){
    mViewFlipper.showNext();
  }
}
```

Include tags allow Android to copy and paste the layout files together to form one complete file. For you this means that you can treat each view separately when coding, and it also means that you can see both views in the Layout Editor if you prefer to work in the WYSIWYG mode. Create the two new layout files, `timer_view.xml` and `event_view.xml`:

1. From the File menu, select New ⇨ Other.

2. In the dialog box that pops up, navigate to the Android section.

3. Select Android XML Layout File and click Next.

4. In the File box, enter `timer_view`.

5. Set the Root Element to LinearLayout and click Finish to create your new layout file.

To create the `event_view` layout repeat the above steps, but entering **event_view** instead to create the second view for the ViewFlipper.

The `timer_view` allows the user to set alarms, which when fired make the kitchen lamp light up in a certain pattern.

Give the view a title that tells the user what it does (remember the Android Design Guidelines and keep all text brief). The time for the alarm will be set using something called a NumberPicker, which is available in the Advanced drawer of the Layout Editor palette. To actually set the alarm you'll use a Button, place the button under the NumberPickers.

Add the `TextView`, the two `NumberPicker` elements and the `Button` to your `timer_view` layout, as shown in Listing 10-8.

LISTING 10-8: Build the timer_view layout

```
<?xml version="1.0" encoding="utf-8"?>
<LinearLayout xmlns:android="http://schemas.android.com/apk/res/android"
  android:layout_width="match_parent"
```

```
    android:layout_height="match_parent"
    android:orientation="vertical" >
    <TextView
      android:id="@+id/timer_title"
      android:layout_width="match_parent"
      android:layout_height="wrap_content"
      android:layout_margin="10dp"
      android:text="Timer View"
      android:textAppearance="?android:attr/textAppearanceLarge" />
    <TextView
      android:id="@+id/timer_text"
      android:layout_width="wrap_content"
      android:layout_height="wrap_content"
      android:layout_margin="10dp"
      android:text="Select minutes and seconds, then press Set Alarm."
      android:textAppearance="?android:attr/textAppearanceMedium" />
    <LinearLayout
      android:layout_width="wrap_content"
      android:layout_height="wrap_content"
      android:layout_gravity="center_horizontal"
      android:layout_margin="10dp" >
      <NumberPicker
        android:id="@+id/picker_minutes"
        android:layout_width="wrap_content"
        android:layout_height="wrap_content" />
      <NumberPicker
        android:id="@+id/picker_seconds"
        android:layout_width="wrap_content"
        android:layout_height="wrap_content" />
    </LinearLayout>
    <Button
      android:id="@+id/button_timer"
      android:layout_width="wrap_content"
      android:layout_height="wrap_content"
      android:layout_gravity="center_horizontal"
      android:text="Set Alarm"
      android:onClick="setAlarm" />
  </LinearLayout>
```

The finished `timer_view` should look something like Figure 10-7.

Notice the `onClick` attribute set in the button; if you prefer, you can use an `OnClickListener` within your activity instead. However, using the `onClick` attribute produces less code in the activities, which is a good thing. Go ahead and add the `setAlarm` method to your `MainActivity` directly so that you avoid any unnecessary exceptions later. See Listing 10-9.

FIGURE 10-7: The finished timer_view layout

LISTING 10-9: Add the setAlarm method

```
package com.wiley.aoa.kitchen_lamp;
import android.app.Activity;
import android.os.Bundle;
import android.view.View;
public class MainActivity extends Activity {
  @Override
  protected void onCreate(Bundle savedInstanceState) {
    super.onCreate(savedInstanceState);
    setContentView(R.layout.activity_accessory);
  }
  public void setAlarm(View v) {
  }
}
```

RESOURCES AND HARD-CODED VALUES

According to the guidelines, when building Android apps you should always strive to use String resources rather than hard-coded values as in the preceding listings. You should, of course, always follow those guidelines when building applications, but having said that you can avoid using them in this prototype to make the process a bit quicker.

The benefit of using resources becomes very clear when building applications for multiple languages.

The event_view contains three checkboxes, letting the user select what events to listen for. These just register and unregister the broadcast receiver for each event. Add the code in Listing 10-10 to your event_view.xml.

LISTING 10-10: Build the event_view layout

```
<?xml version="1.0" encoding="utf-8"?>
<LinearLayout xmlns:android="http://schemas.android.com/apk/res/android"
  android:layout_width="match_parent"
  android:layout_height="match_parent"
  android:orientation="vertical" >
  <TextView
    android:id="@+id/event_title"
    android:layout_width="wrap_content"
    android:layout_height="wrap_content"
    android:layout_margin="10dp"
    android:text="Event View"
    android:textAppearance="?android:attr/textAppearanceLarge" />
  <TextView
```

```
      android:id="@+id/event_text"
      android:layout_width="wrap_content"
      android:layout_height="wrap_content"
      android:layout_margin="10dp"
      android:text="Listen for the following events:"
      android:textAppearance="?android:attr/textAppearanceMedium" />
  <CheckBox
      android:id="@+id/check_sms"
      android:layout_width="wrap_content"
      android:layout_height="wrap_content"
      android:layout_margin="10dp"
      android:text="SMS messages" />
  <CheckBox
      android:id="@+id/check_phone"
      android:layout_width="wrap_content"
      android:layout_height="wrap_content"
      android:layout_margin="10dp"
      android:text="phone calls" />
  <CheckBox
      android:id="@+id/check_weather"
      android:layout_width="wrap_content"
      android:layout_height="wrap_content"
      android:layout_margin="10dp"
      android:text="weather updates" />
</LinearLayout>
```

The event_view user interface should look something like Figure 10-8.

Building the Kitchen Timer

To build the kitchen timer functionality you use a class called CountDownTimer; this class lets you create an event sometime in the future by entering a number of milliseconds. It then counts down to 0 from that specific time at an interval which you define.

Before you create the CountDownTimer, you should store the references to the UI that will control the time in the future. Add the references to the NumberPickers and then set their respective maximum values, as shown in Listing 10-11.

FIGURE 10-8: The finished event_view UI

LISTING 10-11: Add references to the NumberPickers

```
package com.wiley.aoa.kitchen_lamp;
[...]
import android.widget.NumberPicker;
public class MainActivity extends Activity {
  private ViewFlipper mViewFlipper;
  private Animation next_in, next_out, previous_in, previous_out;
  private NumberPicker minutes, seconds;
  @Override
```

continues

LISTING 10-11 *(continued)*

```
    protected void onCreate(Bundle savedInstanceState) {
      super.onCreate(savedInstanceState);
      setContentView(R.layout.activity_accessory);
      mGestureDetector = new GestureDetector(this, mGestureListener);
      mViewFlipper = (ViewFlipper) findViewById(R.id.viewFlipper1);
      next_in = AnimationUtils.loadAnimation(this, R.anim.transition_next_in);
      next_out = AnimationUtils.loadAnimation(this, R.anim.transition_next_out);
      previous_in = AnimationUtils.loadAnimation(this, R.anim.transition_previous_in);
      previous_out = AnimationUtils.loadAnimation(this, R.anim.transition_previous_out);
      minutes = (NumberPicker) findViewById(R.id.picker_minutes);
      minutes.setMaxValue(60);
      seconds = (NumberPicker) findViewById(R.id.picker_seconds);
      seconds.setMaxValue(60);
    }
    [...]
}
```

Add the `CountDownTimer` instance to your `MainActivity`, and let the method `setAlarm` read how far into the future the alarm is set. See Listing 10-12 for details.

LISTING 10-12: Add the CountDownTimer

```
    package com.wiley.aoa.kitchen_lamp;
    import java.util.concurrent.TimeUnit;
    [...]
    public class MainActivity extends Activity {
      [...]
      private CountDownTimer timer;
      [...]
      public void setAlarm(View v) {
        if (timer != null)
          timer.cancel();
        long min = minutes.getValue() + TimeUnit.SECONDS.toMillis(seconds.getValue()
        long millisInFuture = TimeUnit.MINUTES.toMillis(min);
        timer = new CountDownTimer(millisInFuture, Constants.TIMER_COUNTDOWN) {
          @Override
          public void onTick(long millisUntilFinished) {
          }
          @Override
          public void onFinish() {
          }
        }.start();
      }
      [...]
    }
```

You'll notice that there's another constant called `TIMER_COUNTDOWN`; add it to the `Constants` class with a value of 250 milliseconds. See Listing 10-13 for details. You can change the value of this constant to something that feels alright for you; remember, though, that these updates will be sent to the accessory as well, so don't update too often!

LISTING 10-13: Add the TIMER_COUNTDOWN constant

```
package com.wiley.aoa.kitchen_lamp;
public class Constants {
  public static final int MIN_SWIPE_LENGTH = 100;
  public static final int TIMER_COUNTDOWN = 250;
}
```

When the timer updates it's always a good idea to give some sort of feedback to the user. In this project you update the Kitchen Lamp itself, but you should also update the user interface on the application. Add the `updateTime` method in your activities as shown in Listing 10-14.

LISTING 10-14: Let the CountDownTimer update the NumberPickers

```
[…]
public class MainActivity extends Activity {
  […]
  public void setAlarm(View v) {
    if (timer != null)
      timer.cancel();
    long millisInFuture = TimeUnit.HOURS.toMillis(hours.getValue())
        + TimeUnit.MINUTES.toMillis(minutes.getValue())
        + TimeUnit.SECONDS.toMillis(seconds.getValue());
    timer = new CountDownTimer(millisInFuture, Constants.TIMER_COUNTDOWN) {
      @Override
      public void onTick(long millisUntilFinished) {
        updateTime(millisUntilFinished);
      }
      @Override
      public void onFinish() {
        updateTime(0);
      }
    }.start();
  }
  […]
  private void updateTime(long millis){
    int m = (int) TimeUnit.MILLISECONDS.toMillis(millis);
    minutes.setValue(m);
    int s = (int) TimeUnit.MILLISECONDS.toMillis(millis);
    seconds.setValue(s);
  }
}
```

Responding to Phone Calls

Android has a large number of various system-generated events; some of these events are related to the phone. You'll tap into this functionality in your Kitchen Lamp application to send notifications to the accessory when the phone is ringing.

Start by creating the `BroadcastReceiver` used to detect phone calls. Add the code from Listing 10-15 to your `MainActivity`.

LISTING 10-15: The BroadcastReceiver for the phone state events

```java
import android.content.BroadcastReceiver;
[...]
public class MainActivity extends Activity {
  [...]
  private BroadcastReceiver phoneReceiver = new BroadcastReceiver() {
    @Override
    public void onReceive(Context context, Intent intent) {
    }
  };
}
```

The broadcast ACTION_PHONE_STATE is sent whenever the state of the phone changes. This isn't limited to when the phone is ringing, so you need to add extra filtering methods in your receiver. See Listing 10-16 for details.

LISTING 10-16: Listen only to the phone state RINGING

```java
[...]
private BroadcastReceiver phoneReceiver = new BroadcastReceiver() {
  @Override
  public void onReceive(Context context, Intent intent) {
    String state = intent.getExtras().getString(TelephonyManager.EXTRA_STATE);
    if (state.equals(TelephonyManager.EXTRA_STATE_RINGING)) {
    }
  }
};
[...]
```

To register this receiver you need an IntentFilter, and because you want to be able to register and unregister throughout the lifetime of the application you should create a method that handles these actions for you. See Listing 10-17.

LISTING 10-17: Create the method to register and unregister the phoneReceiver

```java
import android.content.IntentFilter;
import android.telephony.TelephonyManager;
[...]
public class MainActivity extends Activity {
  private IntentFilter phoneFilter;
  [...]
  private void registerPhone(boolean register) {
    if (phoneFilter == null) {
      phoneFilter = new IntentFilter();
      phoneFilter.addAction(TelephonyManager.ACTION_PHONE_STATE_CHANGED);
    }
    if (register) {
      registerReceiver(phoneReceiver, phoneFilter);
    } else {
```

```
          unregisterReceiver(phoneReceiver);
      }
   }
   private BroadcastReceiver phoneReceiver = new BroadcastReceiver() {
     @Override
     public void onReceive(Context context, Intent intent) {
     }
   };
}
```

With the receiver set and the registration method created, all you need to do is call the register-Phone method and pass the correct state to toggle the listener on or off. You toggle the state from an OnCheckedChangeListener (see Listing 10-18).

Notice that there's another boolean variable introduced in this listing called phoneRegistered; this is only to track the changes in the listeners and, if a certain listener is registered by the time the application hits the onDestroy method, that receiver has to be unregistered.

LISTING 10-18: Add the OnCheckedChangedListener

```
[…]
import android.widget.CompoundButton;
import android.widget.CompoundButton.OnCheckedChangeListener;
public class MainActivity extends Activity {
  private CheckBox chkPhone;
  private IntentFilter phoneFilter;
  private boolean phoneRegistered;
  @Override
  public void onCreate(Bundle savedInstanceState) {
    super.onCreate(savedInstanceState);
    setContentView(R.layout.activity_accessory);
    […]
    chkPhone = (CheckBox) findViewById(R.id.check_phone);
    chkPhone.setOnCheckedChangeListener(checkboxListener);
  }
  @Override
  protected void onDestroy() {
    super.onDestroy();
    if (phoneRegistered)
      registerPhone(false);
  }
  […]
  private void registerPhone(boolean register) {
    if (phoneFilter == null) {
      phoneFilter = new IntentFilter();
      phoneFilter.addAction(TelephonyManager.ACTION_PHONE_STATE_CHANGED);
    }
    if (register)
      registerReceiver(phoneReceiver, phoneFilter);
    else
      unregisterReceiver(phoneReceiver);
  }
```

continues

LISTING 10-18 *(continued)*

```java
    private BroadcastReceiver phoneReceiver = new BroadcastReceiver() {
      @Override
      public void onReceive(Context context, Intent intent) {
        String state = intent.getExtras().getString(TelephonyManager.EXTRA_STATE);
        if (state.equals(TelephonyManager.EXTRA_STATE_RINGING)) {
        }
      }
    };
    private OnCheckedChangeListener checkboxListener = new OnCheckedChangeListener() {
      @Override
      public void onCheckedChanged(CompoundButton buttonView,
          boolean isChecked) {
        if (buttonView.getId() == R.id.check_phone) {
          registerPhone((phoneRegistered = isChecked));
        }
      }
    };
  }
```

Your app is now ready to receive phone state broadcasts when the user selects the correct checkbox from the UI. One thing is missing, though. As is common on Android, many actions and services require a specific permission; this is a safety measure that allows the user to see clearly what parts of the device your application have access to. Listening to the phone state broadcasts is one of those things. Add the `<uses-permission>` tag to the `AndroidManifest.xml`, as shown in Listing 10-19.

LISTING 10-19: Ask for permission to listen to phone state events

```xml
<manifest xmlns:android="http://schemas.android.com/apk/res/android"
    package="com.wiley.aoa.kitchen_lamp"
    android:versionCode="1"
    android:versionName="1.0" >
    <uses-sdk
        android:minSdkVersion="12"
        android:targetSdkVersion="15" />
    <uses-permission android:name="android.permission.READ_PHONE_STATE" />
    <application
        android:icon="@drawable/ic_launcher"
        android:label="@string/app_name"
        android:theme="@style/AppTheme" >
        <activity
            android:name=".MainActivity"
            android:label="@string/title_activity_main" >
            <intent-filter>
                <action android:name="android.intent.action.MAIN" />
                <category android:name="android.intent.category.LAUNCHER" />
            </intent-filter>
        </activity>
    </application>
</manifest>
```

Listen for SMS Events

SMS events, just like the phone state events, are broadcast by the system openly so that any application that wants to listen for new SMS messages can. However, there is one catch. There is no constant defined in the `TelephoneManager` class for the `SMS_MESSAGE` event. You'll have to either type the correct string in or create another constant in the `Constants` class. The latter is recommended because it makes the code a little bit more readable. Add the `SMS_RECEIVED` constant as shown in Listing 10-20.

LISTING 10-20: Add the **SMS_RECEIVED** constant

```
package com.wiley.aoa.kitchen_lamp;
public class Constants {
  public static final int MIN_SWIPE_LENGTH = 100;
  public static final int TIMER_COUNTDOWN = 250;
  static final String SMS_RECEIVED = "android.provider.Telephony.SMS_RECEIVED";
}
```

Add another broadcast receiver to your `MainActivity.java`; this receiver listens specifically for `SMS_RECEIVED` events, which are sent only when a new SMS has been received. You don't have to add any extra filtering inside the receiver. See Listing 10-21 for details.

LISTING 10-21: The **SMS_RECEIVED** listener

```
public class MainActivity extends Activity {
  [...]
  private BroadcastReceiver smsReceiver = new BroadcastReceiver() {
    @Override
    public void onReceive(Context context, Intent intent) {
    }
  };
}
```

Add the `registerSms` method, which is almost identical to the `registerPhone()` method. Listing 10-22 highlights the differences.

LISTING 10-22: Create the registerSms method

```
import android.content.IntentFilter;
import android.telephony.TelephonyManager;
[...]
public class MainActivity extends Activity {
  private IntentFilter phoneFilter, smsFilter;
  [...]
  private void registerSms(boolean register) {
    if (smsFilter == null) {
      smsFilter = new IntentFilter();
      smsFilter.addAction(Constants.SMS_RECEIVED);
```

continues

LISTING 10-22 *(continued)*

```
      }
      if (register)
        registerReceiver(smsReceiver, smsFilter);
      else
        unregisterReceiver(smsReceiver);
    }
    private BroadcastReceiver smsReceiver = new BroadcastReceiver() {
      @Override
      public void onReceive(Context context, Intent intent) {
      }
    };
  }
```

Call the registerSms method from the OnCheckedChangeListener, as shown in Listing 10-23.

LISTING 10-23: Call the registerSms method

```
  [...]
  public class MainActivity extends Activity {
    [...]
    private CheckBox chkPhone, chkSms;
    private IntentFilter phoneFilter, smsFilter;
    private boolean phoneRegistered, smsRegistered;
    @Override
    public void onCreate(Bundle savedInstanceState) {
      super.onCreate(savedInstanceState);
      setContentView(R.layout.activity_main);
      [...]
      chkPhone = (CheckBox) findViewById(R.id.check_phone);
      chkPhone.setOnCheckedChangeListener(checkboxListener);
      chkSms = (CheckBox) findViewById(R.id.check_sms);
      chkSms.setOnCheckedChangeListener(checkboxListener);
    }
    @Override
    protected void onDestroy() {
      super.onDestroy();
      if (phoneRegistered)
        registerPhone(false);
      if (smsRegistered)
        registerSms(false);
    }
    [...]
    private OnCheckedChangeListener checkboxListener = new OnCheckedChangeListener() {

      @Override
      public void onCheckedChanged(CompoundButton buttonView, boolean isChecked) {
        if (buttonView.getId() == R.id.check_phone) {
          registerPhone((phoneRegistered = isChecked));
        } else if (buttonView.getId() == R.id.check_sms) {
          registerSms((smsRegistered = isChecked));
```

```
        }
      }
    };
    private void registerPhone(boolean register) {
      if (phoneFilter == null) {
        phoneFilter = new IntentFilter();
        phoneFilter.addAction(TelephonyManager.ACTION_PHONE_STATE_CHANGED);
      }
      if (register)
        registerReceiver(phoneReceiver, phoneFilter);
      else
        unregisterReceiver(phoneReceiver);
    }
    private void registerSms(boolean register) {
      if (smsFilter == null) {
        smsFilter = new IntentFilter();
        smsFilter.addAction(Constants.SMS_RECEIVED);
      }
      if (register)
        registerReceiver(smsReceiver, smsFilter);
      else
        unregisterReceiver(smsReceiver);
    }
    private BroadcastReceiver phoneReceiever = new BroadcastReceiver() {
      @Override
      public void onReceive(Context context, Intent intent) {
        String state = intent.getExtras().getString(TelephonyManager.EXTRA_STATE);
        if (state.equals(TelephonyManager.EXTRA_STATE_RINGING)) {
          // TODO
        }
      }
    };
    private BroadcastReceiver smsReceiver = new BroadcastReceiver() {
      @Override
      public void onReceive(Context context, Intent intent) {
        // TODO
      }
    };
}
```

Just like the phone event listener, you need to ask for permission to receive SMS events. Add the uses-permission to your AndroidManifest.xml file, as shown in Listing 10-24.

LISTING 10-24: Add the uses-permission to receive SMS events

```
<manifest xmlns:android="http://schemas.android.com/apk/res/android"
  package="com.wiley.aoa.kitchen_lamp"
  android:versionCode="1"
  android:versionName="1.0" >
  <uses-sdk
    android:minSdkVersion="12"
    android:targetSdkVersion="15" />
```

continues

LISTING 10-24 *(continued)*

```xml
    <uses-permission android:name="android.permission.RECEIVE_SMS" />
    <uses-permission android:name="android.permission.READ_PHONE_STATE" />
    <application
      android:icon="@drawable/ic_launcher"
      android:label="@string/app_name"
      android:theme="@style/AppTheme" >
      <activity
        android:name=".MainActivity"
        android:label="@string/title_activity_main" >
        <intent-filter>
          <action android:name="android.intent.action.MAIN" />
          <category android:name="android.intent.category.LAUNCHER" />
        </intent-filter>
      </activity>
      <activity android:name="Usb12Activity" >
      </activity>
      <activity android:name="Usb10Activity" >
      </activity>
    </application>
</manifest>
```

Connecting to the WroxAccessory

Adding the WroxAccessories code is a simple task, thanks to your previous work in developing the WroxAccessories library. Follow these steps to add the WroxAccessories library to your project:

1. From the Project menu, select Properties.

2. In the list on the left side, select Android.

3. Select Add from within the Library panel.

4. In the new dialog box, select the WroxAccessories library and click OK.

5. Click Apply and then click OK.

Having added the library as part of the build path you can now add the needed code to your `MainActivity.java` file. First add the needed WroxAccessory objects, as shown in Listing 10-25.

LISTING 10-25: Add the needed WroxAccessory objects

```java
import com.wiley.wroxaccessories.UsbConnection12;
import com.wiley.wroxaccessories.WroxAccessory;
import android.hardware.usb.UsbManager;
[…]
public class MainActivity extends Activity {
  private WroxAccessory mAccessory;
  private UsbManager mUsbManager;
  private UsbConnection12 connection;
  […]
  @Override
```

```java
public void onCreate(Bundle savedInstanceState) {
  […]
  mUsbManager = (UsbManager) getSystemService(USB_SERVICE);
  connection = new UsbConnection12(this, mUsbManager);
  mAccessory = new WroxAccessory(this);
}
[…]
}
```

Override the onResume lifecycle method and then send the connect message to the accessory as shown in Listing 10-26.

LISTING 10-26: Perform the connect

```java
@Override
protected void onResume() {
  super.onResume();
  try {
    mAccessory.connect(WroxAccessory.USB_ACCESSORY_12, connection);
  } catch (IOException e) {
    e.printStackTrace();
  }

}
```

Then, in the onDestroy lifecycle method you should disconnect the accessory, which will gracefully send a disconnect message and unregister all subscriptions. As shown in Listing 10-27.

LISTING 10-27: Disconnect in the onDestroy method

```java
@Override
protected void onDestroy() {
  super.onDestroy();
  if (phoneRegistered)
    registerPhone(false);
  if (smsRegistered)
    registerSms(false);
  try {
    mAccessory.disconnect();
  } catch (IOException e) {
    e.printStackTrace();
  }
}
```

The only thing missing now is to publish the right messages to the correct topic. Start with the CountDownTimer, which publishes a message to the Kitchen Lamp topic, abbreviated to "kl" in this project, with a two-byte payload; the first byte marks what message you're sending (timer, SMS, or phone call), and the second byte contains the percent (0–100), which is only applicable to the timer in this example, but you can expand on this project and re-use that message for other kinds of events too. See Listing 10-28 for details.

LISTING 10-28: Publish **VU_EVENT** message

```
[...]
@Override
public void onTick(long millisUntilFinished) {
  setTime(millisUntilFinished);
  float percent = ((float) millisUntilFinished / (float) timer_max) * 100;
  byte[] buffer = new byte[2];
  buffer[0] = Constants.VU_EVENT;
  buffer[1] = (byte) percent;
  try {
    mAccessory.publish("kl", buffer);
  } catch (IOException e) {
    e.printStackTrace();
  }
}
[...]
```

The SMS event message contains only one byte. Add the publish call to the smsReceiver as shown in Listing 10-29.

LISTING 10-29: Publish **SMS_EVENT** message

```
[...]
private BroadcastReceiver smsReceiver = new BroadcastReceiver() {
  @Override
  public void onReceive(Context context, Intent intent) {
    byte[] buffer = new byte[1];
    buffer[0] = Constants.SMS_EVENT;
    try {
      mAccessory.publish("kl", buffer);
    } catch (IOException e) {
      e.printStackTrace();
    }
  }
};
[...]
```

Just like the publish message for the SMS event, the phone event contains just one byte; the message type. See Listing 10-30.

LISTING 10-30: Publish **PHONE_EVENT** message

```
[...]
privateBroadcastReceiver phoneReceiver = newBroadcastReceiver(){
  @Override
  publicvoidonReceive(Contextcontext,Intentintent){
    Stringstate=intent.getExtras().getString(TelephonyManager.EXTRA_STATE);
    if(state.equals(TelephonyManager.EXTRA_STATE_RINGING)){
      byte[] buffer = new byte[1];
      buffer[0] = Constants.PHONE_EVENT;
```

```
        try{
          mAccessory.publish("kl", buffer);
        }catch(IOExceptione){
          e.printStackTrace();
        }
      }
    }
  };
  [...]
```

Finally, add the message constants to the `Constants.java` class, as shown in Listing 10-31.

LISTING 10-31: Add all message constants to the Constants.java

```
public class Constants {
    static final String SMS_RECEIVED = "android.provider.Telephony.SMS_RECEIVED";
    protected static final byte VU_EVENT = 0;
    protected static final byte SMS_EVENT = 1;
    protected static final byte PHONE_EVENT = 2;
}
```

FURTHER IMPROVEMENTS

The final installation is shown in action in Figure 10-9. There you see how the system responds to the arrival of a call. But what are some things that you could improve if you had the time? The following sections look at those in detail.

FIGURE 10-9: Kitchen lamp informing you of a phone call

Product-ready Embedded System

We have oversimplified the embedded code to make sure it would be easy to understand how to build the program. However, you could make a couple of improvements to make a better lamp:

➤ It would be interesting to make more functions with more effects that would, for example, fade the light in, instead of going directly from off to on when you turn on the lamp.

➤ You could also imagine adding a dimming function by using a single button that you could press continuously as a way to cycle through different dimming values.

➤ More importantly, once there has been a notification, for example a phone call, it would be good to have a visual reminder on the lamp of missed phone calls or received text messages. You could make one LED turn red for each call, and use yet another color to inform you about every SMS arrival. This would imply using a button to deactivate the notifications on the lamp.

Making a Better App

You can improve the Android app in few very obvious ways. First, you could change the user interface to something easier and definitely something more suitable for its purpose and context:

➤ Moving the accessory-specific code to a `Service` instead would let the user interact with the screen; closing and opening the Kitchen Lamp app as they please. However, pushing the communication to a `Service` isn't as straightforward as just consuming the `ACCESSORY_ATTACHED` event because only activities can receive it. This would also let the timer and `BroadcastRecivers` run in the background so that events can be handled when the app is no longer running in the foreground.

➤ Making the app launch on both versions of the Accessory library would be the next step in broadening the scope of devices capable of connecting to the accessory. You could do this by introducing yet another "hidden" activity with the only task of determining how to proceed; this activity would use the static `Build` class, polling the `SDK_INT` constant and then instantly sending the user to the correct destination.

➤ One of the design guidelines defined by Android is that of saving user-generated data. If the user has selected to listen for an event, you should save this selection in the app's preferences and then load it up again the next time the app is launched.

➤ When improving the user experience you should always consider adding animations and effects as hints of how the user is navigating you application's interface. One of the most obvious places to use animations in Android is the `ViewFlipper`; it even has methods specifically for defining how views should be animated.

➤ The `ViewFlipper` is one of those things in Android where gestures really makes sense; using a `GestureDetector`, you can detect when the user swipes across the screen with their fingers and then change views with a smooth animation (as mentioned above). This creates a much smoother user experience.

SUMMARY

Building prototypes is one thing, but making them for other people who will use them in a real setting requires a slightly different mindset. If you are thinking about how cool it would be to have a lamp or any other electric appliance controlled by the phone, also consider whether it will make sense without the phone. The life expectancy of a kitchen lamp is far longer than the one of a phone (maybe 10 or 15 times as much).

You can probably imagine a whole series of accessories that require using a phone, like in project 1 (Chapter 9), where you used the high-speed camera on the phone to make animations. In that case, the whole construction would make no sense without the phone. On the other hand, in some cases the object needs to also work on its own without a phone.

Creating an accessory that can work with or without a phone will mark the kind of embedded software you create for the accessory. It needs to have a default mode and a connected one. Once you hook up the phone, it will start commanding the object, augmenting its features.

On Android many system events such as phone calls or text messages are broadcast to the entire system, meaning you can listen in on them and react to them in any fashion you want — for example letting a special pattern be displayed on a large wall-mounted LED lamp.

Working with broadcasts is fairly easy, the only catch is to register them and unregister them at the best times. You should think of the following when working with broadcast receivers:

➤ Always make sure that all `BroadcastReceivers` are unregistered in either `onPause` or `onDestroy`, depending on if you want to receive broadcasts while your application is paused or not.

➤ You can register to listen for broadcasts during run time if you wish; however, there's no list of what broadcasts your application has registered too. In order to unregister the correct `BroadcastReceivers`, you'll need to track that on your own. In this project you used two `boolean` variables for this purpose.

There are multiple ways of working with multi-view applications, in this project you got a little bit acquainted with the `ViewFlipper`, which lets you load multiple layouts within the same `Activity`, and then select the currently active layout. There are a few benefits of working with a `ViewFlipper` like this:

➤ You don't need to set up and maintain the accessory connection for each individual view; they all share the same connection since they are all parts of the same `Activity`.

➤ `ViewFlipper` contains built-in methods for animating between different views.

There is of course some downsides to this way of working as well, the code in the single `Activity` can easily grow quite large. In a more modern setting you would have likely used `Fragments` instead, which would have made the code more readable and manageable.

11

Mr. Wiley

WHAT'S IN THIS CHAPTER?

➤ Autonomous intelligent robots

➤ Computer vision through OpenCV

➤ Pre-assembled robotics platforms

➤ Using multiple serial ports

➤ Color filtering

➤ Contour detection

➤ Self-made wooden shields

WROX.COM CODE DOWNLOADS FOR THIS CHAPTER

The wrox.com code downloads for this chapter are found at www.wrox.com/remtitle .cgi?isbn=1118454766 on the Download Code tab. The code is in the Chapter 11 download and individually named according to the names throughout the chapter.

You are going to create a robot called Mr. Wiley, which is capable of following objects using computer vision. Mr. Wiley is made of merging together the Arduino Robot platform with an Android device. The camera on your Android will be capturing images that the phone will analyze to decide how to react. The Arduino Robot platform is an inexpensive and easy-to-hack robotics platform that can be reprogrammed in full using the Arduino IDE.

Computer vision is born from the meeting between computers and cameras. In this project you use your phone or tablet to detect an object — a red ball in this case — and make a robot turn towards it. The Basic Robot you made out of two servo motors in Chapter 8 would suffice to implement this project, but it would be too slow. Therefore, we suggest using the Arduino Robot platform, which uses DC motors and moves much faster.

In this chapter you create a program that captures images and filters them to detect an object. It then decides whether or not the object is in front of the robot. If not, the robot turns until the object is in front of it. Although the original design is not for this robot to follow the ball, implementing such functionality requires adding just a couple extra lines to the code presented in this chapter.

THE CONCEPT

Given an existing robot that enables you to control its motors with easy commands like "turn left" or "move forward," you can hack it to add computer vision capabilities. Ideally, you could go on expanding this platform for as long as you want, so you should look for a platform that is not too limited.

If you were to make your own robot, the one presented in Chapter 8 would suffice. It is slow and lacks a phone holder, but you can figure out ways to place the phone or tablet on it somehow. Servo motors (the ones used for that project) can carry a lot of weight, and you should have no problem adding the Android device on top of the motors, Arduino board, and battery holder.

However, to push the design further, we suggest you take whatever robotics platform you have on hand that you can command via a serial port or a series of digital input/output pins. You should use your Arduino Mega ADK to translate the messages coming from the phone into the commands understood by your robot.

We have chosen to use the Arduino Robot (see Figure 11-1), an educational device created by Arduino that can be fully hacked and that offers all of its blueprints for study (it is open source hardware). The robot has two boards: the control board and the motor board. Each one carries its own processor. The control board needs computing power to drive a screen, some buttons, a potentiometer, a compass, and whatever other sensors you might add to it. The motor board implements a bunch of line-following sensors, two DC motors, a motor driver (H-bridge), and a circuit to recharge the batteries and power up the whole robot.

FIGURE 11-1: The Arduino Robot

You need only the motor board, because the rest of the intelligence is brought in by the phone. The Arduino Mega ADK will take the place of the control board on the robot and translates the MQTT commands sent by the phone into something the robot can understand. In this case, the Arduino Robot motor board has a connector offering a serial port, power, and ground to feed the whole robot + ADK + phone combo.

THE DESIGN BRIEF

The final brief for this project requires few electronics (because you are using a ready-made platform), some mechanics, and a serious amount of coding inside the phone. Also, we would like to distinguish between three different pieces of software:

➤ **Firmware** — The software running in your robot. If you use the Arduino Robot as we suggest, you will write the firmware using Arduino's IDE. If you choose to use another robot platform for this, you might find that the firmware is not made for the Arduino IDE, or even that it isn't released under an open source license. As long as it offers you hooks (both software and hardware) where you can hijack the robot's motors, it should be no problem.

➤ **Software (embedded)** — This is the software running on the Arduino Mega ADK. It can read MQTT commands published by the phone, and extract the payload to use it on the robot.

➤ **App** — The app executes the computer vision algorithms on your Android device and sends commands to the Arduino Mega ADK.

Taking into account the different aspects you need to consider to make the robot possible, your task list is as follows:

➤ Create a robot capable of turning towards an object, in this case a tennis ball.

➤ Build the robot's intelligence into an Android device.

➤ Use a computer vision (CV) framework, such as OpenCV, to simplify the CV-related operations.

➤ Make the robot autonomous; this means no interaction with humans. It should follow the ball and eventually stop when it is close enough to it.

➤ Design a phone/tablet holder. You need to make sure the device lays on top of the robot with the camera pointing to the front. We suggest a construction like the one in Figure 11-2. You can find the blueprints for it in the downloads section on the website for this chapter.

FIGURE 11-2: Robot with phone on top

THE ARDUINO SIDE

Because the robotics platform is ready-made and off-the-shelf, you should look at it as yet another component in your project. You could think of it as another peripheral to your Arduino Mega ADK like a potentiometer or a servo motor, but with enhanced functionalities. This approach simplifies the way to think about this project.

THE ARDUINO ROBOT

Back in 2010, the robotics association Complubot, from Alcala de Henares, Spain, suggested that the Arduino team create an educational robot. Complubot, in addition to having many years of experience in teaching robotics to kids, had won four world championships in robotics soccer B at the RoboCup Junior. If you aren't familiar with the RoboCup competition, it is an annual meeting where roboticists from all over the world compete to solve different tasks with their machines. Soccer playing is just one of them.

RoboCup participants have to play the game in a fair way; before competing, they have to explain to their opponents how they are planning to make things happen. The robots are commanded by artificial intelligence (AI) and the main goal behind RoboCup is helping AI to develop further. Therefore, sharing knowledge is a strong component of the competition.

Preparing a robot for one of these competitions is a little like making a Formula One car. You have one year to get ready, and you need to explain to others how you do what you do to prove you are meeting the competition's requirements. At the end of the championship, participants go back to the drawing board to start all over again to make their robots for the following year.

At Arduino, we do not create one-run devices — we try to minimize the economic impact when we make educational tools. Therefore, scale factor is key. Between 2010 and 2012, we spent many months with the two teenagers behind Complubot, transforming those "Formula One" robots (sometimes worth thousands of Euros) into affordable devices (in the range of hundreds of Euros) for use in educational programs.

The result of this adventure is the Arduino Robot, designed by two teens and meant for teens to learn about technology. In this case, it is a great tool to create your computer vision robot.

The Hardware

Figure 11-3 shows the parts needed to build this project.

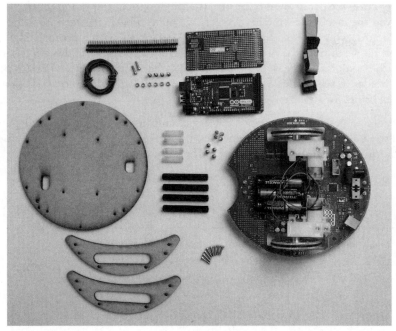

FIGURE 11-3: Parts needed in the CV robot project

The list of parts for this project is as follows:

➤ Arduino Mega ADK + micro USB cable for your processor

➤ Arduino prototyping shield for Arduino Mega

➤ Pin headers, both male-only and female with long pins

➤ The motor board for the Arduino Robot

➤ AA rechargeable batteries (2450 mAh or more preferred)

➤ Self-made wooden platform to carry the phone and the Arduino Mega ADK on top of the motor board

The schematic for the project is shown in Figure 11-4. The most important part is to understand the pin-out on the connector coming from the robot platform. This provides the power for the Arduino Mega ADK and supplies a serial port to connect the ADK to the robot.

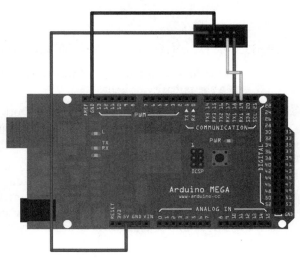

FIGURE 11-4: Project schematic

Because you might choose to work with your own platform, we are not going to put too much emphasis on the way we solved the mechanics for this project. We made a basic platform to affix on top of the robot's motor board, where we placed the Arduino Mega ADK with a prototyping shield and a series of wooden pieces to hold the phone. If you are using a Samsung Galaxy S III or a Galaxy Nexus, as we did, the holder we suggest will be enough. Otherwise, you should revise the shape and size of the phone holder to see if it fits your needs. Please refer to the downloads section on the website to find the blueprints for this part.

The power for the whole system comes from the robot's battery circuit. It is a complex voltage pump (technically known as DC-DC converter). We simply added a wire to the 5 V pin on the shield (and another to the GND pin) to draw power from the same batteries as the robot.

DC-DC CONVERTERS

These circuits (DC-DC converters) transform whatever voltage they have at their input to a very clean, constant output. In the case of the Arduino Robot, there is a battery set that has two modalities — 3 or 4 AA batteries — which means 4.5 V or 6 V.

As the batteries discharge, the voltage drops; the DC-DC converter keeps it stable at 9 V. A voltage regulator then adjusts it to the needed 5 V.

This is a common trick in robotics, because it helps feed the motors the right way: having a constant voltage and draining current as needed. The only disadvantage is that the system will give the impression of suddenly running out of battery power. When the voltage level on the batteries goes too low, the DC-DC converter will stop working in an instant. It will not start acting strange or run the motors slower, it will just stop working. It will then be time to charge the batteries.

Besides the DC-DC converter, the robot board contains the following:

➤ **Line-following sensors** — Infrared sensors pointing to the ground that detect simple changes in the intensity of light.

➤ **H-bridge** — A circuit that can drive both direction and speed of the two motors on the board simultaneously. It uses PWM coming from the processor to run the motors at different speeds.

➤ **DC motors with gearboxes** — Two motors with gearboxes. The gears make a transformation in the factor 1:48; the speed is reduced in a 48 to 1 factor, but the strength made by the motor increases in the same amount. DC motors spin very quickly, but they have little strength. The gears slow them down, transforming their kinetic energy to allow them to carry more weight.

➤ **Placeholders for sensors** — A series of connectors to plug in extra sensors as well as an on-board multiplexor.

➤ **Completely reprogrammable intelligence** — The robot board is controlled using an ATMega32U4, the same processor as on an Arduino Leonardo, one of the Arduino proto-typing boards. Thanks to this, you can completely reprogram the board to tailor-fit your needs.

In essence, the robot board is an Arduino Leonardo with augmented features. When building robots, it is convenient to have distributed intelligence. In this case, the robot has three processing units: the robot platform, the Arduino Mega ADK, and the Android device. If the robot platform allowed the accessory mode connection to the phone, you could also run the whole system without the Mega ADK.

As Figure 11-5 shows, we soldered everything together onto a prototyping shield. You see a ribbon cable, coming from the robot board. That cable carries a serial port, power and ground, and some other signals. The signals feed the Arduino Mega ADK.

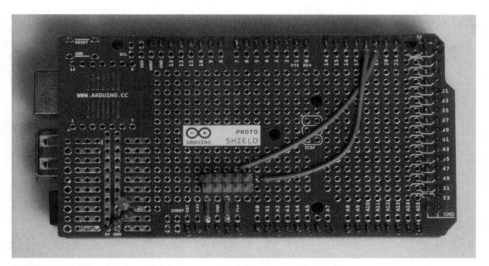

FIGURE 11-5: View of the shield on top of Arduino once soldered

The Firmware (on the Robot Board)

The robotics platform comes with its own firmware that can perform operations on all the sensors it carries onboard. You could spend some time learning how it works, but part of the beauty of this platform is that it is fully hackable and that you can introduce your own simple firmware in it using the Arduino IDE.

Therefore, we suggest you build your own firmware from scratch, given that the whole design of the robot is open source and you have full access to its blueprints. Figure 11-6 shows a simplified version of the robot's schematics (taking out the battery-charging units and some other components) where you can see the way the H-bridge connects to the microcontroller (a note later in this section explains what an H-bridge is). This is everything you need to know to create a simple firmware for the robot to move forward/backward and turn left/right.

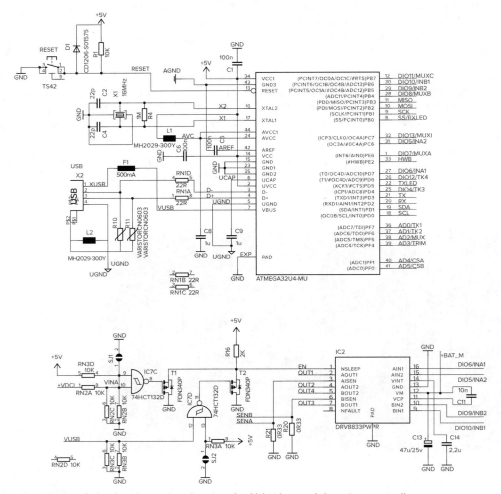

FIGURE 11-6: Robot's schematics showing the H-bridge and the microcontroller

The robot has two motors, labeled motor A and motor B. The relevant pins to use to control those are:

➤ **Digital pin 5** — Determines motor A's direction; 0 means forward, 1 means backward

➤ **Digital pin 6** — Determines motor A's speed; using PWM you can set how quickly this motor will turn

➤ **Digital pin 9** — Determines motor B's direction

➤ **Digital pin 10** — Determines motor B's speed, again using PWM

This platform will talk over a serial port to the Arduino Mega ADK mounted on top. The ATMega 32U4, the processor commanding the robot's board, can easily be controlled using that serial port.

Therefore, all that your code on the robot will do is read the serial port and upon arrival of data, change the behavior of the motors.

The following is a list of behaviors you want the robot to do:

➤ Check whether or not there is a serial connection.

➤ If there is serial connection, wait until a command arrives. Filter the command and perform an action on the motors.

➤ If the serial communication breaks or no data arrives for X seconds, stop the motors.

The robot is a moving entity, and it could eventually get damaged by crashing against something. Therefore, you need to define a timeout X in the firmware to stop the robot from moving.

Creating the Program's Skeleton

The program's skeleton reflects the above-mentioned list of behaviors more or less directly. Listing 11-1 shows a transcription of the behavior list in pseudo code. Because no libraries need to be instantiated, the code very much resembles the text.

LISTING 11-1: Program's skeleton

```
int declareSomeVariables;
int declareMotorPins;
void setup() {
  initSerialComm(); // to communicate with the ADK
  initMotorPins;
}
void loop() {
  if(!Serial OR timeout) executeCommand(STOP);
  if(Serial && Serial.available()) executeCommand(Serial.read());
}
void executeCommand(int com) {
  switch (com) {
    case LEFT:
      turnLeft();
      break;
    case RIGHT:
      turnRIGHT();
      break;
    case STOP:
      turnOffMotors();
      break;
  }
}
```

Firmware as Arduino Code

This program is really straightforward. You can transcribe the meta-code almost literally into C once you know which pins are performing which functions on the robot. We explained earlier that digital pins 5, 6, 9, and 10 are the ones moving the motors. You need to declare those as ouputs and then go on writing the different functions to make the motors move forward, backward, and so on.

WHAT ARE H-BRIDGES?

An H-bridge is a circuit that allows you to apply a voltage on a motor (and any other kind of load) in any direction. In other words, imagine you have a voltage source, like a battery providing a constant voltage value. Applying the voltage in one way (for example, motor pin A to the battery's positive pin and motor pin B to the battery's negative pin) makes the motor spin in one direction, and connecting the pins in the opposite way makes it turn in the other direction.

With H-bridges it is possible to do this electrically, by making it possible for digital circuits to take control of it without having to rewire the circuit. The H-bridge on the Arduino Robot controls not one, but two motors! This is possible because it carries two H-bridges inside.

You control a single motor inside an H-bridge through four transistors that have to be activated in pairs. Therefore, you have two pins to control each motor. With some extra logic, it is possible to achieve the functionality we see on the Arduino robotics platform: One pin takes care of the direction, and the other one controls the speed of the motor.

Listing 11-2 shows the final version of the firmware for the robot's motor board.

LISTING 11-2: Translate the meta into code

```
#define LEFT      0
#define RIGHT     1
#define STOP      2
int pinDirMotorA = 5;
int pinDirMotorB = 9;
int pinSpeedMotorA = 6;
int pinSpeedMotorB = 10;
void setup() {
  // configure Serial port
  Serial.begin(9600);
  // declare direction motor pins as outputs
  pinMode(pinDirMotorA, OUTPUT);
  pinMode(pinDirMotorB, OUTPUT);
}
void loop() {
  if(!Serial) executeCommand(STOP);
  if(Serial && Serial.available()) executeCommand(Serial.read());
}
void executeCommand(int com) {
  switch (com) {
    case LEFT:
      turnLeft();
      break;
    case RIGHT:
      turnRIGHT();
      break;
```

```
      case STOP:
        turnOffMotors();
        break;
    }
  }
void turnRight() {
  //Motor A at 50%
  digitalWrite(pinDirMotorA,0);
  analogWrite(pinSpeedMotorA,127);
  //Motor B at 50%
  digitalWrite(pinDirMotorB,0);
  analogWrite(pinSpeedMotorB,127);
}
void turnLeft() {
  //Motor A at 50%
  digitalWrite(pinDirMotorA,1);
  analogWrite(pinSpeedMotorA,127);
  //Motor B at 50%
  digitalWrite(pinDirMotorB,1);
  analogWrite(pinSpeedMotorB,127);
}
void turnOffMotors() {
  //Motor A at 0%
  digitalWrite(pinDirMotorA,0);
  analogWrite(pinSpeedMotorA,0);
  //Motor B at 0%
  digitalWrite(pinDirMotorB,0);
  analogWrite(pinSpeedMotorB,0);
}
```

Adding Some Timing Safety

The final aspect to consider on the motor board is to stop the board from moving if nothing has happened for a while. Listing 11-3 adds a timer as well as a way to check it out in the code.

LISTING 11-3: Add a timer

```
#define TIMEOUT   5000
[...]
long timer = 0;
void setup() {
  [...]
  // init timer
  timer = millis();
}
void loop() {
  if(!Serial || millis() - timer > TIMEOUT) executeCommand(STOP);
  if(Serial && Serial.available()) executeCommand(Serial.read());
}
void executeCommand(int com) {
  [...]
  timer = millis(); // restart timer
}
[...]
```

Creating Software for the Mega ADK Board

The Mega ADK board interfaces the robotics platform with the phone. You need to have a program on it that:

➤ Checks whether or not an Android device is connected

➤ If no Android device is connected, sends a stop command to the robot

➤ If there is an Android device, subscribes to its information feed and listens to data published by it

➤ Pipes the data inside the MQTT packages and sends them through serial to the robot

---

TWO HARDWARE SERIAL PORTS? UP TO FOUR!

In this example, the Mega ADK board makes use of two serial ports:

➤ One debugs so that things are working as expected. This is a common functionality, and you have been doing it throughout all the examples in this book.

➤ One communicates with the robotics platform.

The Arduino Mega ADK, just like the normal Arduino Mega, has four serial ports. This means you could connect up to four devices to your board using this type of communication and get them to send data back and forth. The way to channel data through them within Arduino is using the predefined objects: `Serial`, `Serial1`, `Serial2`, and `Serial3`.

Creating the Program's Skeleton

In this case, your ADK board is going to be a mere proxy. Listing 11-4 is an illustration of the code you will be implementing to get this part of the project to work.

LISTING 11-4: ADK's program skeleton

```
#include <libraries_Communication>
int declareSomeVariables;
libComm mqtt = mqttConstructor();
void setup() {
  initSerialComm();  // to debug that things are going ok
  initSerialComm2(); // to send data to the robot platform
  mqtt.initMqttComm(); // to establish the communication towards the Android device
}
void loop() {
  if(!connected) serial2.send(STOP);
  if(connected && !subscribed) subscribed = mqtt.subscribe();
  if(subscribed) {
    if(mqtt.publishArrived()) serial2.send(mqtt.getPayload());
  }
}
```

Adding All Those Serial Ports

It is good to start by adding the serial ports. You could use this technique to test that the communication works between the Arduino Mega ADK and the robot, preprogram some basic functions on one of the boards and control it remotely from the other, and so on.

Listing 11-5 shows how to do this.

LISTING 11-5: Program using two serial ports

```
void setup() {
  Serial.begin(9600);
  Serial1.begin(9600);
}
void loop() {
  if(Serial.available() > 0) {
    Serial1.write(Serial.read());
  }
}
```

The code inside the loop will proxy whatever arrives through the serial port you use to debug information on your Arduino Mega ADK as well as to the serial port 1, corresponding to pins 18 and 19 on your board.

Adding the P2PMQTT Library

Besides issuing the commands from the serial interface, you might be interested in sending commands after parsing them from data sent from the phone. Listing 11-6 looks into decoding the MQTT packages to channel the information inside their payloads to the right port.

LISTING 11-6: Communication libraries and payload analysis

```
#include <AndroidAccessory.h>
#include <P2PMQTT.h>

P2PMQTT mqtt(true);  // add true to see debug info over the serial port
boolean subscribed = false;

void setup() {
  Serial.begin(9600);
  Serial1.begin(9600);
  Serial.println("ready");
  mqtt.begin("Mr Wiley");
}
void loop() {
  int firstByteMSB = mqtt.getType(mqtt.buffer);
  int payload = 0;

  switch(firstByteMSB) {
    case CONNECT:
      Serial.println("connected");
```

continues

LISTING 11-6 *(continued)*

```
        if(!subscribed) subscribed = mqtt.subscribe("mw");
        break;

    case PUBLISH:
        payload = mqtt.getPayload(mqtt.buffer,PUBLISH)[0];
        Serial.println(payload);
        Serial1.write(payload);
        break;

    default:
        // do nothing
        break;
    }
}
```

Periodically Checking whether the Android Device Is Connected

Finally, as in all of the other projects, you need to ensure you have a way to safely solve the situation if the communication between the robot and the phone breaks. In any unexpected scenario, the robot should stop moving. You can achieve this by checking whether there is a connection between the phone and the robot, and in case there is none, you can program the ADK to send the stop command (a zero), as shown in Listing 11-7.

LISTING 11-7: Ensuring the robot stops if the phone disconnects

```
#include <AndroidAccessory.h>
#include <P2PMQTT.h>

#define TIMEOUT 1000
[...]
long timer = 0;

void setup() {
  [...]
  timer = millis();
}
void loop() {
  if((millis() - timer > TIMEOUT && !mqtt.isConnected())) {
     Serial1.write(2);
     timer = millis();
  }
  [...]
}
```

BUILDING THE ANDROID APP

Because the Android device acts as the brains of the robot and can react to the environment in a special way (chasing that red ball), you must create the "intelligence" for your robot. This "intelligence" is also the biggest hurdle to pass on the Android side of things because it involves a fairly advanced topic called computer vision.

COMPUTER VISION

A key characteristic of animals is their vision, which enables them to quickly analyze their surroundings to find food and shelter, determine threats, and act accordingly by either running away or taking a defensive stance. In short, vision enables animals to build an internal model of the external world that defines how they act.

Computer vision is a very large field, and you can find applications of it in many artifacts used on a daily basis, as well as advanced medical equipment and industrial machines. If you've ever used a camera that can stitch multiple photographs into one 360-degree panoramic photo, you've definitely come in contact with this topic.

Sketching the Application Layout

The Android project is fairly small in this case, consisting of only three classes. One of these classes is a straight copy from an available sample, just as in the Bike Ride Recorder project. Figure 11-7 shows a rough sketch of the project.

Creating the Mr. Wiley Project

You'll be controlling Mr. Wiley with a red ball rather than a traditional user interface, like the one you built in the mini project called Basic Robot, so you can jump directly to the application logic. Follow these steps to create your Mr. Wiley project:

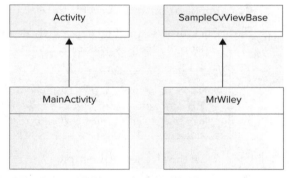

FIGURE 11-7: UML sketch of the Mr. Wiley project

1. Open the File menu and select New ➪ Android Application Project.
2. Enter **Mr Wiley** as the Application Name.
3. Enter **Mr Wiley** again as the Project Name.
4. As the Package Name, enter **com.wiley.aoa.mr_wiley**.
5. Set the Minimum Required SDK to 12.
6. Click Next.
7. Choose a launcher icon image or clipart that matches your preferences.
8. Click Next and allow Eclipse to create a BlankActivity.
9. Set the title of the MainActivity to **Mr Wiley**.
10. Click Finish to create your project.

Giving the Gift of Sight

You can add OpenCV to your Android projects in two ways. You can build the image-processing parts of your application directly in native code using the Android NDK (Native Development Kit), or you can use the Java API, which calls all the native methods for you.

In this project you implement the computer vision algorithm using the OpenCV Java API; by doing this you completely avoid having to build any native code in your project. However, you should note that building the computer vision algorithm using the Java API is far more expensive than building it in native code, so you're definitely encouraged to explore that option if you build performance-critical OpenCV applications in the future.

To add OpenCV functionality to your project follow these steps:

1. Download the Android OpenCV library from `http://opencv.org/`.

2. In the Eclipse File menu, select Import.

3. Select Existing Project.

4. Import from an archive file by selecting the Select archive file radio button.

5. Click Browse and find your newly downloaded file. When this book was written, the latest version of OpenCV was 2.4.2 and the filename was `OpenCV-2.4.2-android-sdk.zip`.

> **NOTE** *The archive file contains both the OpenCV library and multiple sample projects with which you can explore OpenCV; however, for this project to work you only need to import the library.*

6. Click the Deselect All button.

7. Then select the checkboxes titled OpenCV Library — 2.4.2 (Java) and OpenCV Tutorial 2 — Use OpenCV Camera.

8. Click Finish to import OpenCV to your workspace.

9. Open the File menu and select Properties.

10. Select Android, and in the Library panel click Add.

11. Select OpenCV Library — 2.4.2 in the dialog box that pops up.

12. Click OK.

Your project should now have the OpenCV library added and you're ready to start coding computer vision algorithms — almost. The way OpenCV for Android works (without programming in native code) is by using an app called OpenCV Manager, which provides and updates the best possible native library for your device. All your image processing will be handled by this external application.

Open `MainActivity.java` and add the highlighted code from Listing 11-8; this will automatically try to connect to the binary packages of OpenCV, and if they're not available it will attempt to install them from Google Play Store.

LISTING 11-8: Load the binary OpenCV packages

```java
package com.wiley.aoa.mr_wiley;
import org.opencv.android.BaseLoaderCallback;
import org.opencv.android.LoaderCallbackInterface;
import org.opencv.android.OpenCVLoader;
import android.app.Activity;
import android.os.Bundle;
import android.util.Log;
public class MainActivity extends Activity {
  protected static final String TAG = "MrWiley";
  @Override
  public void onCreate(Bundle savedInstanceState) {
    super.onCreate(savedInstanceState);
    if (!OpenCVLoader.initAsync(OpenCVLoader.OPENCV_VERSION_2_4_2, this,
        mOpenCVCallBack)) {
      Log.i(TAG, "Couldn't connect to OpenCV");
    }
  }
  private BaseLoaderCallback mOpenCVCallBack = new BaseLoaderCallback(this) {
    @Override
    public void onManagerConnected(int status) {
      if (status == LoaderCallbackInterface.SUCCESS) {
        Log.i(TAG, "Connected to OpenCV");
      } else {
        super.onManagerConnected(status);
      }
    }
  };
}
```

This code will only load the OpenCV library, though; you still need to add the code to handle the camera frames, and more specifically the image-processing algorithm that makes Mr. Wiley know how to follow the red ball.

Much like the Bike Ride Recorder, Mr. Wiley uses a `SurfaceView` to draw the camera preview into — you're lucky that most of the work has already been solved for you. Open the project you imported earlier called OpenCV Tutorial 2 — Use OpenCV Camera. There's a Java class called `SampleCvViewBase.java`, which has been prepared for projects just like the one you're about to build; copy that file to your project. Make sure to place it inside the package `com.wiley.aoa.mr_wiley`.

1. In the Package Explorer, expand the project called OpenCV Tutorial 2 — Use OpenCV Camera.

2. Expand the package called `org.opencv.samples.tutorial2` and select the file named `SampleCvViewBase.java`.

3. In the Edit menu, select Copy.

4. Expand your Mr Wiley project and select the package called `com.wiley.aoa.mr_wiley`.

5. From the Edit menu, select Paste.

If you view the `SampleCvViewBase.java` class you'll notice that it's an abstract class, meaning you can't directly instantiate an object of it. Instead, you should create a subclass that extends the `SampleCvViewBase` class.

1. From the File menu, select New Class.

2. Enter **com.wiley.aoa.mr_wiley** as the Package.

3. In the Name box, enter **MrWiley**.

4. Where it says Superclass, enter **com.wiley.aoa.mr_wiley.SampleCvViewBase**.

5. Select the Constructors from superclass and Inherited abstract methods checkboxes.

6. Click Finish.

This is where you'll define the behavior of Mr. Wiley — chasing that red ball he just loves so much. You need only three methods inside the `MrWiley.java` class: `surfaceCreated` to initialize the needed objects, `run` to deallocate the initialized objects, and `processFrame` for your image-processing algorithm. Before you continue, make sure your `MrWiley` class looks like Listing 11-9, and don't forget the synchronized blocks, which you need for all `SurfaceView` implementations.

The `processFrame` method and the constructor should have already been added automatically by Eclipse. The other two you'll need to override yourself.

LISTING 11-9: The beginning of MrWiley

```
package com.wiley.aoa.mr_wiley;
import org.opencv.highgui.VideoCapture;
import android.content.Context;
import android.graphics.Bitmap;
import android.view.SurfaceHolder;
public class MrWiley extends SampleCvViewBase {
  public MrWiley(Context context) {
    super(context);
  }
  @Override
  public void surfaceCreated(SurfaceHolder holder) {
    super.surfaceCreated(holder);
    synchronized (this) {
    }
  }
  @Override
  protected Bitmap processFrame(VideoCapture capture) {
    return null;
  }
  @Override
  public void run() {
    super.run();
    synchronized (this) {
    }
  }
}
```

The next step is initializing `MrWiley` inside your `MainActivity`. This involves a few things you should remember: Release the camera related to `MrWiley` inside `onPause`. In `onResume` attempt to load the camera, and if that fails immediately quit the application — no camera, no brains. If you successfully loaded OpenCV, attempt to load the camera too. You do this inside the `BaseLoaderCallback`.

Listing 11-10 shows how to do all of these steps.

LISTING 11-10: Init MrWiley

```
package com.wiley.aoa.mr_wiley;
import org.opencv.android.BaseLoaderCallback;
import org.opencv.android.LoaderCallbackInterface;
import org.opencv.android.OpenCVLoader;
import android.app.Activity;
import android.os.Bundle;
import android.util.Log;
public class MainActivity extends Activity {
  protected static final String TAG = "MrWiley";
  private MrWiley mrWiley;
  @Override
  public void onCreate(Bundle savedInstanceState) {
    super.onCreate(savedInstanceState);
    if (!OpenCVLoader.initAsync(OpenCVLoader.OPENCV_VERSION_2_4_2, this,
        mOpenCVCallBack)) {
      Log.i(TAG, "Couldn't connect to OpenCV");
    }
  }
  @Override
  protected void onResume() {
    super.onResume();
    if (mrWiley != null && !mrWiley.openCamera())
      finish();
  }
  @Override
  protected void onPause() {
    super.onPause();
    if (mrWiley != null)
      mrWiley.releaseCamera();
  }
  private BaseLoaderCallback mOpenCVCallBack = new BaseLoaderCallback(this) {
    @Override
    public void onManagerConnected(int status) {
      if (status == LoaderCallbackInterface.SUCCESS) {
        Log.i(TAG, "Connected to OpenCV");
        mrWiley = new MrWiley(mAppContext);
        setContentView(mrWiley);
        if (!mrWiley.openCamera())
          finish();
      } else {
        super.onManagerConnected(status);
      }
    }
  };
}
```

Because this application uses the camera, you need to ask for permission to use the Camera. Add the following code to your manifest:

```
<uses-permission android:name="android.permission.CAMERA"/>
```

While you're inside the manifest, go ahead and lock the orientation of the `MainActivity` to landscape; this correctly rotates the camera and you'll avoid unnecessarily slow orientation changes when the app is running:

```
<activity
   android:name=".MainActivity"
   android:label="@string/title_activity_main"
   android:screenOrientation="landscape">
```

Building the Computer Vision Algorithm

Making Mr. Wiley follow a red ball is not a simple task. First it needs the intelligence to understand what constitutes a red ball; there's no method in any programming language that is called `followTheRedBall`. You need to instruct Mr. Wiley what "red ball" means, and you'll do this through computer vision.

You can solve the problem of creating a computer vision algorithm in several ways. Two of the best documented are: feature detection and color filtering. Feature detection is very expensive because it often deals with many features that need to be filtered through special algorithms (for example, line detection) and you often want to run these algorithms on detailed images so that no resolution is lost.

Color filtering is less expensive than feature detection because its first objective is to limit the amount of information in an image to a minimum through thresholds — for example, the color red — and to create a binary image of that result (an image containing only black or white pixels).

Loading the Image Data into the Matrix

Begin by loading the image data from the VideoCapture object; this image data has to be stored inside a matrix object, called `src` here. The one thing you can't do with a matrix in OpenCV is display it on screen, even if it's containing image data — before you can display that image on screen you'll need to convert it to a `Bitmap` using the `matToBitmap` function. See Listing 11-11 for details.

> **NOTE** `Mat` *is the most common container for data in OpenCV; it can store all kinds of images, vectors, matrices, and other interesting data commonly used when doing computer vision.*

LISTING 11-11: Load the image data into a matrix

```
package com.wiley.aoa.mr_wiley;
import org.opencv.android.Utils;
import org.opencv.core.Mat;
import org.opencv.highgui.Highgui;
import org.opencv.highgui.VideoCapture;
import android.content.Context;
```

```
import android.graphics.Bitmap;
import android.view.SurfaceHolder;
public class MrWiley extends SampleCvViewBase {
  private Mat src;
  public MrWiley(Context context) {
    super(context);
  }
  @Override
  public void surfaceCreated(SurfaceHolder holder) {
    super.surfaceCreated(holder);
    synchronized (this) {
      src = new Mat();
    }
  }
  @Override
  protected Bitmap processFrame(VideoCapture capture) {
    capture.retrieve(src, Highgui.CV_CAP_ANDROID_COLOR_FRAME_RGBA);
    Bitmap bmp = Bitmap.createBitmap(src.cols(), src.rows(), Bitmap.Config.ARGB_8888);
    Utils.matToBitmap(src, bmp);
    return bmp;
  }
  @Override
  public void run() {
    super.run();
    synchronized (this) {
      if (src != null)
        src.release();
      src = null;
    }
  }
}
```

This should give you a simple standard camera preview window, like the one shown in Figure 11-8.

Converting the Extracted Frame to the HSV Space

When filtering colors, the HSV color space is far superior to the RGB space (which you're currently using) because colors are limited to just one variable instead of three; your next step in building the algorithm, then, is to convert the extracted frame to the HSV space. You use a static method called cvtColor inside the Imgproc class, as shown in Listing 11-12.

FIGURE 11-8: Displaying the raw camera frame

LISTING 11-12: Convert the camera frame to the HSV color space

```
package com.wiley.aoa.mr_wiley;
import org.opencv.android.Utils;
import org.opencv.core.Mat;
import org.opencv.highgui.Highgui;
import org.opencv.highgui.VideoCapture;
import org.opencv.imgproc.Imgproc;
import android.content.Context;
import android.graphics.Bitmap;
```

continues

LISTING 11-12 *(continued)*

```
import android.test.PerformanceTestCase.Intermediates;
import android.view.SurfaceHolder;
public class MrWiley extends SampleCvViewBase {
  private Mat src, hsv;
  public MrWiley(Context context) {
    super(context);
  }
  @Override
  public void surfaceCreated(SurfaceHolder holder) {
    super.surfaceCreated(holder);
    synchronized (this) {
      src = new Mat();
      hsv = new Mat();
    }
  }
  @Override
  protected Bitmap processFrame(VideoCapture capture) {
    capture.retrieve(src, Highgui.CV_CAP_ANDROID_COLOR_FRAME_RGBA);
    Imgproc.cvtColor(src, hsv, Imgproc.COLOR_RGB2HSV);
    Bitmap bmp = Bitmap.createBitmap(src.cols(), src.rows(), Bitmap.Config.ARGB_8888);
    Utils.matToBitmap(src, bmp);
    return bmp;
  }
  @Override
  public void run() {
    super.run();
    synchronized (this) {
      if (src != null)
        src.release();
      src = null;
      if (hsv!= null)
        hsv.release();
      hsv = null;
    }
  }
}
```

You shouldn't even bother trying to display the resulting image from this conversion; the image will look very weird because of the differences between the HSV and the final bitmap color space (ARGB). Instead, continue with the color filtering using the inRange method.

HSV COLOR SPACE

The HSV color space in OpenCV is different from that found in image software, such as Photoshop or GIMP. This means that you can't use those software solutions to find the correct color values when filtering your images in OpenCV.

However, you can use a tool that is freely available, called ColorWheelHSV, to find the correct OpenCV HSV values from any image. You can find it at http://www .shervinemami.info/colorConversion.html#colorWheelHSV.

Listing 11-13 shows how to filter an HSV image using `inRange` with thresholds using `Scalar` objects.

> **NOTE** *In OpenCV the* `Scalar` *is an object defining an ordered set of numbers (also called Tuples). In the example below you'll use* `Scalar` *to define thresholds in the HSV color space, the first number represents the hue, the second is the saturation and the third is the value.*

LISTING 11-13: Apply the color filter

```
package com.wiley.aoa.mr_wiley;
import org.opencv.android.Utils;
import org.opencv.core.Core;
import org.opencv.core.Mat;
import org.opencv.core.Scalar;
import org.opencv.highgui.Highgui;
import org.opencv.highgui.VideoCapture;
import org.opencv.imgproc.Imgproc;
import android.content.Context;
import android.graphics.Bitmap;
import android.view.SurfaceHolder;
public class MrWiley extends SampleCvViewBase {
  private Mat src, hsv, dst;
  public MrWiley(Context context) {
    super(context);
  }
  @Override
  public void surfaceCreated(SurfaceHolder holder) {
    super.surfaceCreated(holder);
    synchronized (this) {
      src = new Mat();
      hsv = new Mat();
      dst = new Mat();
    }
  }
  @Override
  protected Bitmap processFrame(VideoCapture capture) {
    capture.retrieve(src, Highgui.CV_CAP_ANDROID_COLOR_FRAME_RGBA);
    Imgproc.cvtColor(src, hsv, Imgproc.COLOR_RGB2HSV);
    Core.inRange(hsv, new Scalar(0, 10, 110), new Scalar(6, 255, 255), dst);
    Bitmap bmp = Bitmap.createBitmap(dst.cols(), dst.rows(), Bitmap.Config.ARGB_8888);
    Utils.matToBitmap(dst, bmp);
    return bmp;
  }
  @Override
  public void run() {
    super.run();
    synchronized (this) {
      if (src != null)
        src.release();
```

continues

LISTING 11-13 *(continued)*

```
            src = null;
            if (hsv != null)
              hsv.release();
            hsv = null;
            if (dst != null)
              dst.release();
            dst = null;
          }
        }
      }
```

The result should resemble Figure 11-9; notice that the pixels that lie in between the two threshold values are white, whereas everything else is black. This is a binary image.

You should experiment with the values in the inRange method on your own. See what suits your red ball — perhaps you want to use a green ball instead? A hue of around 75 would probably work fairly well for green.

The binary image makes the position of the ball really obvious; however, you have a lot of small pixels all over the screen — these will all register as "red balls" too unless they're removed.

FIGURE 11-9: Applying a "red" color filter

Removing Pixel Noise

You have a couple of ways to remove the noise all over the screen. The easiest is probably to use a method called erode, which changes the color of a pixel based on its neighboring pixels; you can make the erode function behave in slightly different ways depending on the matrix you tell it to erode according to, in the code below you'll use a standard 9-by-9 matrix for the erode. This matrix should always have the same number of rows as columns. See Listing 11-14 for details.

LISTING 11-14: Remove the noise by using erode

```
package com.wiley.aoa.mr_wiley;
import org.opencv.android.Utils;
import org.opencv.core.Core;
import org.opencv.core.Mat;
import org.opencv.core.Scalar;
import org.opencv.core.Size;
import org.opencv.highgui.Highgui;
import org.opencv.highgui.VideoCapture;
import org.opencv.imgproc.Imgproc;
import android.content.Context;
import android.graphics.Bitmap;
import android.view.SurfaceHolder;
public class MrWiley extends SampleCvViewBase {
  private Mat src, hsv, dst, intermediate;
  public MrWiley(Context context) {
```

```
      super(context);
    }
    @Override
    public void surfaceCreated(SurfaceHolder holder) {
      super.surfaceCreated(holder);
      synchronized (this) {
        src = new Mat();
        hsv = new Mat();
        dst = new Mat();
        intermediate = new Mat();
      }
    }
    @Override
    protected Bitmap processFrame(VideoCapture capture) {
      capture.retrieve(src, Highgui.CV_CAP_ANDROID_COLOR_FRAME_RGBA);
      Imgproc.cvtColor(src, hsv, Imgproc.COLOR_RGB2HSV);
      Core.inRange(hsv, new Scalar(0, 10, 110), new Scalar(6, 255, 255), intermediate);
      Mat erode = Imgproc.getStructuringElement(Imgproc.MORPH_ERODE, new Size(9, 9));
      Imgproc.erode(intermediate, dst, erode);
      Bitmap bmp = Bitmap.createBitmap(dst.cols(), dst.rows(),
          Bitmap.Config.ARGB_8888);
      Utils.matToBitmap(dst, bmp);
      return bmp;
    }
    @Override
    public void run() {
      super.run();
      synchronized (this) {
        if (src != null)
          src.release();
        src = null;
        if (hsv != null)
          hsv.release();
        hsv = null;
        if (dst != null)
          dst.release();
        dst = null;
        if (intermediate != null)
          intermediate.release();
        intermediate = null;
      }
    }
  }
```

FIGURE 11-10: Remove the noise using erode

Your result should look something like Figure 11-10.

Defining the Algorithm Using Dilate

If the area of white pixels became very small after you applied the erode you can use a method called dilate, which will perform the opposite of the erode. Add code from Listing 11-15 to perform an erode on your image.

LISTING 11-15: Add the dilate method to your algorithm

```
package com.wiley.aoa.mr_wiley;
[...]
public class MrWiley extends SampleCvViewBase {
  [...]
  @Override
  protected Bitmap processFrame(VideoCapture capture) {
    capture.retrieve(src, Highgui.CV_CAP_ANDROID_COLOR_FRAME_RGBA);
    Imgproc.cvtColor(src, hsv, Imgproc.COLOR_RGB2HSV);
    Core.inRange(hsv, new Scalar(0, 10, 110), new Scalar(6, 255, 255), intermediate);
    Mat erode = Imgproc.getStructuringElement(Imgproc.MORPH_ERODE, new Size(9, 9));
    Imgproc.erode(intermediate, dst, erode);
    Mat dilate = Imgproc.getStructuringElement(Imgproc.MORPH_DILATE, new Size(9, 9));
    Imgproc.dilate(dst, intermediate, dilate);
    Bitmap bmp = Bitmap.createBitmap(intermediate.cols(), intermediate.rows(),
      Bitmap.Config.ARGB_8888);
    Utils.matToBitmap(intermediate, bmp);
    return bmp;
  }
  [...]
}
```

Hopefully, you'll get an image similar to Figure 11-11.

This is a fairly clean image.

Adding Contour Data

Now that you have a fairly clean binary image (only black and white pixels) you can start looking for contours in it. In computer vision you'll often read something called blobs; a blob is a collection of pixels that together form a coherent space in an image. In this example your white pixels form a blob on your image, defined by a contour around them.

FIGURE 11-11: Result of the dilate filter

Each blob has a number of attributes that come in handy when dealing with this sort of basic computer vision algorithms; it has an area and a center, both of which come in handy in this example. Add the call to findContours as shown in Listing 11-16.

There's no point in displaying another image onscreen in this step because you're finding contour data, not applying an image filter. So, you can go ahead and create the returned bitmap based on the src matrix again to make it show the original camera preview, just like you did in the very first step.

LISTING 11-16: Find the contour data

```
package com.wiley.aoa.mr_wiley;
import java.util.ArrayList;
import org.opencv.android.Utils;
import org.opencv.core.Core;
import org.opencv.core.Mat;
import org.opencv.core.MatOfPoint;
```

```
import org.opencv.core.Scalar;
import org.opencv.core.Size;
import org.opencv.highgui.Highgui;
import org.opencv.highgui.VideoCapture;
import org.opencv.imgproc.Imgproc;
import android.content.Context;
import android.graphics.Bitmap;
import android.view.SurfaceHolder;
public class MrWiley extends SampleCvViewBase {
  private Mat src, hsv, dst, intermediate, hierarchy;
  private ArrayList<MatOfPoint> contours;
  public MrWiley(Context context) {
    super(context);
  }
  @Override
  public void surfaceCreated(SurfaceHolder holder) {
    super.surfaceCreated(holder);
    synchronized (this) {
      src = new Mat();
      hsv = new Mat();
      dst = new Mat();
      intermediate = new Mat();
      hierarchy = new Mat();
      contours = new ArrayList<MatOfPoint>();
    }
  }
  @Override
  protected Bitmap processFrame(VideoCapture capture) {
    capture.retrieve(src, Highgui.CV_CAP_ANDROID_COLOR_FRAME_RGBA);
    Imgproc.cvtColor(src, hsv, Imgproc.COLOR_RGB2HSV);
    Core.inRange(hsv, new Scalar(0, 10, 110), new Scalar(6, 255, 255), intermediate);
    Mat erode = Imgproc.getStructuringElement(Imgproc.MORPH_ERODE, new Size(9, 9));
    Imgproc.erode(intermediate, dst, erode);
    Mat dilate = Imgproc.getStructuringElement(Imgproc.MORPH_DILATE, new Size(9, 9));
    Imgproc.dilate(dst, intermediate, dilate);
    Imgproc.findContours(intermediate, contours, hierarchy, 0, 2);
    Bitmap bmp = Bitmap.createBitmap(src.cols(), src.rows(), Bitmap.Config.ARGB_8888);
    Utils.matToBitmap(src, bmp);
    if( contours != null)
      contours.clear();
    return bmp;
  }
  @Override
  public void run() {
    super.run();
    synchronized (this) {
      if (src != null)
        src.release();
      src = null;
      if (hsv != null)
        hsv.release();
      hsv = null;
      if (dst != null)
        dst.release();
      dst = null;
```

continues

LISTING 11-16 *(continued)*

```
        if (intermediate != null)
          intermediate.release();
        intermediate = null;
        if (hierarchy != null)
          hierarchy.release();
        hierarchy = null;
        contours = null;
      }
    }
  }
```

At this point you've stored the contours in a `ArrayList`. The only thing you need to do now is find the largest contour and assume that is the red ball; of course, this is a very simplistic approach and you have much better ways of determining what (if anything) is a red ball.

Luckily for you, OpenCV has built-in methods for calculating areas and bounding rectangles of contours. Listing 11-17 shows how to find the largest contour based on its area.

LISTING 11-17: Find the largest contour

```
package com.wiley.aoa.mr_wiley;
[...]
public class MrWiley extends SampleCvViewBase {
  [...]
  @Override
  protected Bitmap processFrame(VideoCapture capture) {
    capture.retrieve(src, Highgui.CV_CAP_ANDROID_COLOR_FRAME_RGBA);
    Imgproc.cvtColor(src, hsv, Imgproc.COLOR_RGB2HSV);
    Core.inRange(hsv, new Scalar(0, 10, 110), new Scalar(6, 255, 255),intermediate);
    Mat erode = Imgproc.getStructuringElement(Imgproc.MORPH_ERODE, new Size(9, 9));
    Imgproc.erode(intermediate, dst, erode);
    Mat dilate = Imgproc.getStructuringElement(Imgproc.MORPH_DILATE, new Size(9, 9));
    Imgproc.dilate(dst, intermediate, dilate);
    Imgproc.findContours(intermediate, contours, hierarchy, 0, 2);
    int largestContour = -1;
    double area = 0;
    for (int i = 0; i < contours.size(); i++) {
      double cArea = Imgproc.contourArea(contours.get(i));
      if (cArea > area) {
        area = cArea;
        largestContour = i;
      }
    }
    Bitmap bmp = Bitmap.createBitmap(src.cols(), src.rows(), Bitmap.Config.ARGB_8888);
    Utils.matToBitmap(src, bmp);
    if( contours != null)
      contours.clear();
    return bmp;
  }
  [...]
}
```

Now that you know which contour is the largest, you can simply extract the bounding rectangle for that contour; when you know the bounding rectangle it's a simple process to calculate in what direction Mr. Wiley should turn (if any). Extract the bounding rectangle and draw it on the source image, as shown in Listing 11-18.

LISTING 11-18: Extract the bounding rectangle

```
package com.wiley.aoa.mr_wiley;
[...]
public class MrWiley extends SampleCvViewBase {
  [...]
  @Override
  protected Bitmap processFrame(VideoCapture capture) {
    capture.retrieve(src, Highgui.CV_CAP_ANDROID_COLOR_FRAME_RGBA);
    Imgproc.cvtColor(src, hsv, Imgproc.COLOR_RGB2HSV);
    Core.inRange(hsv, new Scalar(0, 10, 110), new Scalar(6, 255, 255),intermediate);
    Mat erode = Imgproc.getStructuringElement(Imgproc.MORPH_ERODE, new Size(9, 9));
    Imgproc.erode(intermediate, dst, erode);
    Mat dilate = Imgproc.getStructuringElement(Imgproc.MORPH_DILATE, new Size(9, 9));
    Imgproc.dilate(dst, intermediate, dilate);
    Imgproc.findContours(intermediate, contours, hierarchy, 0, 2);
    int largestContour = -1;
    double area = 0;
    for (int i = 0; i < contours.size(); i++) {
      double cArea = Imgproc.contourArea(contours.get(i));
      if (cArea > area) {
        area = cArea;
        largestContour = i;
      }
    }
    Rect r = null;
    if (largestContour > -1)
      r = Imgproc.boundingRect(contours.get(largestContour));
    if (r != null)
      Core.rectangle(src, r.tl(), r.br(), new Scalar(255, 255, 255), 5);
    Bitmap bmp = Bitmap.createBitmap(src.cols(), src.rows(), Bitmap.Config.ARGB_8888);
    Utils.matToBitmap(src, bmp);
    if( contours != null)
      contours.clear();
    return bmp;
  }
  [...]
}
```

Determining Object Direction

The only thing remaining now is to determine if the ball is on the left side or the right side of the screen; however, instead of testing left or right you actually test if it's above or below the middle. You have to do this because the camera is rotated 90 degrees by default (see Listing 11-19).

LISTING 11-19: Determine where Mr Wiley should go

```
package com.wiley.aoa.mr_wiley;
[...]
public class MrWiley extends SampleCvViewBase {
  [...]
  @Override
  protected Bitmap processFrame(VideoCapture capture) {
    capture.retrieve(src, Highgui.CV_CAP_ANDROID_COLOR_FRAME_RGBA);
    Imgproc.cvtColor(src, hsv, Imgproc.COLOR_RGB2HSV);
    Core.inRange(hsv, new Scalar(0, 10, 110), new Scalar(6, 255, 255), intermediate);
    Mat erode = Imgproc.getStructuringElement(Imgproc.MORPH_ERODE, new Size(9, 9));
    Imgproc.erode(intermediate, dst, erode);
    Mat dilate = Imgproc.getStructuringElement(Imgproc.MORPH_DILATE, new Size(9, 9));
    Imgproc.dilate(dst, intermediate, dilate);
    Imgproc.findContours(intermediate, contours, hierarchy, 0, 2);
    int largestContour = -1;
    double area = 0;
    for (int i = 0; i < contours.size(); i++) {
      double cArea = Imgproc.contourArea(contours.get(i));
      if (cArea > area) {
        area = cArea;
        largestContour = i;
      }
    }
    Rect r = null;
    if (largestContour > -1)
      r = Imgproc.boundingRect(contours.get(largestContour));
    if (r != null) {
      Core.rectangle(intermediate, r.tl(), r.br(), new Scalar(255, 255, 255), 5);
      if ((r.y + r.height/2) < this.getHeight() / 2) {
        // Move right
      } else {
        // Move left
      }
    }else{
      // Stop
    }
    Bitmap bmp = Bitmap.createBitmap(src.cols(), src.rows(), Bitmap.Config.ARGB_8888);
    Utils.matToBitmap(src, bmp);
    if( contours != null)
      contours.clear();
    return bmp;
  }
  [...]
}
```

Connecting to the WroxAccessory

Connecting to the modified Arduino robot requires you to first add the WroxAccessory library, you've done this many times already so it should be a breeze:

1. From the Project menu, select Properties.

2. In the list on the left side, select Android.

3. Select Add from within the Library panel.

4. In the new dialog box, select the WroxAccessories library and click OK.

5. Click Apply and then OK.

Adding the Required WroxAccessory Objects

Connecting to the accessory requires three objects: the WroxAccessory object which handles the communication, the Connection object that defines what kind of connection you're interested in, and the UsbManager that lets you connect to USB accessories.

You connect to the WroxAccessory as shown in Listing 11-20.

LISTING 11-20: Add the required WroxAccessory objects

```java
package com.wiley.aoa.mr_wiley;
import org.opencv.android.BaseLoaderCallback;
import org.opencv.android.LoaderCallbackInterface;
import org.opencv.android.OpenCVLoader;
import com.wiley.wroxaccessories.UsbConnection12;
import com.wiley.wroxaccessories.WroxAccessory;
import android.app.Activity;
import android.hardware.usb.UsbManager;
import android.os.Bundle;
import android.util.Log;
public class MainActivity extends Activity {
  protected static final String TAG = "MrWiley";
  private MrWiley mrWiley;
  private WroxAccessory mAccessory;
  private UsbManager mUsbManager;
  private UsbConnection12 connection;
  @Override
  public void onCreate(Bundle savedInstanceState) {
    super.onCreate(savedInstanceState);
    if (!OpenCVLoader.initAsync(OpenCVLoader.OPENCV_VERSION_2_4_2, this,
      mOpenCVCallBack)) {
      Log.i(TAG, "Couldn't connect to OpenCV");
    }
    mUsbManager = (UsbManager) getSystemService(USB_SERVICE);
    connection = new UsbConnection12(this, mUsbManager);
    mAccessory = new WroxAccessory(this);
  }
  [...]
}
```

Sending the Connect Message

In the onResume method, send the connect message to the accessory as shown in Listing 11-21.

LISTING 11-21: Perform the connect

```
package com.wiley.aoa.mr_wiley;
[...]
public class MainActivity extends Activity {
  [...]
  @Override
  protected void onResume() {
    super.onResume();
    if (mrWiley != null && !mrWiley.openCamera())
      finish();
    try {
      mAccessory.connect(WroxAccessory.USB_ACCESSORY_12, connection);
    } catch (IOException e) {
      e.printStackTrace();
    }
  }
  [...]
}
```

Disconnecting the Accessory

When the app is no longer alive you should shut down the communication. To do so you should call the accessory's `disconnect` method in the activity's `onDestroy` method, as shown in Listing 11-22.

LISTING 11-22: Disconnect and close the connection

```
package com.wiley.aoa.mr_wiley;
[...]
public class MainActivity extends Activity {
  [...]
  @Override
  protected void onDestroy() {
    super.onDestroy();
    try {
      mAccessory.disconnect();
    } catch (IOException e) {
      e.printStackTrace();
    }
  }
  [...]
}
```

Adding the Handler

Make sure to publish the correct messages to the correct topic. To do this, add a `Handler` interface between `MrWiley.java` and `MainActivity.java`. Add the `Handler` in `MainActivity.java` as shown in Listing 11-23.

LISTING 11-23: Add the Handler to your activity

```
package com.wiley.aoa.mr_wiley;
[...]
import android.os.Handler;
public class MainActivity extends Activity {
  protected static final byte ACTION_LEFT = 0;
  protected static final byte ACTION_RIGHT = 1;
  protected static final byte ACTION_STOP = 2;
  [...]
  private Handler mHandler = new Handler(){
    @Override
    public void handleMessage(Message msg) {
      switch(msg.what){
      case ACTION_LEFT:
        break;
      case ACTION_RIGHT:
        break;
      case ACTION_STOP:
        break;
      }
    }
  };
}
```

Adding the Publishing Calls

Add the publish calls to the corresponding action inside the switch statement. See Listing 11-24 for details.

LISTING 11-24: Publish the events

```
package com.wiley.aoa.mr_wiley;
[...]
public class MainActivity extends Activity {
  protected static final byte ACTION_LEFT = 0;
  protected static final byte ACTION_RIGHT = 1;
  protected static final byte ACTION_STOP = 2;
  [...]
  private Handler mHandler = new Handler() {
    @Override
    public void handleMessage(Message msg) {
      byte[] buffer = new byte[1];
      switch (msg.what) {
      case ACTION_LEFT:
        buffer[0] = ACTION_LEFT;
        break;
      case ACTION_RIGHT:
        buffer[0] = ACTION_RIGHT;
        break;
      case ACTION_STOP:
        buffer[0] = ACTION_STOP;
        break;
```

continues

LISTING 11-24 *(continued)*

```
        }
        try {
          mAccessory.publish("mw", buffer);
        } catch (IOException e) {
          e.printStackTrace();
        }
      }
    };
  }
```

Passing the Handler Reference to Mr. Wiley

The final thing before you're done is to pass the `mHandler` reference to your `MrWiley.java` class, enabling it to send the messages at the proper time. See Listing 11-25 for how to pass the reference to `MrWiley.java`.

LISTING 11-25: Pass the mHandler reference to MrWiley

```
package com.wiley.aoa.mr_wiley;
[...]
public class MainActivity extends Activity {
  [...]
  private BaseLoaderCallback mOpenCVCallBack = new BaseLoaderCallback(this) {
    @Override
    public void onManagerConnected(int status) {
      if (status == LoaderCallbackInterface.SUCCESS) {
        Log.i(TAG, "Connected to OpenCV");
        mrWiley = new MrWiley(mAppContext, mHandler);
        setContentView(mrWiley);
        if (!mrWiley.openCamera())
          finish();
      } else {
        super.onManagerConnected(status);
      }
    }
  };
  [...]
}
```

Passing Messages Using the mHandler Reference

Listing 11-26 shows how to pass the messages from `MrWiley` to the `MainActivity`.

LISTING 11-26: Send the messages from MrWiley

```
package com.wiley.aoa.mr_wiley;
[...]
import android.os.Handler;
public class MrWiley extends SampleCvViewBase {
  private Mat src, hsv, dst, intermediate;
```

```
private ArrayList<MatOfPoint> contours;
private Mat hierarchy;
private Handler mHandler;
public MrWiley(Context context, Handler mHandler) {
  super(context);
  this.mHandler = mHandler;
}
[...]
@Override
protected Bitmap processFrame(VideoCapture capture) {
  capture.retrieve(src, Highgui.CV_CAP_ANDROID_COLOR_FRAME_RGBA);
  Imgproc.cvtColor(src, hsv, Imgproc.COLOR_RGB2HSV);
  Core.inRange(hsv, new Scalar(0, 10, 110), new Scalar(6, 255, 255), intermediate);
  Mat erode = Imgproc.getStructuringElement(Imgproc.MORPH_ERODE, new Size(9, 9));
  Imgproc.erode(intermediate, dst, erode);
  Mat dilate = Imgproc.getStructuringElement(Imgproc.MORPH_DILATE, new Size(9, 9));
  Imgproc.dilate(dst, intermediate, dilate);
  Imgproc.findContours(intermediate, contours, hierarchy, 0, 2);
  int largestContour = -1;
  double area = 0;
  for (int i = 0; i < contours.size(); i++) {
    double cArea = Imgproc.contourArea(contours.get(i));
    if (cArea > area) {
      area = cArea;
      largestContour = i;
    }
  }
  Rect r = null;
  if (largestContour > -1)
    r = Imgproc.boundingRect(contours.get(largestContour));
  if (r != null) {
    Core.rectangle(intermediate, r.tl(), r.br(), new Scalar(255, 255, 255), 5);
    if ((r.y + r.height/2) < this.getHeight() / 2) {
      // Move right
      mHandler.obtainMessage(MainActivity.ACTION_RIGHT).sendToTarget();
    } else {
      // Move left
      mHandler.obtainMessage(MainActivity.ACTION_LEFT).sendToTarget();
    }
  }else{
    // Stop
    mHandler.obtainMessage(MainActivity.ACTION_STOP).sendToTarget();
  }
  Bitmap bmp = Bitmap.createBitmap(src.cols(), src.rows(),Bitmap.Config.ARGB_8888);
  Utils.matToBitmap(src, bmp);
  if( contours != null)
    contours.clear();
  return bmp;
}
[...]
}
```

MAKING FURTHER IMPROVEMENTS

You can do a couple of things to further develop this project. We are in love with the idea that things are never completely finished, and here is what we suggest you explore to make Mr. Wiley the best ball-hunting robot in the hood!

Electronics

➤ You should consider making this robot not just look at the ball but follow it. That requires adding some extra safety measures as well as a couple of functions the system hasn't implemented yet. You need the following: functions to move forward and backward, and some distance sensors to determine the distance to a wall; you don't want your robot to crash when moving around hunting a ball.

➤ You could enable the robot to push the ball around and carry it. You could then add a sensor (for example, infrared) to detect whether the ball is being carried by the robot.

Making a Better App

➤ Because you have no user interface in this project, most of the improvements are related to the computer vision algorithm. You can do the following: Create a better detection algorithm than the simplistic one developed in this chapter — an algorithm with not just color filtering and blob detection, but extended to include feature tracking and object detection. After refining the computer vision algorithm for finding that lovely red ball, you can reduce the number of native calls by moving the algorithm to native code and calling just one method from your Java API. You want to do this because, generally, calling native methods like you've done in this project is really expensive.

➤ To avoid flooding the communication, keep track of the last send message and avoid resending that message.

SUMMARY

Robotics is not such a novel field; you can find many ready-mades to use in your projects. If you are interested, you could even form a robotics team to compete in international championships. You can become a roboticist and learn more about the field from your home.

To drive DC motors, you could make the robot with discrete components like relays or transistors, but chips are available that minimize the amount of space needed on your board to make this. The technique that enables controlling the direction a motor turns using a single voltage source is called an H-bridge. The integrated H-bridges control not only direction of turn, but also the motor's speed.

Working with the camera of your Android device can be a difficult task, both for you and the phone; adding image processing on top of that makes it even more complex, especially when you do a lot of pixel-heavy operations like you've done in this project. OpenCV is a framework that helps you overcome these difficulties and use Android's camera in a good way.

INDEX

M

MAKE THE **10 EXAMPLES** FROM PART ONE IN THIS BOOK **BY GETTING**

THE ARDUINO ADK KIT

ARDUINO.CC/ADKkit

WITH THIS KIT YOU CAN:

Use your **ARDUINO MEGA ADK (usb cable included)** to connect an Android™ device. Mount all your experiments on the **breadboard** and join your components using your **wire kit**. Build visual indicators using some of the **40 LEDs** in the kit; you have them in **4 different colors**. Build your own physical controller to your phone using some **potentiometers(you get a total of 10)**. Make a simple robot using **2 continuous rotation servo motors**. Measure the amount of light using some of the **5 light sensors** included. Display texts and small graphics on the **2 bicolor dot matrix LED display (32 x 16 LEDs)**. Control your physical world with a **relay module (wires included).** Check if your project is upside down with the **tilt module**. Make a small keyboard out of the **5 push buttons.** Play small melodies using the **piezo speaker**. Measure the distance using the **ultrasound sensor**. Power up your projects with the **5V voltage regulator**. Determine the precise amount of degrees using the **temperature sensor module**. And don't forget you get the **176 pcs resistor kit** for your prototypes.

Find more information about the **ARDUINO™** Open Source Hardware Project at **ARDUINO.CC**
Get your ADK and **ARDUINO™** devices at:

STORE.ARDUINO.CC